RADIO CAROLINE
The Pirate Years

by
Ralph C. Humphries

THE OAKWOOD PRESS

© Oakwood Press & Ralph C. Humphries 2003
Revised and updated 2018.

British Library Cataloguing in Publication Data
A Record for this book is available from the British Library
ISBN 978 0 85361 276 6

Typeset by Oakwood Graphics.
Repro by Ford Graphics, Ringwood, Hants.
Printed by Inkon Printers Ltd, Yateley, Hants.

Dedication

Audrey Humphries 8th January, 1928-31st May, 2003

This book is dedicated, with all my love, to my Mum. She was so very proud when I
told her that this book was to be published. Unfortunately she died the day before I was
to show her the final proof copy. Having my first book published is for me a very special
occasion which I want to share with a very special lady.

Title page: About 9.00 pm on 19th January, 1966, the Coastguard at Walton-on-Naze
noticed that the *Mi Amigo* was drifting in a stormy wind and rough seas. In spite of
attempts to contact the ship, the Coastguard could get no reply from the radio ship.
Eventually the *Mi Amigo* ran aground, but the local Coastguard rescue team saved the
radio staff, leaving the captain and his crew aboard.
   This view shows the ship 50 metres from the beach the following morning. Fortunately
no one was hurt, and the damage done to the *Mi Amigo* was not too serious.
   Those involved with the ship looked on the incident in a more positive way. They liked
to think that the *Mi Amigo* had its own personality, and that she was looked over. So
instead of feeling sad that the incident had happened, they feel that someone was looking
over them that night. Why?
   The beach had groynes along its length, set at regular intervals, except where the
Mi Amigo came ashore. Due to the ship's length, this was the only area that she would fit
in, without being impaled.
   This original drawing of the *Mi Amigo*, on the beach, shows just how close it came to
one of those groynes It was drawn by Radka Chocholousova, from the Czech Republic in
January 2003.

Published by The Oakwood Press (Usk), 54-58 Mill Square, Catrine, KA5 6RD.
E-mail: sales@stenlake.co.uk   telephone: 01290 551122
Website: www.stenlake.co.uk

Contents

Acknowledgements

This story, about Radio Caroline, started way back in 1976. I was serving in the uniform branch of Trinity House, and apart from any other duties, I compiled weather reports for the Met Office. These reports were compiled 24 hours per day, 365 days of the year, by the duty officer.

The completed reports were sent hourly, in coded form, to the Weather Centre at Southampton, by telephone. Whilst passing one such report, I heard music in the background. In reply to my question, 'What station are you listening to?', I was told that it was Radio Caroline.

I was intrigued to hear that she was still on the air, as the last time I had heard her had been back in early 1968. I tuned to her frequency, but reception was very poor, due to my being stationed near to a high powered Morse code, coastal radio station. It was, however, at that moment, during the middle watch, that this project started.

I wrote to several magazines, requesting information, totally unprepared for the response that I got! Letters poured in from around Europe, including Sweden, Denmark, Holland, Belgium and, literally nationwide from this country. It got to the point that the postman reckoned that I should negotiate a pay rise for him!

Through this incredible response I was led to Buster (Roland C. Pearson), and his *Monitor* magazine. We never met, although we did converse on several occasions. He was quite an extraordinary man, who had to be Radio Caroline's most devoted listener.

I choose not to use the term 'Anorak' to describe him, for he was far more than that. Not only did he have a wealth of information about his favourite station, he was well loved, and respected, by those who worked for Caroline. Sadly he is no longer with us, but I bet that whichever cloud he is sitting on, he is listening to Caroline tapes.

Over the intervening years I had many postings, during one such move most of the original cuttings and letters were lost. Fortunately, I had packed my notes separately, so all was not lost.

It does mean, however, that I can not thank every individual who has helped me with this project, and for that I apologise.

I can thank FotoFlite, Guernsey Press, Roger 'Twiggy' Day, E. Houwerzijl, David Moore, E. Varley , Ron van den Bos, Jane de Rose, Ben Bradley, and Philip Matcham the senior licensing manager for the Official UK Charts Company. Former Trinity House colleagues, Jane Wilson, Clive Biggs, Peter Halil, and the late Steve McClary; Steve was lost overboard from the Seven Stones light vessel, on Saturday 5th March, 1980.

I would like to extend my special thanks, to Harry Spencer, who had some funny stories to tell, and not just about Radio Caroline. Last, but by no means least, thank you to Ronan, and all who worked for Radio Caroline, without whom there would be no story to tell.

Introduction

Way back in the 1800s, signals were sent by means of the electric telegraph. An American painter, and inventor, Samuel Finley Breese Morse (1791-1872) devised a means of sending signals through the telegraph. The signals consisted of a code, which became known as Morse code.

Each letter of the alphabet was represented by a series of dots and/or dashes. For example: A was transmitted as one short dot, and one long dash. Z was represented by two long, and two short. To send these signals the transmitter had to be connected to the receiver, by means of a wire.

An Italian physicist, Guglielmo Marchese Marconi (1874-1937), then developed a form of transmission which did not rely on a wire, to connect the transmitter to the receiver. The radio transmissions were enhanced by means of an aerial, the contents of the signal comprising Morse code. The first broadcast was made in 1895, followed by trans-Atlantic signals in 1901.

Marconi was determined to transmit the spoken word, which he achieved in 1914. He also wanted to develop the new wireless contraption for entertainment (so that he could listen to his early Rolling Stones records). In 1920 he started the Marconi Company, which was based in Chelmsford, Essex.

On 23rd February, 1920, the company commenced test transmissions, which lasted for two weeks. The signals, which comprised music and song, were of one hour duration, and were heard over a distance of 1,400 miles. These broadcasts proved so popular that regular transmissions commenced during 1921.

The Marconi Company moved to new premises, in the Strand, from where the transmissions were made, using the call sign, '2LO London'. Two regional stations quickly followed, which used the call signs '2ZY Manchester', and '5IT Birmingham'. The Government decided that they only wanted to have one radio company, unlike in America where a plethora of radio stations were being opened.

On 18th October, 1922, the British Broadcasting Company Ltd was created. Within one year they had nine regional transmitters, each with a range of about 30 miles, which broadcast for four hours per day. In 1924 they tested a long wave transmitter, which had the call sign '5XX Daventry'. These tests were highly successful, and were followed by regular transmissions commencing in July 1925.

In 1926 the Government's broadcasting policy was reviewed, by the Crawford Committee, which made some recommendations. The most important was that a public monopoly, responsible to the Government, was the best way to ensure quality in radio broadcasts.

The British Broadcasting Company Ltd did not have its licence renewed, when it expired at the end of 1926. The company was replaced by the British Broadcasting Corporation (BBC), in 1927. Established by Royal Charter, the BBC became solely responsible for broadcasting in this country.

The BBC was financed by revenue from a licence fee, which was paid by one million licence holders in 1926. They also received a grant-in-aid, from the Government, to develop an overseas service. The Government also reserved the right to take control of those broadcasts, during times of national emergencies, a right which has not been claimed to this date.

The O'Rahilly

Sing of the O'Rahilly,
Do not deny his right,
Sing a 'The' before his name;
Allow that he, despite
All those learned historians,
Established it for good;
He wrote out the word himself.
He christened himself with blood.
How goes the weather?

Sing of the O'Rahilly
That had such little sense
He told Pearse and Connolly
He'd gone to great expense
Keeping all the Kerry men
Out of that crazy fight;
That he might be there himself
Had travelled half the night.
How goes the weather?

'Am I such a craven that I should not get the word
But for some travelling man
Had heard I had not heard?'
Then on Pearse and Connolly
He fixed a bitter look:
'Because I helped wind the clock I came to hear it strike'.
How goes the weather?

What remains to sing about
But of the death he met
Stretched under a doorway
Somewhere off Henry Street;
They that found him found upon
The door above his head 'Here died the O'Rahilly
R.I.P' writ in blood.
How goes the weather?

William Butler Yeats

The Variorum Edition of the Poems of W.B. Yeats
Courtesy of A.P. Watt Ltd on behalf of Michael B. Yeats

The State monopoly was a traditionalist, but basically flawed, concept, which allowed broadcasting to stagnate. Meanwhile, in America (and other countries) a comprehensive network of local commercial stations were developed.

The BBC had to cater for a very large audience, and all tastes had to be catered for. It was just not possible for the BBC to keep pace with the cultural, and musical, changes that were taking place.

In 1935 the Ullswater Committee refused to advocate the introduction of commercial radio, or television, wishing to maintain the State monopoly. The Beveridge Committee, of 1949 and 1951, also discussed the topic, and once again they advocated a monopoly situation. Some members, however, did feel that there was a need to break that monopoly.

The pressure for commercial television increased, so that within four years the Independent Television Authority (ITA) was formed. The ITA started in 1955, with finance for its activities coming from advertisers who paid to have commercials transmitted.

The nation now had a choice in viewing, but not in their radio entertainment, with the BBC maintaining its monopoly. The interest in records and music was increasing, it was now the 1950s, the Rock and Roll era had commenced. The Government authorised yet another committee to discuss the future policy in sound broadcasting. The Pilkington Committee sat in 1960, they recommended that a sustained trial for commercial radio was justified, but they added that there was no demand for such a service.

The Government issued a White Paper, in July 1962, in which they declared that they would like to gauge public opinion before reaching a decision. As they had not issued a new licence to a broadcaster, and the BBC did not carry commercials, it was impossible to gauge reaction to something that did not exist.

A second White Paper was issued in December 1962, in which the Government admitted that there might be a latent interest in local commercial radio. They also added that they would consider the subject again, at a later date, as it was not an important issue.

It was against this background, of sitting on the fence, that an ambitious young man left his native Ireland, to make his fortune in London. That man was Ronan O'Rahilly, who moved to this country in 1961. He was the son of an Irish businessman who operated a ferry linking Preston to Greenore, a port which he later purchased from British Railways.

Ronan's grandfather had been shot dead by British soldiers, during an uprising in Dublin, during 1916. Such was his notoriety that the Irish poet and dramatist, William Butler Yeats (1865-1939), wrote a poem about him. That poem, *The O'Rahilly*, is reproduced opposite.

Ronan's main interests were music and acting, on arrival in this country he established an actors school called Studio 61. He also opened the Scene Club, which soon became the place to be. Alexis Korner played there, as did the, as yet unknown, Rolling Stones.

Ronan was trying to get airtimefor another unknown (who went on to fame and fortune), Georgie Fame. Ronan soon found that the recording industry was governed by four major companies, EMI, Decca, Pye and Phillips.

These four companies also controlled radio air time, and record distribution. He approached each of the companies, in turn, to see if they would record Georgie, but he met with no success.

He decided to make his own recording, and approached Radio Luxembourg (Fab 208) to see if they would play the record. They refused, saying that they could not play a record from an independent label as all of their air time was sponsored by the major companies.

Down, but not defeated, Ronan approached the BBC, but they told him that they only played the music of established artists. Now here was a dilemma, if a major company will not record you, and existing radio stations would not give air time to independents, how could you become established?

A chance conversation informed Ronan of the existence of a pirate radio station, broadcasting from a ship, which was anchored off the Dutch coast. Ronan found out all that he could regarding this unusual radio station, which was called Radio Veronica.

As for Georgie Fame, his first record *Yeh Yeh* entered the Top 40 on 11th December, 1964, at number 26. It spent a total of 12 weeks in the charts, with two of those at number 1, from 7th January, 1965. He went on to have 12 more records in the Top 40, including two more number 1s: *Get Away* in June 1966, and *The Ballad of Bonnie and Clyde*, in December 1967.

Ronan O'Rahilly.   *Doug Mackenzie*

Chapter One

Arrival of the Pirate Ships

Offshore radio came to Europe in 1958, and in terms of popularity, with its listeners, it could not have been more successful. The various Governments of Europe were, however, united in their determination to rid the airwaves, of these latter day pirates.

A group of Danish businessmen set up a company to oversee the project. An advertising agency, based in Liechtenstein, purchased a small ship, which they registered in Panama. The ex-German fishing vessel, of 107 tons, was converted in total secrecy at a Danish port.

Whilst the conversion was taking place, a studio was constructed in Copenhagen. The ship was ready, and on Friday 11th July, 1958 she sailed to an anchorage in international waters, off Copenhagen. The ship, which had been named *Cheeta*, commenced test transmissions using the callsign 'Radio Mercur'.

Using a 1½ kilowatt transmitter, the tests were made on 93.12 mHz VHF. A directional aerial was mounted on top of the mast, and was kept pointing in the right direction by means of a manual control in the control room.

During the evening of Thursday 17th July, the radio ship lost its anchor and drifted, eventually running aground on the coast of Sweden, near Malmo. The *Cheeta* was refloated, by a salvage tug, which then towed her into the port of Limhamn, for repairs.

The *Cheeta* returned to her anchorage, having been repaired, and commenced regular broadcasts on Saturday 2nd August. The Danish authorities were far from happy with the situation and requested that Radio Mercur cease broadcasts, not surprisingly they did not comply.

The station did, however, change frequency to 89.55 FM, when the owners found out that they were causing interference to a Swedish radio station. On Friday 29th August Panama withdrew registration of the *Cheeta*, at the request of the Danish Government.

This action, far from deterring Radio Mercur, seemed to prompt them. Just two days later, on Sunday 31st August, the station commenced a Swedish language programme, which was aired from midday until 2 pm, using the callsign 'Skanes Radio Mercur'.

The Danish authorities became increasingly annoyed with the station, as it grew in popularity, but there was nothing that they could do. Radio Mercur had started attracting advertising contracts, which helped to finance better quality programmes and increase the efficiency of the transmissions.

The success of Europe's first offshore radio station did not go unnoticed by others, and in 1959 a group of Dutch businessmen held a meeting in an Amsterdam hotel. The result of this meeting was that they formed a Liechtenstein-based company, Vrije Radio Omroep Nederland(VRON) which purchased an ex-German lightship.

The *Borkum Riff* was converted for her new role. When the work was completed she was towed out of the German port of Emden, to an anchorage off the Dutch resort of Katwijk ann Zee.

Europe's first pirate radio ship, the 107 ton *Cheeta*, which commenced broadcasting on 11th July, 1958. The directional aerial can be seen at the top of the mast. *Scandia Photopress*

Test transmissions from Radio Veronica commenced on Wednesday 30th March, 1960, on 185 metres (1640 kHz). Regular broadcasts commenced on Friday 6th May, but the transmissions caused interference to Dutch coastal communications. In retaliation the Dutch authorities authorised the jamming of Radio Veronica.

The station moved to 182 metres (1640 kHz), but this made the situation even worse, so the station shut down. Transmissions resumed on Sunday 15th May, on 192 metres (1562 kHz), which solved the problem. However, the station was experiencing financial problems; in spite of having in excess of 5 million listeners, advertisers could not be persuaded to use the station, causing financial hardship.

In the meantime, Radio Mercur was going from strength to strength. The station was now making so much, from advertising, that it was able to purchase a second radio ship. The 450 ton ship was renamed *Cheeta II*, and it commenced broadcasting on Tuesday 31st January, 1961, using 88 mHz FM.

Three weeks later, a third radio ship commenced test broadcasts from the Baltic. The *Bon Jour* was anchored in international waters, off the coast of Stockholm, and was called Radio Nord.

The project had started way back in November 1959, but it had been beset with problems right from the outset. In May 1960 the promoters had purchased a small coaster called the *Olga*, which was for sale in the German port of Kiel. The ship had been built as a three-masted schooner, in 1921, by Deutsche Werke A.G., Kiel. In 1927 she underwent major rebuilding, when she was converted from sail, and her length was increased by 36 feet to 134 feet; at the same time she was renamed *Margarethe*.

Conversion work started at the German port of Hamburg where the ship was renamed *Bon Jour*, and she was registered in Nicaragua. After two months, the German authorities started to take an interest in the ship, so it was decided to leave and she sailed to Copenhagen.

The ship was fitted with a 125 ft mast, and equipped with two 10 kilowatt transmitters, which were flown in from Continental Electronics in America. The ship sailed on 20th December, 1960, but it experienced all kinds of problems. Just five days later the crew abandoned ship when they encountered heavy seas, thinking the mast was going to collapse. The crew rejoined ship the next day, and eventually it was taken to a port in Finland for repairs.

Repairs were completed, and the *Bon Jour* sailed on Saturday 4th February, but once again the ship encountered heavy seas, which caused damage to the aerial. She entered the port of Stockholm three days later to have repairs carried out, and whilst there they very cheekily broadcast a test transmission.

On Tuesday 21st February, 1961 test transmissions were broadcast which continued for a few days, but once again there were problems with the aerial, which necessitated another visit to port. The ship returned to its anchorage on Wednesday 1st March, which was just as well, because the very next day the Swedish Government introduced legislation that empowered them to seize any ship with unauthorised transmitting equipment, if it entered territorial waters.

Radio Nord commenced test transmissions on 495 metres (606 kHz) where they encountered interference, so they made a slight change to 498 metres (602 kHz) but continued to advertise the fact that they were on 495.

The *Cheeta II* was Europe's third pirate radio ship when it commenced radio broadcasts on 31st January, 1961. The ship was home to Radio Mercur, who then sold it to Mrs Wadner, and it became home for Radio Syd. Of the four ships to have broadcast from the Baltic, she was the only one to survive after 16th August, 1962. This view shows the ship whilst anchored off the coast of England. *Sky Fotos*

Whilst these tests were in progress, Nicaragua withdrew the ship's registration, at the behest of the Swedish Government. Undeterred the owners applied for Panamanian registration. Panama agreed, but the ship had to change its name, the owners selecting *Magda Maria*. Radio Nord then commenced normal programming, from Wednesday 8th March, 1961, at 10 am.

Meanwhile, at Radio Mercur things were not going very smoothly. Members of staff were not agreed on broadcasting policy, which led to a parting of the ways. The breakaway group purchased a 240 ton coaster, which they renamed *Lucky Star*, anchoring the radio ship off the Danish coast, near Copenhagen.

The new station was called Danmarks Commercielle Radio (DCR), and it commenced broadcasts on 93.97 mHz FM on Friday 15th September. The programmes were pre-recorded in a Copenhagen studio, and then taken to the ship for broadcasting. The content comprised a mix of light music, opera and plays, the station being on the air for seven hours per day, starting at 3 pm.

Radio Mercur, meanwhile, had sent the *Cheeta* to Norway for repairs and servicing. She recommenced broadcasts on Saturday 25th November, from a location between the islands of Zeeland and Fünen. During stormy conditions, in December, the aerial collapsed. Repairs were made but the *Cheeta* exchanged places with the *Cheeta II*, for a more protected anchorage.

December 1961 proved to be a very stormy month. Radio Mercur had, as we have just seen, experienced problems with the *Cheeta I*, it was Radio Nord's turn next. During the morning of Wednesday 6th December, the *Magda Maria* parted from her anchor, allowing the ship to drift. Radio Nord continued to broadcast, even though the ship's engine could not be started! During the evening they eventually managed to start the engine, but in the meantime one of the aerial support wires had broken.

In spite of the Swedish legislation, the ship had to enter port, so that repairs could be carried out. Proving that the Swedish Government were not party wreckers, they decided not to impound the ship and allowed the repairs to continue. The *Magda Maria* was allowed to sail, two days later, and Radio Nord resumed transmissions.

The programmes from DCR were not proving to be very popular, so the operators held discussions with Radio Mercur, which resulted in the two stations merging, on Monday 29th January, 1962. Just two weeks later, the *Cheeta I* got into difficulties during stormy weather.

A tug responded to her calls for assistance, towing the stricken ship into Copenhagen on Monday 12th February, where it was detained by the Danish authorities. Having acquired the *Lucky Star*, as a result of the merger with DCR, Radio Mercur used that ship to replace the *Cheeta I*.

Radio Mercur decided to sell the *Cheeta I*, and it was purchased by Mrs Britt Wadner, who had been programme director for Radio Mercur's Swedish language service. Surprisingly, the Danes allowed the ship to sail, and within a few days it was anchored in international waters, off Malmo. The *Cheeta I* was now the home for Radio Syd, which broadcast on FM 88.3.

On Thursday 14th June, 1962, the Danish Government introduced legislation to outlaw the offshore radio stations, Parliament passing the proposals with a majority of 45. The Swedish Parliament had also made similar legislation, during May 1962. The Danes decided to hold talks with their Scandanavian neighbours, before setting a date for the implementation.

The Swedish Government hosted the discussions, on Tuesday 3rd July, in Stockholm. Representatives from Denmark, Finland, Norway and Sweden agreed to implement the new legislation, in a joint process which would come into force on Wednesday 1st August, 1962.

Radio Nord, which had been planning to introduce an FM service in July decided to cancel the project. The station owners held discussions with some business people who were interested in buying the *Magda Maria*, as a result Radio Nord closed down on Saturday 30th June, 1962. The radio ship remained at anchor for a few days, and then sailed away from the Baltic, arriving in the Spanish port of El Ferrol on Thursday 2nd August.

Radio Mercur ceased broadcasts from the *Cheeta II* on Tuesday 10th July, the ship sailing to a German port where it was sold to Mrs Wadner. The *Cheeta II* then sailed to an anchorage off Malmo, Sweden, to be used by Radio Syd.

The *Lucky Star* continued to broadcast for Radio Mercur, but this station closed down at midnight on Tuesday 31st July. The ship remained at anchor, but on Monday 13th August it resumed broadcasting old Radio Mercur tapes. The owners claimed that they had hired the ship to another operator. Three days later the ship was boarded, and silenced, by Danish police officers.

The ship was escorted into port, where it was detained, until it could be established who owned the vessel. Of the Baltic pirates, only Radio Syd was still broadcasting.

Meanwhile, out on the North Sea, Radio Veronica was becoming very popular, with estimated earnings of £1 million from advertising. In February 1961, the station experimented with an English language service, using the callsign CNBC Commercial Neutral Broadcasting Company.

The programmes were broadcast for two hours daily, commencing at 7 am, although this was extended to five hours, starting at 8 am. The contact address was given as Ross Radio, London W1, although a, recording studio was constructed at Veronica's premises in Holland. CNBC, did not last for long, as their London representative did not obtain sufficient advertising.

In spite of the action taken against the Baltic stations, the Dutch did nothing to stop Radio Veronica which was soon to be joined by another radio ship broadcasting from the North Sea. A Belgium radio engineer purchased the 585 ton supply ship, *Crocodile*. The 70 ft, ex-French Navy vessel, was renamed *Uilenspiegel*, and underwent conversion in the Dutch port of Amsterdam. On completion the ship sailed to an anchorage off Zeebrugge, where transmissions commenced on Friday 12th October, 1962.

This new station was called Radio Antwerpen, and it broadcast on 1492 kHz medium wave from 7 am until midnight. Programmes were in Flemish, except for a short programme in French. Such was the success of the station, the owner commenced broadcasts in the 41 metre short wave band, on 7600 kHz.

In November the aerial mast was damaged, but this was quickly repaired and the station resumed broadcasts. During December, the station owner died and, within a few days, so did his station. Gale force winds lashed the radio ship, waking the staff in the early hours of the morning of Sunday 16th December.

They found that the ship was leaking which had caused damage to the transmitters.

Just after 1 pm when the crew realised that the ship was adrift, they broadcast an emergency message, and within the hour a Belgian lifeboat was alongside. The lifeboat set about rescuing the crew, and it was soon joined by a tug, by which time the radio ship was less than a mile off the shore.

The lifeboat transferred six of the 10 persons from the ship, but it developed engine trouble and had to return to port. The tug, meanwhile, had attached a tow rope, so the crew were not in immediate danger.

In worsening conditions the tow rope parted so the crew of the tug rescued the four persons, leaving the *Uilenspiegel* to its fate. The radio ship eventually ran aground on the Dutch coast, near Cadzand, but was never salvaged. For nine years it was left on the beach, until being blown up by the Dutch authorities.

So, by 1963, the situation was that of the four ships to have broadcast from the Baltic, only one survived, and only one of the two North Sea ships was still on the air. Ronan found that there were plans to establish a pirate station off the English Coast.

Ronan met with an Australian businessman, Allan Crawford, who was a director of Merit Music in London. Mr Crawford had started a company, Project Atlanta, with which he hoped to operate the radio station, so as to broadcast cover versions of chart hits.

Project Atlanta had been negotiating for the ex-Radio Nord ship, the *Magda Maria*, which had sailed to Spain after that station had closed in June 1962. Whilst the ship underwent refurbishment, its name was changed to *Mi Amigo* (my friend).

Backing for this project fell through, so the *Mi Amigo* sailed to Galveston in Texas, where work commenced on decommissioning her soon after her arrival on Saturday 9th March, 1963. With new backers, Mr Crawford's Project Atlanta obtained the *Mi Amigo* from its owners, Atlantic Services Anstalt, Liechtenstein.

On 28th December, the *Mi Amigo* battered its way back across the Atlantic, in appalling conditions, eventually arriving at Gran Canaria's port of Las Palmas on 30th January, 1964. After repairs had been carried out the ship sailed to El Ferrol, on Wednesday 5th February, 1964.

Chapter Two

The British Corsairs,
1964-1968

"I originally had shipbrokers all over the world and eventually we homed in on this ex-Danish ship, the engines and everything were in immaculate condition, and it looked good. We started negotiating with them, but out of the blue they sent a telex basically saying, 'we understand this ship may be used for an offshore radio ship'. They wanted guarantees that the ship would not be used for such a purpose included in the contract, The Danish Government would have been embarassed if Radio Fredericia had started up off the Danish Coast.

We dropped negotiations with those brokers, and went to another company. We convinced them that we were going to carry cattle in the passenger accommodation – it made no sense unless you're a complete loony! They believed it so no clause was inserted into the contract".

Ronan O'Rahilly, January 1973

1964

Top 20 for week commencing Friday 27th March, 1964

1	(8)	*Can't Buy Me Love*	Beatles
2	(1)	*Little Children*	Billy J. Kramer and the Dakotas
3	(2)	*Just One Look*	Hollies
4	(3)	*Not Fade Away*	Rolling Stones
5	(5)	*I Love You Because*	Jim Reeves
6	(11)	*I Believe*	Bachelors
7	(6)	*Bits And Pieces*	Dave Clark Five
8	(10)	*Diane*	Bachelors
9	(7)	*That Girl Belongs To Yesterday*	Gene Pitney
10	(4)	*Anyone Who Had A Heart*	Cilla Black
11	(12)	*Tell Me When*	Applejacks
12	(9)	*Boys Cry*	Eden Kane
13	(16)	*World Without Love*	Peter and Gordon
14	(13)	*Theme For Young Lovers*	Shadows
15	(14)	*I Think Of You*	Merseybeats
16	(21)	*Over You*	Freddie and the Dreamers
17	(15)	*Let Me Go Lover*	Kathy Kirby
18	(20)	*Viva Las Vegas*	Elvis Presley
19	(17)	*Stay Awhile*	Dusty Springfield
20	(23)	*Good Golly Miss Molly*	Swinging Blue Jeans

Floating a Dream

Project Atlanta had thought that Ronan might become an investor, but that was not to be the case. Instead, through his own company, Planet Productions, he set about finding finance for his own station. With backing of £250,000 from Irish, British and Swiss sources, a suitable ship was found

On December 30th 1963 the MV *Fredericia* was purchased by Cross Channel Container Services Ltd (Ronan O'Rahilly) Greenore Harbour, for £20,000. It had been stated that the ship was to be renamed *Iselut,* and be used on an Ireland-UK service. Instead it was transferred to Astrenic S.A. (Ronan o'Rahilly), Panama.

The 693-ton passenger ferry had been built by Frederikshaven Voerft & Flydeok A/S, and launched on November 14th 1929, for the Danish company DFDS (The United Steamship Company). It sailed on services based out of Copenhagen, until finally being laid up on August 8th 1963. On Thursday 13th February 1964, on behalf of her new owners, it was towed from Rotterdam to Greenore.

During the following weeks the port was a hive of industry, as the ship was prepared for its new role, which included adding 300 tons of concrete ballast. The conversion proceeded under a cloak of secrecy, the locals being informed that the ship was for marine/weather research.

Meanwhile, the *Mi Amigo* had been fitted with bilge keels, to increase her stability. Ronan invited Mr Crawford to move his boat to Greenore to try and minimise the risk of the radio ships being detected. The *Mi Amigo* left Spain on Tuesday 3rd March, 1964, and was berthed at the same quay as the *Fredericia.*

Ronan flew to America to purchase transmitters from Continental Electronics, in Dallas, Texas. Whilst on the flight he saw a photograph, in a magazine, of the late President John F. Kennedy playing in the Oval Office with his daughter Caroline. It was at that moment that Ronan decided on the name for his station, Radio Caroline.

The transmitters were flown to Ireland, and installed in the ship, which was also renamed MV *Caroline,* and registered in Panama. Both of the ships were fitted with aluminium masts, which had been designed by Spencer Rigging, from the Isle of Wight.

Both Ronan and Allan knew that the first station to go on the air would make history, and possibly attract more advertisers. Both men wanted their ship to be the first, and both wanted to anchor in the Thames Estuary, so that they could broadcast to London and the South East.

The *Caroline* was fitted with a 168 ft-tall mast, which had been made in Southampton. The mast had to be heavily insulated, against the effects of salt spray and the damp sea conditions. The build up of salt deposits could seriously affect the transmission efficiency, and in extreme conditions stop all broadcasts.

Two, Continental Electronics, 10 kilowatt transmitters were installed, these being crystal controlled so as to avoid, as far as possible, causing interference to other broadcasts. The transmitters were driven by Mercedes Benz generators, two of which had been installed.

The studio was equipped with two, gimble mounted, transcription record players, two Ampex tape machines, and a mixer panel. Following a night time raid of the *Mi Amigo,* three Spotmaster cassettes suddenly appeared.

Radio Atlanta had taken expert advice into the frequency on which they were to broadcast, and the position in which the *Mi Amigo* would anchor. The frequency was to be 197 metres (1520 kHz), and the location was off Clacton on Sea. The frequency of 197 was chosen because it was near to Radio Veronica on 192, and the nearest other transmitter on that frequency was in Spain and another in Czechoslovakia.

The *Caroline* was to broadcast on 201 metres (1495 kHz); very cheekily a test transmission was broadcast whilst still in port, but this caused heavy

The MV *Caroline* prepares to leave the port of Greenore in March 1964.

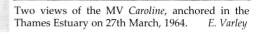

Two views of the MV *Caroline*, anchored in the Thames Estuary on 27th March, 1964.　　*E. Varley*

interference to Irish television. Caroline's very first broadcast consisted of music from Ray Charles.

The race really was on, both organisations were trying to mislead each other as to the state of readiness. As the work continued the *Mi Amigo* had to leave its berth to make way for a coaster, owned by Ronan's father. For a week the ship lay at anchor, during which time a storm blew up causing the ship to drag its anchor, and it very nearly ran aground.

Inevitably, leaks about the two radio ships fitting out in Ireland reached the ears of the British Government. Their first reaction was to proclaim such a venture illegal, to which Ronan replied, 'We have taken legal advice, our company is registered in Switzerland, under international law they cannot touch us'.

Under the supervision of Arthur Carrington, who had worked for the BBC and the Marconi Company, all of the radio equipment was installed. Mr Carrington was an acknowledged expert who had been responsible for Britain's first undersea and aerial television broadcasts.

The engineers were instructed to make six-hourly checks, on at least 40 measurements to ensure that peak performance was maintained. Modulation had to be constantly monitored, to ensure that there were no peaks above 90%, which could distort Caroline's signal, or cause spurious transmissions to interfere with other stations.

The Panamanian-registered MV *Caroline* had a Dutch crew of 10, which included the captain, cook and stewards. They worked a rota of six weeks on, one week off. The first skipper was Captain Baeker, who left after a short time, to be replaced by Captain G.E. Mackay.

Bill Scaddon was appointed as the Harwich agent, and Anglia Marine Agencies Ltd were contracted to service the ship from the Essex port. The tender *Offshore 1*, a converted Dutch fishing vessel, was used to exchange DJs and deliver supplies and mail. The tender also made regular crossings to Holland, to exchange crew, and to obtain duty free items.

Every aspect of the operation was checked, so that nothing was left to chance. Some decisions, such as how much fuel, food and water would be consumed, could only be made once the ship was at anchor.

To handle the day to day running of the ship, and to organise mail and advertising, an office with a small recording studio was opened at 52 Fetter Lane, London. The building was also occupied by *Queen* magazine whose owner, Mr Jocelyn Stevens, became a director of Planet Productions.

Almost everything was now ready, jingles and station ID tapes had been recorded, the music library was well stocked, and the DJs had signed on. The ship had been fuelled, and water and provisions had been stowed. Ronan had completely mislead Allan Crawford, so it came as a big surprise when the *Caroline* slipped her moorings and sailed away into the history books.

The radio ship sailed from Greenore on Monday 23rd March, giving Spain as her destination, but she rounded Land's End, and headed into the English Channel. A Royal Navy warship escorted her for a short time, but it turned away near Plymouth, the rest of the voyage was uneventful.

At 7 pm on Good Friday, 27th March, the MV *Caroline* anchored 3½ miles off Felixstowe, in an area known as the Wallet Channel. It was a dark and stormy

Portrait of Chris Moore.   *Author's Collection*

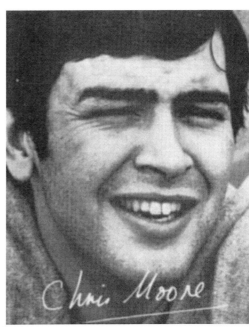

Portrait of Simon Dee.   *Author's Collection*

night that greeted the *Caroline*, gale force winds had made for a rough sea, and there was driving rain.

Two test transmissions were made that night, one lasting for 15 minutes, the second lasting for an hour. Chris Moore was the first voice to be heard, during those tests which were broadcast on 201 metres (1495 kHz), and the first record was *Around Midnight* by Jimmy McGriff.

Radio Caroline officially opened at midday, on Saturday 28th March, 1964, but on a new wavelength, 197 metres (1520 kHz). Simon Dee announced, 'This is Radio Caroline on 199, your all day music station. We are on the air every day, from 6 in the morning, until 6 at night. The time right now is 1 minute past 12, which means it's time for Christopher Moore.'

'Hello, and Happy Easter, to all of you. This is Christopher Moore, with the first record programme on Radio Caroline. The first record is by the Rolling Stones, and I'd like to play it for all of the people who worked to put the station on the air, and particularly Ronan.'

That first record was Not Fade Away, Radio Caroline had won the race to become Britain's first offshore radio station. To rub salt into Radio Atlanta's wound, Caroline was even using the frequency that they had planned to use.

During the afternoon transmissions stopped, and it was not until midday on Sunday 29th March that the station returned. Simon Dee re-opened the station. 'Good afternoon Ladies and Gentlemen, you are tuned to Radio Caroline on 199, your all day music station. We will be on the air until 6 o'clock.' The first record to be played was *Can't Buy me Love*, by the Beatles.

On Monday 30th March, Trinity House complained that Caroline was causing interference to lightship communications. As a direct result ship to shore radio telephone services for the MV *Caroline* were withdrawn, except for emergencies.

During that first week of broadcasting the International Telecommunications Union (ITU), who control the world's broadcasting frequencies, met with Panamanian officials. This led to Panama withdrawing the MV *Caroline's* registration, on Tuesday 7th April.

On the same day, a statement was read by the Postmaster General in the House of Commons. He informed the House that the Government were considering a number of options, including the jamming of Caroline's broadcasts.

One Conservative MP asked who the station was harming. The Postmaster replied that Caroline had caused interference to maritime broadcasts in this country, and in the area of Antwerp. The Belgian Government had registered a complaint, on the same day as Trinity House.

The Government may not have taken to this pirate of the airwaves, but the listeners could not have been more pleased. Within the first few days, Caroline had achieved more than anyone could have imagined. On Wednesday 1st April, Caroline's tender delivered nine sacks of mail, more then 20,000 letters. This is made even more astounding, when you consider the almost total secrecy surrounding preparations.

Concerned at the reports that Caroline had been causing interference, Mr Carrington went out to the ship to see if he could assist the engineers to solve the problems. Radio Caroline is not the only station to have caused interference, even the BBC has had problems. But it was obvious that Caroline, as a new and

The *Margarethe* was built in 1921 by Deutsche Werft AG, Kiel, West Germany. She was a three-masted schooner, her steel hull was 98 ft in length, and she was 156 tons. In 1927 she was sold, and converted to a motor vessel, her hull was cut and a new 36 ft section was inserted, increasing her tonnage to 274 tons. She was renamed *Olga*. During World War II she was commandeered by the German Navy, and was used used as a landing craft, complete with bow door. She was in service from 1941 to 1943 before resuming her career. In 1959 she was sold to the Superior Shipping Corp., who renamed her *Bon Jour*, and registered her in Nicaragua. The ship was converted for use as a radio ship, partly in Hamburg, and completed in Copenhagen. Transmissions from Radio Nord commenced in February 1961. The ship's registration was revoked in Nicaragua, so she was reregistered with Panama and renamed *Magda Maria*. Radio Nord closed in 1962 and sold the ship, which was renamed *Mi Amigo*. She started broadcasts with Radio Atlanta in April 1964, and passed to Radio Caroline two months later.

Coastal Cards

unauthorised station, would come in for heavy criticism. It also became clear that the radio ship's anchorage was not so good, she was not on good holding ground, and she was too near the shipping lanes, so the ship was moved by about 1 mile, in April.

The *Offshore 1*, which was owned and operated by the Dutch salvage company, Wijsmuller, was also meeting with some problems. The Customs and Immigration services enforced the ruling that, as the radio ship was outside territorial waters, the personnel were technically leaving the country and passports had to be shown.

Meanwhile, whilst Radio Caroline was basking in the glory, Radio Atlanta was still at Greenore. The new mast had been delivered and preparations were being completed. The *Mi Amigo* finally sailed on Monday 20th April, stating that her destination was Spain.

Right from the start, things had not gone smoothly for Project Atlanta, and they were soon to encounter more problems. The ship encountered heavy seas off Land's End, which resulted in damage to the rigging of the mast. The mast had been swaying so much that a shackle broke and the mast was in danger of collapse.

The Captain tried to make a link call to Ireland, but the Post Office radio station at Land's End refused to handle the call. The skipper called the French station, Brest Radio, who allowed the call to be made.

The *Mi Amigo* entered the port of Falmouth, where rigger Harry Spencer made the necessary repairs, the ship leaving on 23rd April. On Monday 27th April the *Mi Amigo* anchored 3½ miles off Walton on Naze, 14 miles from the MV *Caroline*.

At 6 pm that same day a test transmission was made on the frequency used by Radio Caroline, 197 metres. The test started as Caroline closed down for the night. Listeners were informed that this was a test transmission from Radio Atlanta, and that normal programming would soon commence, on 201 metres.

The station still had many problems to overcome, and it was not until Saturday 9th May that testing resumed. Radio Atlanta officially opened on Tuesday 12th May. Australian Tony Withers welcomed listeners to Radio Atlanta, 'On our very first day, our champers day, bringing you brighter broadcasting, with some of the finest sounds around'.

Radio Caroline, meanwhile, was becoming increasingly popular, to such an extent that broadcasting hours were increased by four hours, the new timings being from 6 am until 10 pm. The hours were changed again so that the station was on the air from 6 am until 9 pm and again from midnight until 3 am.

In spite of this meteoric climb to fame, the station had yet to broadcast its first advert. It was not until Friday 1st May that Woburn Abbey became Caroline's first client. An opinion poll was published on Saturday 9th May, which revealed that Radio Caroline had a staggering 7 million listeners over the age of 18.

As a result of the poll, potential advertisers decided not to wait any longer. On the very day that Radio Atlanta commenced broadcasting, Radio Caroline obtained £30,000 of advertising contracts.

Nobody could have imagined the incredible response that Caroline had evoked, but it was hardly surprising; there was a cultural revolution taking place, but no one was catering for it. There had, of course, been the night time broadcasts from Radio Luxembourg on 208, but the reception was pretty diabolical.

Radio Invicta was Britain's fourth pirate radio station, broadcasting on 306 metres. The station took over the long abandoned Red Sands Fort. *Sky Fotos*

The other problem with Luxembourg was that they only played part of the record, maybe a minute or a minute and a half, and just as you started to enjoy the record it was stopped. The station was also commercial, who can forget such adverts as, Horace Bachelor, Keynsham, that's K-E-Y-N-S-H-A-M, Bristol?

Now there was not just one, but two, alternatives broadcasting for 12 hours each day. During May, just eight weeks from opening, Caroline doubled her power, from 10 to 20 kilowatts, the same as Radio Atlanta.

With the increase in power, Radio Caroline agreed to pay royalties to the Performing Rights Society, who look after the interests of composers, artists and publishers, for copyright protection. Radio Atlanta also made the same agreement, on 26th May.

One of the many criticisms levelled against the pirate stations was that, unlike their onshore counterparts, they had no restrictions on needle time. That is to say that some time should be devoted to live broadcasts, and it was felt that this could seriously affect the live performers.

To stop this particular complaint, Radio Caroline decided to try a live broadcast. During May, Ronan had a meeting with keyboard player Jimmy Smith. He agreed to perform on board the *Caroline*, with fellow musicians, Tony Thorpe and Tony Crombie. Their instruments, a Hammond organ, a set of drums and a guitar were carefully crated, and loaded onto the tender.

The musicians climbed onto the radio ship, and the crates were winched aboard, where it was found that the organ was too large to fit through the doors, into the accommodation. Having come this far, no one was willing to admit defeat, so the musicians agreed to do the concert out on the open deck.

Luckily, the weather remained fine, so that at 5 pm that evening the first live music was broadcast from the MV *Caroline*. In spite of the obvious disadvantages, of performing in the open air, it proved a successful venture. However, due to the technical problems that were encountered, live broadcasts were not attempted again.

Just two weeks after Radio Atlanta had officially opened, Britain's third pirate station set sail. In a blaze of publicity, pop singer Screaming Lord Sutch (who later went on to found the Monster Raving Loony Party, and who died in 1999) sailed down the River Thames, in a 60 ft fishing vessel.

His manager, Mr Reg Calvert, insisted that this was no publicity stunt, they were going to start a radio station. They had invested £4,000 in the project, which they were estimating to cost around £300 per week.

The next day the fishing vessel was tied alongside the long disused Army fort, at Shivering Sands, in the Thames Estuary. Radio Sutch commenced broadcasts the next day, Wednesday 27th May, transmitting on 194 metres (1542 kHz) for 7 hours each day.

Pirate number four started test transmissions one week later, on Wednesday 3rd June, from the Red Sands Fort. During the tests, Radio Invicta tried many wavelengths, opting for 306 metres when regular programming commenced on Friday 17th July.

Both of these fort-based stations were low powered, and on a small budget, and could not hope to compete against Radio Caroline or Radio Atlanta. It was, however, the start of an offshore radio boom the like of which had never been seen before, or after. The corsairs were gathering for an assault on the airwaves, and the eardrums of Britain.

Top 20 for week commencing Friday 3rd July, 1964

1	(6)	House Of The Rising Sun	Animals
2	(25)	It's All Over Now	Rolling Stones
3	(5)	Hold Me	P.J. Proby
4	(2)	Someone Someone	Tremeloes
5	(1)	It's Over	Roy Orbison
6	(4)	Ramona	Bachelors
7	(3)	You're No Good	Swinging Blue Jeans
8	(12)	I Won't Forget You	Jim Reeves
9	(8)	Hello Dolly	Louis Armstrong
10	(17)	Kissin' Cousins	Elvis Presley
11	(10)	Nobody I Know	Peter and Gordon
12	(9)	My Guy	Mary Wells
13	(31)	On The Beach	Cliff Richard
14	(11)	Can't You See That She's Mine	Dave Clark Five
15	(7)	You're My World	Cilla Black
16	(14)	Here I Go Again	Hollies
17	(13)	Shout	Lulu and the Luvvers
18	(-)	I Just Don't Know What To Do With Myself	Dusty Springfield
19	(15)	Rise and Fall of Flingel Bunt	Shadows
20	(18)	Hello Dolly	Frankie Vaughan

The Merger

With four stations broadcasting, the Liberal MP for North Devon, Mr Jeremy Thorpe, proposed taking action against the stations, and their listeners. Mr Thorpe tried to introduce a Bill, which had the support of a handful of MPs of all political persuasions.

He told the House that all commercial radio stations should be registered by the Government. He told the Postmaster General that by not withdrawing the licences of those who listened to the pirates, he was in fact condoning their actions.

Mr Thorpe added that as Panama had withdrawn registration, the radio ships could be seized, as they were no longer protected by Panamanian laws. He added that everyone found on the ships should be prosecuted, for being connected with illegal broadcasts.

The Bill, not surprisingly, did not get Government backing, and therefore did not succeed. To revoke the licence of the listeners it would have to be proved that they had deliberately tuned into the broadcast, for if they had found the station by accident they could not be prosecuted. At the time there were over 7 million listeners, to have proved every case would have been almost impossible, it was an unworkable proposition.

If Mr Thorpe had hoped to intimidate the offshore stations it did not work, in fact it was business as usual. At the same time, rumours circulated that Caroline and Atlanta were going to merge; both stations were competing for the same audience, so it made sense to try and reach a deal.

On Thursday 2nd July, a joint statement was released to the press which read:

The Directors of Project Atlanta and Planet Productions Ltd, today issued a joint statement, announcing a merger between Radio Atlanta and Radio Caroline. The companies are responsible for the advertising, and selling of time, on the two offshore commercial radio stations.

Mr Allan Crawford, Managing Director of Project Atlanta, and Mr Ronan O'Rahilly, Managing Director of Planet Productions, will become joint Managing Directors of the new operation.

The ship broadcasting the present Radio Caroline programmes, MV *Caroline*, will sail to the Isle of Man tomorrow morning, to a position 5 miles from Ramsey, Isle of Man. It will continue to broadcast Radio Caroline on the way to its destination, and will remain on 199 metres medium wave.

The ship MV *Atlanta* will continue broadcasting to the Greater London area, and south-east England, under the national callsign Radio Caroline.

It was stated that the reason for the merger had been the result of 'The enormous interest from the public and advertisers, in other parts of England, outside the original broadcasting area'.

Many years later, Ronan said that Radio Atlanta had run into serious money problems, and that the Wijsmuller company, who operated the tender and supply service, were considering closing the station down. They intended to sell the *Mi Amigo* to recoup some of what they were owed, but before taking such drastic action they asked Ronan if he would take over the project.

Whatever the real reason for the merger, Radio Atlanta closed at 8 pm on Thursday 2nd July, 1964. The MV *Caroline* raised anchor and sailed to the *Mi Amigo*, so that DJs and equipment could be exchanged. Ronan and Allan both went out to the *Mi Amigo*, that evening, to explain the finer details.

Whilst on the radio ship it was explained that the MV *Caroline* that would sail to the new position, off the Isle of Man. It was the larger of the two ships, and it could expect to experience rougher conditions than the *Mi Amigo* would have to endure.

As from 6 am on Friday 3rd July, Radio Caroline South started broadcasting from the *Mi Amigo*. The station kept Atlanta's frequency of 201 metres (1493 kHz), broadcast hours were 6 am until 8 pm, using the callsign 'Caroline on 199'.

The MV *Caroline* commenced her voyage, from the Thames, at midnight and started broadcasting at 6 am, giving details of the voyage and her location. Transmissions were on 197 metres (1520 kHz), using the 20 kW transmitter, and the callsign 'Caroline' on 199.

On Sunday 5th July, the *Caroline* passed the north Cornish coast, the next day she crossed the Irish Sea, to a position off Dublin. She then sailed to a position five miles off Ramsey, anchoring on the Bahama Bank, on Monday 13th July.

To undertake the day-to-day running of the two ships, it was decided to move to a new office, suitable premises being found at 6 Chesterfield Gardens, London W1. The building was renamed Caroline House, and a small studio was constructed, for the recording of adverts and jingles.

The mailing address for Radio Caroline North was PO Box 3, Ramsey, Isle of Man, and a northern office was opened at 61 Lord Street, Liverpool 2. In September, a survey revealed that Caroline North had an audience of 17 million, whilst Caroline South had 15 million.

Radio Caroline was going from strength to strength, but over in the Baltic, life was getting hard for Radio Syd. In 1962, the station owner, Mrs Wadner, had been

Two views of the MV *Caroline* sailing from the Thames Estuary for the last time on 3rd July, 1964. In her new location, off the Isle of Man, she was even more popular then when she had been broadcasting to London.   *E. Varley*

prosecuted and fined for operating the station. In 1963 some of the station's advertisers had been prosecuted, and in October Mrs Wadner had been prosecuted again.

In March 1964, Mrs Wadner was prosecuted, for a third time, and five months later she was in court again. On this occasion she was sentenced to four weeks' imprisonment; due to the terms of her incarceration, she was able to record radio programmes from her cell.

On Thursday 17th September, 1964, severe storms raged through the Baltic, giving the two radio ships a pounding. At the height of the storm, the *Cheeta I* broke adrift, and ran aground near Malmo. For two days the diminutive ship was stranded on the shore, until she was pulled clear and taken into the port of Malmo for repairs. The ship was berthed at the Kockums repair dock, where she sank on Wednesday 7th October, her hull having been damaged below the waterline.

It was also during September 1964 that Radio Sutch stopped broadcasting. The station was taken over by Reg Calvert, who changed the station name to Radio City. The station opened on Wednesday 30th September, on a new frequency of 238 metres (1262 kHz). During December the station changed to 290 metres (1034 kHz), with a second transmitter broadcasting on 187 metres (1605 kHz).

On Thursday 19th November, 1964, the MV *Galaxy*, a converted mine sweeper anchored in the Thames Estuary. The 780 ton 185 ft-long ship, which had been called *Manoula*, was built in Florida during 1945. The ship had been purchased by Marine Investment Inc., Freeport Grand Bahama, and had been converted to a radio ship in Miami, sailing on Thursday 22nd October. The ship commenced test transmissions but it was anchored inside territorial waters, until Radio Caroline put them wise.

The *Galaxy* was moved to a new anchorage, restarting testing an Saturday 5th December, on 266 metres (1125 kHz). Tests were also carried out on 265 and 277 metres, but these were not so successful. The station officially opened on Wednesday 23rd December, 1964, using the callsign 'Radio London'.

The station had American backers who had invested £500,000 in the station, which opened its office at 17 Curzon Street, London W1, in fashionable Mayfair, and just round the corner from Caroline House.

The ship was fitted with a mast which was 212 feet high and initial broadcasts were made with a power of 17 kilowatts, which was soon increased to 40 kilowatts. Radio London had a very slick, highly Americanised format, which soon made it very popular, earning the nickname 'Wonderful Big L'. The *Galaxy* was anchored off Walton on the Naze, just one mile from the *Mi Amigo*. The two stations were very competitive rivals, but Radio London just failed to unseat Caroline as the nation's favourite.

Radio London's top 10, for the last week of December 1964, brings back many happy memories.

1.	*Go Now*	Moody Blues
2.	*Yeh Yeh*	Georgie Fame
3.	*Girl Don't Come*	Sandie Shaw
4.	*I Feel Fine*	The Beatles
5.	*Somewhere*	P.J.Proby
6.	*Ferry Cross The Mersey*	Gerry and the Pacemakers
7.	*Terry*	Twinkle
8.	*Walk Tall*	Val Doonican
9.	*Downtown*	Petula Clark
10.	*Cast Your Fate To The Wind*	Sounds Orchestral

MV *Galaxy* anchored of the Essex coast, near the Shivering Sands fort. Radio London was a highly slick and professional Americanised radio station which became very popular. Radio London's format was the shape of things to come. *Sky Fotos*

December 1964 may have seen the start of Radio London, but it also saw the demise of two other stations. Radio Invicta, which had been broadcasting from the Red Sands Fort, closed after three personnel were drowned. The men had been returning to the shore from the fort on Wednesday 16th December. Later that evening a body was washed ashore, near Whitstable, and several weeks later another body was found in Spain. After such a long period in the water, the body was never identified, but with it was a Radio Invicta programme tape.

During 1963 a Dutch consortium of six with backing from ship builder Cor Verlome, authorised the construction of a structure similar to an oil rig. Construction was carried out at Verlome's shipyard in Cork, and had parts transported to a site six miles off Noordwijk, Holland. It was equipped with a helipad, and an aerial mast which was 360 feet above sea level.

The station commenced broadcasts, testing on 280, 202 and 214 metres, from Sunday 19th July, 1964, using the callsign 'Radio Noordzee'. The official opening was on 29th July, on 214 metres(1400 kHz), with Dutch language programming.

TV Noordsee started test transmissions on Saturday 15th August, with regular broadcasts commencing on Tuesday 1st September. TV programmes were in Dutch, but they also included English language programmes, such as *The Saint* and *Robin Hood*, which were subtitled.

Radio and TV Noordzee became very popular with listeners and advertisers. Within the first month the owners, Reklame Exploitatie Maatschappij (REM), had taken revenue in excess of £100,000.

Popular it may have been, but not with the Dutch Government; just 16 days after TV broadcasts had commenced, moves were afoot to close the station. The Dutch Parliament discussed introducing legislation that would permit Dutch laws to apply to all structures, standing in the North Sea, on the Dutch part of the Continental Shelf.

The important part of this legislation was that even if the structure was outside Territorial Waters, the new law could still be enforced. The REM Island, as the structure had become known, was well in International Waters, but it was covered by the legislation when it became law, on Saturday 12th December.

On Monday 14th December, the TV station came under new ownership, High Seas TV, a company based in London, but it immediately closed down. The radio station continued to broadcast, but the ownership of the REM Island passed to a Panamanian company.

In spite of the fact that foreign nationals now owned the island the Authorities raided it at 09:00 on Thursday 17th December 1964. The nine people on board did not try and stop the raid, and the transmitter was switched off partway through a record.

High Seas TV condemned the raid, adding that they had a reasonable chance that they may be allowed to resume broadcasts. As the Amsterdam Prosecutor, in the name of his Queen, had sealed the transmitters, and officially claimed the island as Dutch territory, there was no chance of resuming broadcasts.

At the time of the raid, TV Noordzee had been broadcasting on Channel 11, and had been so successful that it had earned a substantial profit. Dutch state

TV, on the other hand, carried no advertising but it was not long before it copied the pirate's lead.

The new law did not apply to Radio Veronica, which was anchored in international waters, but it was a warning of what was to come. Life on a radio ship was inherently dangerous, but there was to be no safe refuge for those who took to the forts, or other fixed structures.

As 1964 came to a close, the Postmaster General, Anthony Wedgwood Benn, announced that he was going to seek legislation which would make it an offence to supply the stations with food, fuel and records, It would also be illegal to advertise on the stations, so they could be prosecuted in the way that Radio Syd's clients had been.

Ronan, however, was not in the slightest deterred, the ships were in international waters, and were not registered in Britain, so British laws did not apply. Ronan announced that the only way the British Government could silence his two ships was to declare war on the country who had registered the ships!

1965

Top 20 for week commencing Friday 1st January, 1965

1	(1)	I Feel Fine	Beatles
2	(17)	Yeh Yeh	Georgie Fame
3	(2)	Downtown	Petula Clark
4	(12)	Terry	Twinkle
5	(4)	Walk Tall	Val Doonican
6	(3)	I'm Gonna Be Strong	Gene Pitney
7	(13)	Girl Don't Come	Sandie Shaw
8	(10)	Somewhere	P.J. Proby
9	(9)	I Could Easily Fall	Cliff Richard
10	(27)	Go Now	Moody Blues
11	(7)	No Arms Could Ever Hold You	Bachelors
12	(5)	I Understand	Freddie and the Dreamers
13	(16)	What Have They Done To The Rain	Searchers
14	(31)	Ferry Across The Mersey	Gerry and the Pacemakers
15	(14)	Message To Martha (Kentucky Bluebird)	Adam Faith
16	(8)	Little Red Rooster	Rolling Stones
17	(23)	Cast Your Fate To The Wind	Sounds Orchestral
18	(18)	There's A Heartache Following Me	Jim Reeves
19	(19)	All Day And All Of The Night	Kinks
20	(28)	Genie With The Light Brown Lamp	Shadows

Ships and Forts

Radio Caroline had mixed fortunes at the beginning of 1965. In January they exhibited their Team Brabham at the Racing Car Show. Later, they organised a championship in the Clubmans Sports Car, with the help of the British Racing and Sports Car Club. Interviews were recorded at the Earl's Court Boat Show, and were later broadcast from Caroline South.

It was not all happy news for the station; during the evening of Wednesday 13th January, severe gale force winds swept through the Irish Sea. The MV *Caroline* took a beating, which proved too much for her starboard anchor chain, which snapped under the strain.

The port anchor proved too light, allowing the ship to drift, dragging its anchor. The captain and his crew had the situation under control, preventing the ship from getting into any extreme danger. Within a week the ship had been fitted with a new anchor and chain, the combined weight of which was 6 tons.

When a ship is at anchor, during heavy seas, it is important to pay out more chain than is actually required. Under normal conditions it is usual to have the sea depth, times three, of cable out but much more in rough conditions, or if the seabed is sandy. In this way, the excess chain lies on the seabed, and when the ship does rise and fall the chain moves with the motion, rather then put all the strain on the chain or the anchor. If the chain is too short the ship will snag at the chain, the anchor will be dragged, or even worse the chain will snap.

With the radio ships remaining at anchor for very long periods, the chain takes terrific punishment; not only does the ship rise and fall, it also swings round due to the effect of wind and tide. It is essential to have the chain fitted with swivels, to prevent it from becoming knotted, which would greatly reduce the life of the chain. Following this incident the ship was fitted with a 1½ ton anchor, with 41 tons of chain.

A new station took to the air in March 1965, this was KING Radio, which broadcast from the Red Sands Fort. The station had taken over from Radio Invicta, and commenced test transmissions in March 1965. The station officially opened on Wednesday 24th March, broadcasting on 236 metres. KING Radio was on the air from 7 am until 7 pm using a sweet music format, it was low powered, and no threat to Caroline or London.

In March Caroline celebrated her first birthday, with special programming, and recorded messages from top bands and artists of the day which read like a who's who of 1960s pop hall of fame. Messages from the following artists were also played: Bobby Vee, Cliff Richard, Donovan, Dusty Springfield, Eden Kane, Frankie Vaughan, Peter and Gordon, Roy Orbison, Stevie Wonder and Tom Jones.

To further mark the occasion Ronan introduced the Bell Awards. The ship's bell featured on advertising literature, and was a familiar sound during broadcasting as it was featured in the station ID jingles. Four Bell Awards were made:

Petula Clark - Best Female vocal - for *Down Town*
Tom Jones - Best Male vocal - *It's not Unusual*
The Animals - Best Group - *House of the Rising Sun*
The Beatles - The best and most consistent group

During April the tender, *Offshore 1*, was on its way to exchange DJs and land stores at Radio London and Radio Caroline South. As the tender approached Radio London, an American Air Force jet, flying nearby, developed engine trouble. The pilot of the F101 jet was forced to eject, leaving his plane to crash into the sea.

The MV *Caroline* at anchor off Ramsey, Isle of Man on Monday 13th July, 1964 The ship was home to Radio Caroline North, with a mailing address of P.O. Box 3, Ramsey, I.O.M. and offices at 61 Lord Street, Liverpool.   *NPO Ltd, Belfast*

The tender immediately diverted to where the parachute had landed, Radio London DJ Pete Brady diving into the water to support the pilot, who had injured his back. Willing hands soon lifted both men back to the safety of the ship.

The exchange of DJs and the landing of stores at both radio ships was completed, before the *Offshore 1* returned to Harwich. The skipper had informed the authorities ashore, so an ambulance was waiting to take the injured airman to hospital, where he made a full recovery.

There is no doubt that without the vigilance and prompt action of the *Offshore 1*, the pilot would have drowned in the cold waters of the North Sea as, apart from his injuries, all of his life saving equipment had been lost.

Both Radio Caroline and Radio London broadcast special bulletins about the incident , which resulted in an amusing confession from Ronan. He said that he had heard the news whilst listening to his principal rival, Radio London. A record was played for the airman, and two members of the *Offshore 1* crew returned his parachute whilst he was still in the hospital.

On this occasion, proper watch keeping had resulted in the saving of a life, but this was not always the case with the radio ships. It was to play a major factor in the lives, and well being, of all those on board some of the radio ships. It went to prove that an essential part of sea routine, even during the dull monotony of a long period at anchor, proper watch keeping and vigilance must be maintained.

In 1960 the Pilkington Committee had published its findings on the future of broadcasting. In 1962 the Government had issued a White Paper on the subject, which they stated that they would review the situation at a later date. That review did not come until 13th May, 1965, over a year after Radio Caroline had commenced broadcasts.

During 1964 the Labour Government had won the General Election, but they had taken no action against Radio Caroline, or the other stations. In the meantime the broadcasts had become very popular, and the Government did not want to risk losing voters. Although Labour had won the election, they only had a small majority, and so another election could easily follow. If they did take action against the offshore stations, they risked alienating 7 million voters. It was hardly surprising that they decided to take the line of least resistance, and just review the situation.

During a debate, one Conservative MP said that he thought that it was time that commercial radio was introduced. He went on to say that there was a definite need for such stations, using low power transmitters, but that the cost of setting up the stations should not be added to the licence fee. The Independent Television Authority could be given a licence to broadcast and be renamed the Independent Broadcasting Authority.

Mr Benn, the Postmaster General, replied saying that whatever the future for local radio broadcasts the pirate stations would have no part in it. In spite of this debate, no alternative plan was drawn. The Government was still in a weak position and knew that the millions of listeners would not take kindly to any Government who took the stations away; but who offered no alternative. The Conservatives had shown that they were in favour of local radio, which was the only alternative.

During the debate Mr Benn went on to list the crimes of the pirate stations which included that they constituted a threat to shipping, and ship to shore communications. That they stole copyright, and endangered the livelihood of artists by giving unrestricted needle time. They interfered with Continental radio stations, and not least they appropriated frequencies that had not been allocated to them.

Mr Benn had been given extra ammunition to act against the stations because on 21st January, 1965 the Council of Europe had agreed legislation. The Council, comprising 18 countries, had signed an agreement for the prevention of broadcasts from outside Territorial waters. This included all of the pirate stations, and seven members of the Council had signed the agreement. Words were not converted to deeds, and following this indecision other stations soon took to the air.

Radio Caroline received a Royal visitor in June 1965. Prince Richard of Gloucester visited the *Mi Amigo*, with two colleagues, to get information for an article in the Cambridge University magazine, *Granta*. The Royal party were invited to have dinner whilst on board, they eventually left after spending three hours on the radio ship.

One wonders what the crew and DJs on the *Mi Amigo* would have thought if they had seen the sticker, on the Prince's Mini Moke, which proclaimed, 'I prefer BBC Third on 464'.

A new station, which soon proved to be a serious rival to Radio Caroline, commenced transmissions during September 1965. King Radio, which had been broadcasting since March 1965, on 236 metres, had not been very successful. The station had been using a middle of the road format, which did not appeal to the listeners, or potential advertisers. A change in managers led to the close of King Radio on Wednesday 22nd September, and the next day Radio 390 took over.

Radio 390 was based on the Red Sands Fort, the third station to use this fort, after Radio Invicta, and King Radio. The new management had invested heavily in the new station, a mast had been constructed, which was almost 300 feet high, and a second-hand transmitter had been purchased which had a power of 10 kilowatts.

Engineers had refurbished two generators that had been left behind by the army, which provided power for all domestic and transmitting requirements. The tests were so successful that regular programmes commenced on Saturday 25th September, broadcasting hours being from 6.30 am until midnight.

Broadcasting on 388 metres (773 kHz), the station broadcast a light music format, aimed specifically at the housewife. The format was so successful that it later formed the basis for the BBC's Radio 2.

Just four weeks later, yet another station took to the air. Tower Radio was also using one of the old forts. This station had taken over the Sunk Head Fort, and had spent several months preparing it for its new role.

Test transmissions commenced on Friday 22nd October, on 238 metres (1261 kHz). This was a shoestring pirate that had a low powered transmitter and could not hope to compete with the 'big' stations. 'This is Tower Radio, Tower Radio. Tower Radio testing from the Sunk Head Fort, situated 14½ miles from Walton on Naze.'

Radio 390 commenced broadcasts in September 1965 from the Red Sands Fort. The easy listening format proved immensely popular and was to provide the inspiration for BBC Radio 2.   *Sky Fotos*

Test transmissions were intermittent, and on different wavelengths. The owner also claimed that the station would soon be broadcasting TV programmes, but this appears to have been just a hoax. During November the station started using 236 metres, but the station was poorly managed and transmissions ended in December.

During September, yet another fort-based radio station, Radio Essex, was preparing to commence transmissions, from the Knock John Fort, four miles from the Shivering Sands Fort which was home to Radio City. Personnel from Radio City had already landed on the Knock John, but the new station wanted to use it.

Radio Essex landed some men on the fort, but they were later escorted away, by a man from Radio City. The owner of Radio Essex then returned, in force, and ousted the men from Radio City. The skirmishes lasted for about a month, resulting in Radio Essex taking over the fort.

The owner of Radio Essex, Roy Bates, said that he would protect the fort from all comers. He added that, even though Radio City was part of the Caroline Organisation, which Radio Caroline denied, if they wanted a fight they could have one! Radio City decided that discretion was the better part of valour, and made no further attempts to retake the fort.

Mr Bates then prepared the fort for his use: two of the generators, left by the army, were restored to working order, and an old 1 kilowatt transmitter was also refurbished. An aerial was erected, using old bits of scaffolding, which allowed test transmissions to commence on Wednesday 27th October.

Radio Essex officially opened on Sunday 7th November, 1965, on 222 metres (1353 kHz), at 7 am. Programming consisted of light music during the day, and top 40 music in the evening. Once again, this was a low budget station, which only reached the local area.

Knock John Fort was the scene of skirmishes, as two rival pirate stations vied with each other. Radio City was ousted by Radio Essex, which started test transmissions in October 1965.   *Sky Fotos*

The station set out to be a truly local station, for the County of Essex, specialising in advertising for local companies. It was never going to be hugely popular, as its low powered transmissions only covered a small area, but it did have a loyal following, and it later became the first pirate to pioneer 24 hour broadcasting.

There were now seven stations on the air: Caroline North and South; London; City; 390; Essex and Tower (?). Each of them, in their own way, trying to bring about land-based commercial radio (and in the process make lots of money!). The big stations also hoped to play an important part in the new land-based stations, when they were started.

Mr Benn had other ideas though, during December 1965 he made yet another verbal attack on the pirates. He quite categorically rejected any idea for land-based commercial radio, adding that the pirate stations would have no part in any future development of British Radio.

Just a few days after this scathing rebuke, the Prime Minister, Harold Wilson, in answer to questions in the House of Commons, gave Ronan some unexpected pleasure. The PM was being asked questions about the situation in Rhodesia, which later resulted in that country claiming independence (UDI). There was concern for the civil servants working there, as they were unable to learn what they were supposed to do because of locally imposed censorship.

In his reply, Mr Wilson stated that the Government were doing what they could to resolve the situation. It had been suggested that an old aircraft carrier was to be converted into a floating radio station.

The carrier, *Leviathan*, would be anchored in the Indian Ocean, its purpose being to broadcast propaganda into Rhodesia, in an attempt to stop UDI. The PM added that if they had to take advice from the experience of Radio Caroline, he would not hesitate to do so. In the event, the scheme did not proceed.

During December, Ronan's Planet Productions finally acquired the assets of Project Atlanta. Allan Crawford resigned, leaving Ronan to be responsible for all aspects of the day-to-day running of the two radio ships. This move solved many problems, as both ships now had the same owner, and all administrative and financial problems could be dealt with more easily.

The pure logistics of running the two ships was quite phenomenal. Apart from anything else, such as spare parts, the ships needed essential supplies, crew, DJs, records, tapes, and facilities for sorting out the mail.

Both of the ships usually had a Dutch crew of 10, consisting of captain and one deck officer, deck hands, one engineer with engine room ratings and one cook with stewards. The crew worked six weeks on board, followed by one week ashore.

In addition to the crew, there were radio engineers, and of course the DJs. All of them had to be fed and watered, and the ships had to be fuelled. Both ships used about 3 tons of fuel per week, and were supplied with 20 gallons of milk, and 11 tons of fresh water.

The record library was kept updated with new records and tapes and there were 'extras', in the shape of duty free cigarettes and beer, which were supplied from Holland. The *Mi Amigo* had these supplied every three weeks or so whereas the MV *Caroline* was supplied with duty frees every six months, due to the distance involved.

To see out the year, Radio Caroline organised a Gala Night for Caroline Club members. Many artists appeared, making the evening a complete success and a fitting way to celebrate Christmas and the New Year.

Radio London had some moments of drama. On Christmas Eve 1965 they broadcast an urgent appeal for assistance, when one of the Dutch crew ran amok with a knife. The tender, *Offshore 1*, was used to take police officers out to the *Galaxy*, the man was taken ashore and later returned to Holland.

That was not the end of Radio London's problems that Christmas, programmes were again interrupted, by an urgent appeal. DJ Tony Windsor announced, 'Please help us, we have hardly any water'. The main storage tank, containing 50 tons of drinking water, had developed a leak. Two weeks' supply had been lost.

Philip Birch, Radio London's Managing Director said, 'The listeners came to our rescue'. The office telephone lines had been blocked by the volume of calls from concerned listeners.

If Ronan had had his way, Radio Caroline and Radio London would have merged. He had been trying to negotiate a deal, with some of Radio London's backers, which would have resulted in the *Galaxy* being the third ship in Caroline's fleet.

It was Ronan's intention to move the *Galaxy* to The Wash, from where it could transmit a strong signal into the Midlands and the North East. The combination of the three ships would have given Radio Caroline nationwide coverage, but Mr Birch was totally opposed to the idea. He persuaded the backers that it would be better to remain independent.

Meanwhile, over in the Baltic, the end of 1965 had mixed fortunes for Radio Syd. It had been one of those years, for the solitary Baltic pirate. In June several of the advertisers had been prosecuted, but this did not deter Mrs Wadner from embarking on more ambitious plans.

With considerable backing, rumoured to have been in the six figure region, the *Cheeta II* was prepared for broadcasting television programmes. The radio ship was equipped with a new studio, transmitter and a 90 ft mast.

Test transmissions commenced in December, but the success was tainted by the fact that more advertisers and Mrs Wadner were prosecuted. Mrs Wadner was sentenced to a three month term of imprisonment, but Radio and TV Syd continued to broadcast.

Neither these far-off prosecutions, nor Mr Benn's scathing attack, deterred another British pirate from taking to the air, in December 1965. Britain's fourth radio ship was a converted Clyde-built lightship; the 100 ft, 500 ton vessel was towed to St Sampson's Harbour, Guernsey.

With backing of around £300,000 the *Comet* was equipped with a modern studio, two 10 kilowatt transmitters, and a 145 ft mast. When the work had been completed the ship, which had no propulsion motor, was towed to its anchorage, off Dunbar.

During the voyage, the tow rope parted, giving some anxious moments. The tow was re-established, and the radio ship anchored safely in the North Sea, on Thursday 30th December.

Radio Scotland commenced broadcasts, just before midnight, on New Year's Eve. To the sound of the bagpipes, Scotland received its only pirate station, which broadcast on 242 metres (1241 kHz). 'Turn the dial to Radio Scotland, Radio Scotland's calling you. Turn the dial to Radio Scotland, stationed here on 242.'

Above: The tug *Foreman* manoeuvres the *Comet* into a berth at St Sampson's harbour in the Channel Island of Guernsey.   *Guernsey Press*

Right: The conversion is almost complete, the *Comet* being prepared for the long voyage to the North Sea anchorage off Dunbar, near the Firth of Forth. The height of the mast can be appreciated by making a comparison with the man just below the cross tree.
                                        E. Varley

1966

On the Beach

During the second week of January, storms raged through the southern North Sea, giving the two radio ships a pounding. On Wednesday 12th, the Walton Coastguard realised that the *Galaxy* was not in her usual location. They informed the radio ship of the situation, and the crew discovered, to their horror, that the anchor chain had snapped and that the ship was adrift.

The emergency anchor was lowered, but this was not heavy enough to halt the ship which continued to drift for almost four miles. Eventually the crew were able to bring the ship under control, but by this time it was off Clacton, where she was joined by the local lifeboat.

A tug was dispatched from Felixstowe, which towed the *Galaxy* back to her usual anchorage, one mile from the *Mi Amigo*, where Radio London resumed broadcasts that afternoon.

Radio Caroline had not been affected by the storm, and it was business as usual on board the *Mi Amigo*. The new top 10 had been prepared, ready for the week commencing Saturday 15th January, which consisted of:

1.	*Keep On Running*	Spencer Davis Group
2.	*My Ship Is Coming In*	The Walker Brothers
3.	*A Must To Avoid*	Hermans Hermits
4.	*Day Tripper/We Can Work It Out*	Beatles
5.	*Till The End Of The Day*	Kinks
6.	*Spanish Flea*	Herb Alpert
7.	*A Hard Day's Night*	Peter Sellers
8.	*Take Me For What I'm Worth*	The Searchers
9.	*England Swings*	Roger Miller
10.	*Michelle*	The Overlanders

On Wednesday 19th January, Radio Caroline closed down for the evening at 8 pm. It was a dark and stormy night, gale force winds had been accompanied by rain, which was turning to snow.

For the officer on duty at the Walton Coastguard station, it was the kind of night that anything could, and usually did happen. The officer had been checking the position of the two radio ships, when he realised that the *Mi Amigo* was moving.

From the way that the ship was riding the swell, it looked as though the ship was drifting, out of control. There had been no visual or radio distress calls from the *Mi Amigo*, so the Coastguard had to assume that those onboard were unaware of their predicament.

The officer tried to contact the radio ship, but failed, so he telephoned Caroline's Harwich agent Bill Scaddon. He drove down to the beach at Frinton, and tried to contact the ship, by flashing his headlamps, but it was to no avail. The Coastguard, and the local Post Office radio station, were also trying to contact the ship, by radio and visual signals.

It was painfully obvious that no one on the ship was aware of the danger that they were in. The crew had checked the anchor chain earlier, and thought that all was well, but it was not a night to stay out on deck for too long.

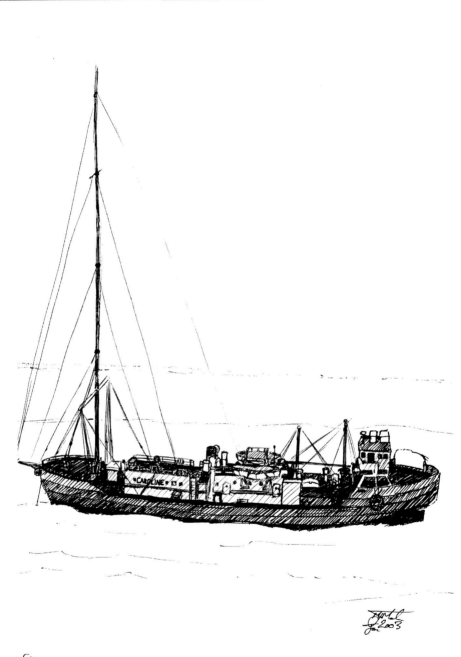

Drawing of the *Mi Amigo* aground on Frinton beach on 19th January, 1966 by Mark Maule.

Mr Scaddon by this time was becoming very anxious, but he thought of another way of letting those on the *Mi Amigo* know of their situation. He knew that the off-duty personnel preferred to watch ITV, so he rang the local TV station.

He asked them if they would broadcast a flash message to the *Mi Amigo*, to warn them of the danger they were in. The TV company were happy to oblige, broadcasting the message at 9.15 pm, which was seen by those on board.

The stricken radio ship continued to drift towards the shore, battered by the heavy swell, whilst the crew tried desperately to start the engine. Meanwhile the Coastguard Rescue company were put on full alert, the local lifeboat had been launched, and the tender *Offshore 1* was on its way.

Eventually the engine started, the crew having to pre-heat it with a blow torch, and the compressed air which was used to start the engine had all but gone. The 220 hp engine, driving the single screw, was not powerful enough to halt the drift, such was the power of the wind and the sea. The *Mi Amigo* finally ran aground, at Holland Haven, just after 12.20 am on Thursday 20th January, broadside onto the waves.

It was far too dangerous for any ship to go alongside, to take the personnel off, so the Coastguard shore team went into action. A parachute flare was launched, so as to illuminate the area, and a rocket line was fired towards the ship; it took a few attempts, but a line was secured.

The breeches buoy equipment was made ready, as the heavy swell crashed into the side of the ship, sending heavy spray cascading over the entire ship. To make an already difficult situation even worse, it had started snowing heavily.

Disc jockey Norman St John was the first to be winched to safety, Tony Blackburn came ashore holding his transistor radio, which was tuned to Radio Luxembourg, and Tom Lodge came ashore clutching a photograph of his wife. Two other DJs, Dave Lee Travis and Graham Webb, were brought ashore, with three radio engineers and a Dutch steward.

Once they were all safely ashore they were taken to the local police station, where they were given dry clothing and a cup of tea. From there they were taken to an hotel for the night, where they were given something a little stronger to help them sleep.

All of the DJs gave interviews, saying how sad they were to see the *Mi Amigo* on the beach, but that they were glad to be safe, and they thanked the rescue team, who were given an award later in the year. Tom Lodge, who had just been appointed as programming director added, 'We shall be back, with bigger and better programmes'.

The Dutch captain, and his crew of six, remained on board the ship throughout the night, and two Coastguards joined them, to offer assistance. The retreating tide left the ship high, but not very dry, on the shore, and it was possible to walk right around the ship.

As the tide returned, the *Mi Amigo* took a beating, the waves trying to push the ship onto one of the concrete groynes. The rescue team stayed on the beach, in atrocious conditions, in case the men had to be taken off the ship. During the afternoon the Wijsmuller tug, *Titan*, arrived, but it was too late to attempt a salvage.

The *Titan* in heavy seas.   *Cees van der Meulen*

A small boat was used to ferry a towing hawser from the *Titan* to the *Mi Amigo*, in preparation for the next high tide, due about midnight. The hawser was five inches in diameter, and nearly two miles in length, as the nearest the *Titan* could get was about 500 yards away.

At high tide, the *Titan* took up the slack, and began pulling, but the 470 ton *Mi Amigo* would not budge. Unfortunately, the tow rope became entangled in a nearby wreck, and parted.

Once again the high water came, and went, leaving the ship firmly on the beach. The *Mi Amigo's* master, Captain Vrury, decided that he was going to try his own rescue attempt. He lowered an anchor, the chain fed over the bows, and waited for the tide to rise.

As the sea started to lift the ship, the anchor chain was winched in, luckily the anchor held, and the ship was pulled round, with the bow pointing out to sea. As the tide rose still further, the wave action began to buffet the ship, causing it to bounce.

The ship's engine was started, and the captain waited his chance, as a large wave passed beneath the bow, the engine was put to full ahead. The wave passed under the hull, lifting the stern, the propeller began to dislodge the sand and gravel that had been holding the ship.

As the propeller bit into the deeper water, it was able to power the ship off the beach, with towing assistance from the Titan. On Friday 21st January the *Mi Amigo* had been saved, by the skill of her captain. The *Titan* towed the radio ship to a safe position, about one mile off shore, to allow divers to go down to inspect the hull. The visibility, below water, was too bad to allow a proper assessment so it was decided to take the ship into dry dock.

It was also discovered that the *Mi Amigo's* engine had been seriously damaged, during the rescue. Sand and gravel had damaged the piston liners and water circulating pipes had become blocked, causing the engine to seize.

Those waiting on the shore, including Ronan, thought that a small price, compared to the salvage of the ship, and the rescue of all personnel, without injury.

As the ship had gained its freedom, Ronan had hugged Bill Scaddon and said, 'What a wonderful sight'. A sentiment echoed by all of those who had been watching, on that cold windswept beach. Not least the Coastguard Team, which were stood down, after 36 hours on standby.

The damaged radio ship was towed to the Dutch port of Zaandam, with pumps running throughout, due to water leaking in through damaged hull plates. The *Mi Amigo* was drydocked on Sunday 23rd January, the radio staff having removed the crystals from the transmitters, which was just as well, because the Dutch authorities insisted that the transmitters had to be removed.

Ronan now had to face the problems of having Caroline South off the air, the loss of advertising revenue, and the loss of listeners to a rival station. Lady Luck was just about to deal a winning hand to Ronan, for his was not the only radio ship to be silenced, by extreme weather.

On Tuesday 18th January, the day before the *Mi Amigo* went adrift, the *Cheeta II* was forced from its anchorage. The Baltic was in the grip of freezing conditions, that had seen the formation of thick pack ice. Radio Syd, the last of the Baltic pirates had been silenced, not by Governmental intervention, but hostile weather. After a period of almost eight years, the Baltic had heard its last pirate.

With all of the prosecutions, Radio Syd was falling on tough times and it had been rumoured that the station was going to close, and that the *Cheeta II* would be used as an offshore station off the coast of Britain.

Mrs Wadner offered the radio ship to Ronan, free of charge, until such time as the *Mi Amigo* could resume broadcasting. This offer had been made because Ronan had written to Mrs Wadner, whilst she was in prison, offering her support and encouragement.

Ronan was now in the fortunate position of being able to announce, that Radio Caroline South would soon be back on the air. The station would, however, be on lower power, just 6 kilowatts, but that this would soon be increased to 10kW.

The *Cheeta II* sailed from the Baltic, arriving off Harwich on Monday 31st January, where she was met by the *Offshore 1*. The tender escorted the radio ship to the *Mi Amigo's* usual anchorage, 3½ miles off Frinton.

The ship needed to undergo alterations, before it could commence transmissions on Radio Caroline's frequency. As Radio Syd had been broadcasting on FM, a medium wave transmitter was required. The *Offshore 1* sailed to Zaandam, where one of the 10 kilowatt transmitters that had been removed from the *Mi Amigo* was taken aboard.

The transmitter was installed on the *Cheeta II*, and it was tuned into a temporary aerial that had been rigged on the ship. The aerial was a crude affair, just consisting of a length of wire, taken to the highest point on the mast.

Strong winds hampered the work of the engineers, and it was not until Sunday 13th February that test transmissions commenced. Power was very low, with night time reception almost impossible, so the transmissions were restricted to 10 am until 4 pm.

The very next day, the lifeboat was requested, as DJ Graham Webb had become ill. The DJ had been rescued from the *Mi Amigo*, and once again he was taken ashore, where he was transferred to an ambulance. He was taken to hospital, in Colchester, where he recovered from a viral infection.

Engineers encountered many problems, which resulted in Caroline South going off air for six days. After two days, transmissions resumed but two days later the station was silent again. This time miracles were performed, which kept the ship silent for another six days. Caroline resumed testing on Sunday 6th March, with increased power.

Radio Caroline began broadcasting her regular hours, but the ship was being pounded by gales and heavy seas. The *Cheeta II* started to flood with water, which forced Caroline off the air again, on Friday 25th March.

The leak was traced to a fractured waste pipe, which was allowing sea water to flood in. A temporary repair was made, but the ship was in need of proper maintenance. The decision was made to take the ship to Lowestoft, so she left her anchorage that afternoon, escorted by the *Offshore 1*.

Sailing under her own power, a fault developed on the ship's engine, which required her to anchor off Lowestoft, for the night. The next morning she was towed into the port, by a local tug assisted by the *Offshore 1*, and berthed at Richards repair yard. The repairs took six days to complete, then the *Cheeta II* sailed back to her anchorage, where transmissions recommenced on Saturday 2nd April.

On Saturday 5th March, Tower Radio restarted test transmissions, using the new callsign of 'Radio Tower'. 'Testing, Testing, Testing - stay tuned to Radio Tower.' 'Get a fix on 236.' The tests, however, were very intermittent, and of poor quality. Radio Tower made further broadcasts, on 234 metres, but was not heard from again, after the second week of May.

North of the border, Radio Scotland had been experiencing problems. On Thursday 10th February, the *Comet* began shipping water during gale force winds with a very heavy swell. The ship's pumps could not cope, so another pump was taken to her.

Reception of the station had been very poor, in some areas, which resulted in the engineers testing on a series of different frequencies. At the end of April it was decided to move the *Comet* to a new location on the west coast of Scotland!

The ship was towed around the north coast, to a new anchorage in Irvine Bay, five miles off Troon. The new location, in the Firth of Clyde, meant that the ship was only a distance of about 30 miles from Glasgow. Reception was improved, but the tow of over 1,000 miles had cost the station a considerable amount, which would have to be recouped from advertising revenue.

Radio Caroline North had also experienced some problems. At its anchorage in Ramsey Bay, the MV *Caroline* had been buffeted by a heavy swell. The ship had lurched violently, which resulted in boiling coffee being accidentally spilt down the back of one of the crew.

The Dutch seaman was taken ashore, by local lifeboat, and treated for scalding in Ramsey hospital. Just a few days later, the lifeboat was summoned again, as one of the crew had been injured. his hand having been crushed in a piece of equipment.

Meanwhile, in the Dutch port of Zaandam, the *Mi Amigo's* hull had been repaired and her engine overhauled. A new 50 kilowatt transmitter had been delivered from Continental Electronics, which would be installed once the ship had sailed.

It was also decided to move to a new frequency, 256 metres (1169 kHz), with a new callsign of 'Caroline on 259'. With the increase of power and the new wavelength it was hoped to attract more listeners, and increase advertising revenue. The new location had been chosen as it was between the BBC, on 247 metres, and Radio London on 266.

The *Mi Amigo* left Zaandam on Tuesday 5th April, and as soon as she left port work started on installing the new 50 kilowatt transmitter. The Dutch had also released the second 10 kW transmitter, which would be used as a back up to the new one.

The ship anchored off Frinton, close to the *Cheeta II*, which was still broadcasting. Engineers installed the new transmitter, and tests commenced on Sunday 17th April, but the aerial could not cope with the 50 kilowatts, which forced the tests to end.

Insulators on the aerial rigging had failed, and some of the stays had been destroyed by arcing. The mast was in danger of collapse, so professional riggers were taken out to the ship to replace the damaged stays and new insulators were fitted.

A fault was still preventing transmissions from resuming, and nobody was prepared to go to the top of the mast to effect repairs as the professionals had left the ship. Ronan decided that he would go to the ship and do the repairs himself, but before he got there Tony Blackburn had managed to do the work.

Tests restarted the next day, on 256 metres, on Wednesday 25th April, but the next day the wavelength was changed to 253 metres (1187 kHz). The two ships were now broadcasting and at times there was a live link up, between the *Cheeta II* on 199, and the *Mi Amigo* on 259.

The *Cheeta II* looking much the worse for wear, under arrest in the River Stour on Saturday 23rd July, 1966.   *Greg Child*

Photographed in January 1971, the *Cheeta II* was being used as a floating restaurant.
                                                                                                                      J. Thompson

Radio Caroline South on 259 commenced regular broadcasts from the *Mi Amigo* at 6 am on Wednesday 27th April, 1966. The station was broadcasting from 6 am until midnight, which was later extended until 2 am. The night time close down allowed the engineers to service and adjust the equipment, but from Saturday 6th August the station started broadcasting for 24 hours.

The *Cheeta II* relayed the broadcasts from the *Mi Amigo* until Sunday 1st May, when her transmitter was switched off at 11 am. The silent radio ship remained at anchor, off Frinton, until Thursday 21st July. The anchor chain had broken, leaving the ship to drift; there were only four persons on board, and they could not lower the emergency anchor.

A tug was dispatched from Felixstowe, which managed to get a line onto the ship, near to the Gunfleet Sands. The tug *Agama* towed the *Cheeta II* to a mooring buoy, in the River Stour, where the Admiralty Marshall and Customs officers boarded.

On Friday 22nd July, the officers attached a writ of arrest to the ship's mast, which prevented the ship sailing, until the writ had been cleared. The salvage company who operated the *Agama* had seized the ship, so as to ensure that their services were paid for.

The salvage company found that they were having problems in identifying the owners of the ship. It was suggested that the *Cheeta II* had been sold, and was to be used for a station that was to anchor off the Welsh Coast.

It was not until November 1966 that the radio ship was released from arrest, but no one tried to move the ship which was re-arrested in January 1967. It was not until the autumn of 1967 that the *Cheeta II* finally sailed.

The ship visited Spain, Morocco, and the Canary Islands, berthing at Tenerife and Las Palmas. The ship then sailed to Bathurst, in the Gambia, where it was decommissioned as a radio ship. The ship was totally refurbished and converted for use as a floating restaurant.

Radio Syd was granted a licence by the Gambian Government and was invited to establish a shore-based radio station. The station commenced broadcasts on 329 metres (910 kHz).

Pirate Armada

As more stations came on the air, and even more were being planned, the Postmaster General came under increasing pressure to silence them. MPs from all parties wanted to know what alternative the Government had, to these illegal broadcasts. Was the Government going to establish a network of low powered local stations?

On Thursday 3rd March, the House of Commons debated broadcasting, once again. Paul Bryan MP, opposition spokesman on broadcasting, stated that everyone was exasperated by the failure of the Government, and Mr Benn in particular, to announce a future policy. He added that a decision was needed soon, because the Government's indecision was very detrimental to broadcasting in general.

Mr Benn replied that the Government intended to introduce legislation against the pirates, but that the popularity of the offshore stations did not prove that there was a demand for local radio.

These were the people who were charged with running our country, and yet they could not understand that millions of people were tuning to the pirate stations, which must mean that they wanted to hear such broadcasts.

On the same day as the debate, the BBC published a pamphlet which came out in favour of local radio. The BBC planned to establish nine local stations which would be run on a trial basis, so that they could gauge public opinion.

In spite of the obvious popularity of all-day pop music, the BBC maintained its opposition to providing such a service. The Government did not react to this proposal, and so once again no decision was made. Due entirely to this indecision, the number of stations was about to multiply, and events would force the Government to take action.

From that very first broadcast by Radio Caroline there had been a lot of talk, but no action. The number of stations was increasing, the operators trying to attract as much advertising as possible, but hoping that the Government would not take action against them.

The Council of Europe had agreed to outlaw pirate broadcasts from outside territorial waters, so they had given official backing to the British Government to take action, but for the time being they were reluctant to do anything.

Running an offshore radio station was a very costly business, and none of the operators wanted to lose money. It was this aspect, the revenue from advertising, which led to the rapid upsurge in the number of new stations. Each operator was trying to outdo the other, in their attempt to woo advertisers.

It had cost almost £700,000 to get Radio Caroline's two ships on the air, with weekly running expenses of £6,500. To obtain the kind of money necessary to cover such costs the station had to be successful, and prove to advertisers that they could sell the sponsors' product or services.

The larger the audience, the more likely it was that the company would benefit from advertising on a particular station. Without the commercials the radio stations could not survive, so it became obvious that rivalry would take place between the pirates who wanted a larger share of the booty.

To handle the advertising, Radio Caroline had a staff of 269 based at Caroline House, and there were sales offices in the USA, Holland and Ireland. The commercials were broadcast for a maximum of 6 minutes, in each hour, and all commercials had to comply with a rigidly enforced code of practice to protect the consumer.

Radio Caroline had an impressive list of clients which included most of the major companies. Another important source of income was from the religious broadcasts, which most of the stations carried. Radio City financed its operation from such broadcasts, which earned in the region of £20,000 per month.

During those early days the charge for a 30 second advert, during peak hours such as 7 am-9 am, was £110 on Caroline South. As the station became more popular the rate for the same period increased to £190.

Caroline was earning in the region of £48,000 per month, and after only 18 months of broadcasting Radio Caroline had received over £750,000 in advertising contracts. All of the pirates needed this source of income, and by 1966 it was estimated that, between them, they were earning over £2 million.

Radio Caroline commissioned a survey, and it proved that advertising could reach millions of listeners and was therefore worthwhile for their clients. The result showed that on a Sunday morning, between 11.30 am and mid-day, there were 4,210,000 listeners to Radio Caroline. With this potential market, Caroline's rates were comparatively cheap, even on peak rate.

By 1967 it was estimated that between 20 and 25 million people were listening to the broadcasts, from one or other of the pirate stations. This was reason enough for the advertisers to be so pleased to be associated with some of the stations. But it was these lucrative contracts that led to the start of the pirate wars.

Radio Caroline's most successful venture into sales was with Caroline Cash Casino, which was on the air every hour, from 9 am until midday, Monday to Friday. The show was introduced by Canadian Bill Hearne, who started off each new quiz with £100 in the kitty.

The basis of the quiz was that listeners had to identify a person, or an object, from clues given in the form of rhyming couplets. The answer had to be sent to Caroline House, with proof of purchase of the sponsor's product, such as a label or a lid.

Three letters were read out each hour, and for every wrong answer £10 was added to the prize total. The highest amount to be won during the 10 competitions was £4,070 for quiz number 5. Cash Casino was run for a period of 27 weeks, finishing on Monday 1st May, 1967.

Cash Casino

No.	Answer	Prize
1.	A camera shutter operating	£460
2.	Geoff Hurst	£3,330
3.	Jean Harlow	£3,020
4.	Ears	£2,490
5.	Mary Quant	£4,070
6.	Old Bill (nickname for WWI London bus)	£2,700
7.	Tommy Cooper's Fez	£2,820
8.	St Paul's Cathedral	£2,110
9.	Margaret Lockwood	£3,870
10.	Louis Bleriot	£1,320

Cash Casino had major sponsors, which included such household names as Findus, Galaxy, Libbys, Shredded Wheat, Weetabix, and Alberta Shampoo. During the course of this promotion over 4 million letters were sent to Caroline House.

Such was the outstanding success of Cash Casino, other competitions quickly followed such as Partners in Profit, sponsored by Weetabix, Lucky Birthday Bonanza sponsored by Golden Wonder and Halex toothbrushes.

During this period, three more stations were preparing to start broadcasting, with hopes of taking a share in the booty. Two of the stations were housed on the same ship, the MV *Olga Patricia*, which anchored in international waters off Walton on the Naze, near to the *Mi Amigo* and the *Galaxy*.

The owners held a press conference in London, on Wednesday 20th April, announcing that the two stations, Radio Britain and Radio England, would commence broadcasts at the end of April. In the event the ship did not arrive from Miami, where she had been converted, until 3rd May.

Radio Britain and Radio England commenced test transmissions that same day, with Britain on 227 metres (1320 kHz), and England on 355 metres (845 kHz). These were the most powerful transmissions, from any of the pirate ships, 55 kilowatts. It was reported that the two stations had American backing, in the region of £1½ million.

The *Olga Patricia* was built in 1944 in New York as a landing craft for the US Navy. The 562 ton ship was 167 ft long, and she was converted at a Miami shipyard. The conversion included the fitting of a 210 ft mast, two studios and a Continental Electronics transmitter which could produce over 50 kilowatts. The ship was later renamed *Laissez Faire*, which means free from restrictions, an individual enterprise with a policy of non-interference. *Sky Fotos*

The testing continued throughout May, but at the beginning of June a fault forced both stations off the air. On the same day, Friday 3rd June, a complaint of interference was received from Italy. A replacement part had to be sent from America before transmissions could resume. When the tests restarted the two stations had changed wavelengths, Radio England was now on 227, whilst Radio Britain was on 355 with a new name, Britain Radio.

Swinging Radio England, 'Where the action is', was another pop station and home for the 'Boss Jocks', broadcasting for 24 hours a day. After a short time the frequency was changed to 225 metres (1331 kHz), in an attempt to improve reception, although the station still announced itself as being on 227.

Britain Radio, 'Hallmark of Quality' transmitted easy listening music, which it was hoped would attract listeners from Radio 390. Both of the stations officially opened on Sunday 19th June, and a celebration reception was held at the Hilton Hotel, London. Britain Radio broadcast for 21 hours per day, and during the night its power was reduced, so as to avoid causing interference to the Italian station.

The third station to commence broadcasts was Radio 270, which was based on a converted Dutch fishing vessel anchored off Scarborough. The *Oceaan VII* was converted in the port of Scarborough, having arrived in February. The ship was equipped with two studios, a 10 kilowatt transmitter, and a 154 foot mast.

Built in 1939, the *Oceaan VII* was 179 tons with a length of 118 feet, she anchored at the beginning of April, but was damaged by rough seas. Part of her mast collapsed, and she had to be towed back into port for repairs. Testing resumed on 4th June, with regular programmes from Thursday 9th June, broadcasting on 269 metres (1115 kHz).

Just 19 days after Radio 270 came on the air, the Post Office made public a list of interference caused by the offshore stations. That list included:

Radio Caroline North:	2 complaints from Belgium, 2 from Czechoslovakia
Radio Caroline South:	2 complaints from France
Radio London:	2 from Belgium, 2 from Yugoslavia
Radio Scotland:	1 from France, 2 from Eire
Radio England:	1 from Italy
Radio 390:	3 from Stockholm
Radio City:	Several maritime radio complaints

Radio City had, in fact, been forced to suspend broadcasts on Monday 27th June, because they had been causing local interference. The engineers made adjustments, which allowed transmissions to resume the next day.

To try and show the successful side of offshore radio, Radio Caroline commissioned a survey, the result of which was published in July. It revealed that almost 40 million listeners were tuning into the stations. The top seven stations were:

1	Radio Caroline	8,818,000
1	Radio Luxembourg	8,818,000
3	Radio London	8,140,000
4	Radio 390	2,633,000
5	Radio England	2,274,000
6	Radio Scotland	2,195,000
7	Britain Radio	718,000

One of the many jingles played by the stations was, 'Just take a lively companion wherever you go, take a portable radio', and that is what just about everybody was doing. Wherever you went, and by whatever means you got there, you were almost certain to hear one of the pirate stations.

'Wherever you go, go, go, with Big L.'

'Caroline South on 259 - The sound of the Nation.'

'Radio City, your host on the coast, the Tower of Power.'

The mid-1960s will long be remembered as a happy, and carefree era. There was the pop explosion, with radio entertainment the like of which had never been heard. To the listener it was fab, great, groovy.

From little radio ships (and forts) we were kept amused by music and lively chat, catchy jingles and adverts. Who can forget the zany humour of Kenny Everett on Radio London, or the brash American Gary Stevens on Radio England.

It seemed that everywhere on the radio dial was a pirate station, waiting to make you happy. For the most part none of the listeners had any idea of what took place behind the scenes, but that was soon to change. The rivalry between the stations was about to become very hostile which would make headlines around the country.

Amid rumours that a propaganda station, Radio Freedom, was about to commence broadcasts, the House of Commons debated the developments in broadcasting.

Boardings and Bullets

Top 20 for week commencing Friday 17th June, 1966

1	(2)	*Paperback Writer*	Beatles
2	(1)	*Strangers In The Night*	Frank Sinatra
3	(3)	*Monday Monday*	Mamas and the Papas
4	(5)	*When A Man Loves A Woman*	Percy Sledge
5	(14)	*Sunny Afternoon*	Kinks
6	(7)	*Don't Bring Me Down*	Animals
7	(11)	*Don't Answer Me*	Cilla Black
8	(12)	*River Deep Mountain High*	Ike and Tina Turner
9	(4)	*Sorrow*	Merseybeats
10	(10)	*Over Under Sideways Down*	Yardbirds
11	(18)	*Nobody Needs Your Love*	Gene Pitney
12	(6)	*Paint It Black*	Rolling Stones
13	(8)	*Promises*	Ken Dodd
14	(21)	*Hideaway*	Dave Dee, Dozy, Beaky, Mick and Titch
15	(9)	*Wild Thing*	Troggs
16	(13)	*Sloop John B*	Beach Boys
17	(16)	*Nothing Comes Easy*	Sandie Shaw
18	(19)	*Once There Was A Time/Not Responsible*	Tom Jones
19	(-)	*Bus Stop*	Hollies
20	(25)	*Opus 17*	Four Seasons

During May, an extension to the law of Piracy was produced in draft form. The idea was to make sure that all of the stations were illegal, and that they should cease broadcasts voluntarily or by force. This failed to get Government approval.

The proposed Radio Freedom was also discussed, as the thought of having an unrestricted propaganda station, broadcasting from off the coast, horrified members of all political persuasions. The House wanted action, and quickly, so as to prevent such a station from getting on the air.

The Postmaster General, Mr Benn, came under fire from all directions. Some MPs wanted swift action to silence the stations, whilst others wanted a suitable alternative, before the stations were closed.

Conservative members were strongly in favour of local commercial radio, under the control of the proposed Independent Broadcasting Authority. Once again though, as had happened so many times before, no definite solution was agreed. Events, however, would soon force the Government to take action.

Several of the existing radio stations were planning to extend their operations. At the end of 1965 it had been rumoured that Radio Caroline was going to take over Radio City, Caroline South would then broadcast from the Shivering Sands Fort.

The *Mi Amigo* would move to one, of two, proposed anchorages. One was in the Bristol Channel, the other was in The Wash, which is where Ronan had wanted to locate the *Galaxy* if he had succeeded in doing a deal with Radio London.

In June, Radio 390 announced that they intended to open a new station called Radio 390 North. The station would be housed on the *Cheeta II*, which would be anchored off the North Wales coast, near Colwyn Bay.

Not to be outdone, Radio London announced, on Thursday 16th June, that they were to take over Radio City and the new station would be called United Kingdom Good Music (UKGM). The *Galaxy* would then move to the North-West coast, where it would broadcast as Radio Manchester, with a power of 75 kilowatts.

Radio Caroline took the threat of a rival to Caroline North seriously, and they announced that power would be increased to 50 kW. Several other stations were planning to start broadcasting with names such as: 365, Ceaser, Cathy, Mayflower and Channel.

Radio 390's plans to use the *Cheeta II* were thwarted, because of the continued uncertainty of the ownership of the ship. Fortunately, for the Government, nothing further was heard of Radio Freedom, or the other proposed stations. It was estimated that by the end of the year there could have been at least 20 pirate stations on the air, with the possibility of even more joining them.

There had been some mystery surrounding the drowning of three Radio Invicta staff, in 1964, and there had been scuffles between men from Radio Essex and Radio City. Now there was a threat against Radio London.

A man claimed to have been approached by two Swiss men, with plans of starting a new station. It soon transpired, however, that the real plan was to silence Radio London.

The plan involved taking a small boat into the vicinity of the *Galaxy*, and transmitting a jamming signal on 266. It appears that a test signal was transmitted, from shore, which blocked Radio London for one hour. Radio London's owners called in the police, which stopped the plot from developing.

Radio City had been relaying Caroline Newsbeat programmes, and a new ten kilowatt transmitter had been promised. The tender *Offshore 1* delivered three large packages to the fort, one of which fell into the sea while being transferred,

Shivering Sands Fort had been the home for Radio Sutch, and then Radio City. It had been raided and silenced, its owner had been shot, it had been prosecuted and finally silenced on 9th February, 1967.

Foto Flite

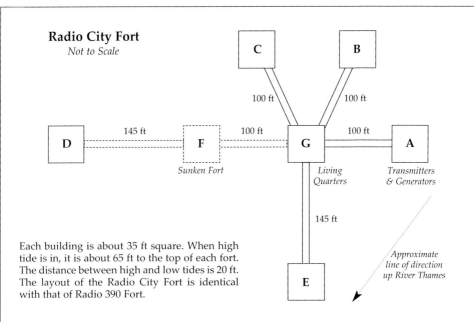

Radio City Fort
Not to Scale

C   B

100 ft   100 ft

D   145 ft   F   100 ft   G   100 ft   A

Sunken Fort   *Living Quarters*   *Transmitters & Generators*

145 ft

Each building is about 35 ft square. When high tide is in, it is about 65 ft to the top of each fort. The distance between high and low tides is 20 ft. The layout of the Radio City Fort is identical with that of Radio 390 Fort.

Approximate line of direction up River Thames

E

but it was successfully recovered.

Radio City engineers had to clean the equipment, before they could start to assemble the transmitter. Radio Caroline sent some staff to the fort, to assist, but they could not get the transmitter to work. Engineers had to overhaul the old equipment to keep the station on the air.

In the early hours of Monday 20th June, four days after Radio London announced that they intended to take over Radio City, twelve men and one woman boarded the station. Major Oliver Smedley, who was a director with Radio Caroline, led the boarding party. He informed the Radio City staff that he was there to prevent the station being taken over.

Major Smedley then returned to shore, leaving the rest of the boarders on the fort. The Major had been a director with Radio Atlanta who owned the transmitter, and was now in a similar role eith the Caroline organisation, as Planet Productions had finally bought out Project Atlanta.

Radio London's managing director immediately pulled out of the discussions, when it was threatened that nerve gas would be used to take the fort back. Apparantly Mr Calvert then approached the owners of Radio 390 to see if they would be interested in a merger with Radio City.

In the meantime Mr Calvert went to the police to complain about the raid on his fort. He also mentioned that the crystal had been removed from the transmitter preventing the station from resuming broadcasts. The police informed Mr Calvert that as the fort was in International Waters, they could take no action.

It seems that Mr Calvert had not paid the £10,000 for the transmitter, which was still not working. He had a very stormy meeting with the Major during the morning of Tuesday 21st of June. Apparantly Mr Calvert threatened to retake the fort, claiming he would use nerve gas!

That evening Mr Calvert went to the house of Major Smedley, and tried to force his way in, a female member of the Major's staff tried to prevent him. The Major heard the fracas and took a shotgun to the door, as he got there he saw that Mr Calvert was about to strike the lady with a statue, so he shot Mr Calvert who died from his injuries. A gas gun was found on Mr Calvert's body.

Major Smedley was charged with murder, and appeared in court on Monday July 18th 1966, when the charge was reduced to manslaughter. At a subsequent hearing, at Chelmsford, the Major was found not guilty, having acted in self-defence.

In spite of Mr Calvert's death, the boarding party remained on the fort, keeping Radio City off the air. On Wednesday 22nd of June Essex police officers visited the fort where they questioned the members of the boarding party. The boarding party left the fort on Sunday 26th of June, and shortly afterwards Radio City resumed broadcasting

The circumstances of the death of Mr Calvert's shocked everyone, including the Government, who decided that they would make plans to close the stations. Following questions about Radio City in the House of Commons, Mr Benn announced that the Government would re-arrange its timetable and introduce a Bill, in draft form, before the Summer recess.

The fate of the offshore stations was soon to be sealed, but in spite of the death of her husband, Mrs Calvert announced that she would keep Radio City on the air.

The 'Tower of Power' would not take part in any merger plans, and would remain as an independent station.

On Friday 1st July, Mr Benn announced that the Bill to silence the stations was almost ready, and that it would definitely be submitted to the House before the recess. He also added that the Government was reviewing its broadcasting policy, and that consideration was being given to providing pop music on a national basis, in addition to a network of local stations. The policy review was not quite ready, but a statement on the proposals could be expected, as soon as possible.

The 24 hour pop music format of the pirate stations was described by Mr Benn as audible wallpaper, when he told the Commons debate that if round the clock music was desired it would best be dealt with by a national station, rather then a multiplicity of commercial stations.

Mr Benn added that four of the pirate stations were broadcasting from within territorial waters, three of these were the fort-based Radio's 390, City and Essex. The fourth station was Radio Scotland, whose ship was anchored off Troon. Mr Benn added that no action would be taken against these stations, as the impending legislation would silence all of the stations, not just these four.

Two days later, on 3rd July, Mr Benn was replaced by Mr Edward Short as the Postmaster General. He told the House, on Wednesday 13th July, that the impending legislation would soon be ready, and that it could be implemented by early 1967. The Bill would make it illegal to work for, or supply, the stations, under guidelines that had been agreed by the Council of Europe.

On Thursday 28th July the Marine etc. Broadcasting (Offences) Bill received its first reading in the House of Commons. The Bill, as had been promised, was wide reaching making it illegal to own or operate an offshore station. It effectively covered every kind of structure including ships and aeroplanes.

The Bill would make it illegal for British citizens to install or maintain equipment to make such broadcasts. It would also be illegal to supply the stations with food, fuel, records and tapes, or to advertise on any pirate station. It would also be against the law to operate a supply tender, or to advertise a station, or to give programme schedules.

This was seen as a move against the freedom of the press, as the word 'advertise' could mean anything, and still to this day causes some confusion. During the research for this book, I was interviewed by police officers, to ensure that I did not contravene the law, as offenders could be sent to prison for two years, with an unspecified fine.

With the first reading of the Bill, which was designed to silence the stations, they began to draw up plans to evade the law by basing their operations overseas. Undeterred by the Bill, Radio Caroline started 24 hour broadcasting, from the *Mi Amigo*, on Saturday 6th August.

All of the big stations, Radio's Caroline, London, Scotland, 270, England and Britain announced that they would continue to broadcast, and that they would obtain advertising from America or the Continent. They would employ foreign nationals on the stations, who would be exempt from the law.

The stations were quite confident that they would be able to continue broadcasting, in spite of the legislation, but they did start 'Save our Station' campaigns. A record was released by a group called The Roaring Sixties, which

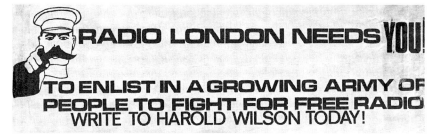

RADIO LONDON NEEDS YOU!

TO ENLIST IN A GROWING ARMY OF PEOPLE TO FIGHT FOR FREE RADIO WRITE TO HAROLD WILSON TODAY!

was entitled *We Love The Pirate Stations*, was given considerable air time. Mr Wilson was sent a copy, but no one was saying whether he played it.

There were many complaints levelled at the pirate stations. Mr Benn as Postmaster General, had said: 'The pirates are a real menace, they don't pay copyright fees, and they don't pay the musicians who record the music. They are making quick money, at the expense of others'.

During their save our station campaign, Radio London answered those charges, in the following manner.

The Postmaster General levels three charges:
1. *We steal our copyrights.*
    This is not true, Radio London pays full royalties for its music.
2. *We interfere with emergency services at sea.*
    Yet in nearly three years of broadcasting, there have been around 3,000 emergency calls around Britain, but not one case of interference has occurred during that time.
3. *We interfere with Continental stations.*
    But in nearly three years Radio London has yet to receive its first complaint.

As to the Postmaster's first charge, it is on record that Radio Atlanta reached agreement with the Performing Rights Society on Tuesday 26th May, 1964. Radio London had entered an agreement with the Society in February 1966.

It is also on record that the Postmaster informed the House of four instances of interference, caused by Radio London. He stated on 28th June that there had been two complaints from Belgium and two from Yugoslavia, but it is not recorded if those complaints were passed on to Radio London.

Radio Caroline produced statistics to show that the offshore radio stations were not the only ones who had usurped frequencies. Caroline claimed that 406 European radio stations were broadcasting on unauthorised frequencies, and that 59 had, by some means such as increased power, altered their agreed characteristics.

There were 191 stations that still adhered to the 1949 Copenhagen Plan, of which Britain was one. Ronan's point was that the stations that had been signatories to the Plan, but had subsequently not adhered to that agreement, were more guilty then Caroline and the other stations who had not been broadcasting in 1949.

The Conservatives, like the stations themselves, were not pleased with the impending Bill. Paul Bryan MP was concerned at the loss of pleasure for the millions of listeners, and advocated the introduction of local commercial radio.

The pirates had proved, by their phenomenal success, that there was a demand for such stations. The many listeners would need, and expect, an alternative. One national station could not provide the kind of service that they would expect.

There had been some mention of the proposed BBC Radio 1, on 247 metres, but the demand was for lively, varied entertainment, with some local content. The Conservatives had recognised that up to 25 million people had, in their own way, shown that there was a need for greater diversity in broadcasting.

Right from the start, through until the Bill became law, the Conservatives fought hard on the listeners' behalf. No doubt they were quick to see that 25 million was a sizeable proportion of the voting electorate.

The first reading of the Bill, in the Commons, had already scored one victory for the Government. Not one of the proposed new stations came on the air; it would have been pointless to invest in a new station, only to have it forcibly closed down soon afterwards. It also curtailed the expansion plans of the existing stations, as they were now too busy fighting for survival.

On 1st July Mr Benn had told the House that four of the stations, under a 1964 Order in Council, were broadcasting from inside territorial waters. He had added that no action would be taken against them. This was just a stay of execution, Radio Scotland was served with a summons on 14th September. Just one week later Radio 390 was served with a summons, relating to the Wireless Telegraphy Act.

The next day, Wednesday 21st September, the station's Managing Director was also served with a summons, for unlawful use of a transmitter. In spite of the impending legal action against him, and his station, he announced that Radio 390 would remain on the air.

Radio Essex received the same treatment, just eight days later, when the station owner, Roy Bates, was served with a summons for using a radio transmitter without a licence. Mr Bates stated that he would fight all the way, and added that the station was to change its name. Radio Essex closed on 4th October, to be replaced on Wednesday 5th October by Britain's Better Music Station (BBMS).

The life of the fort-based stations had already been shown to be precarious, with scuffles between Radio City and Radio Essex, and the boarding and silencing of Radio City. There was also a report that Radio 390 was to have been silenced, in September 1966. Now it was not just pirate fighting pirate, the Government were stepping in with legal guns blazing!

It was the beginning of the end of the good times, but to dispel the gloom and doom Radio Caroline North was just about to make history. The only marriage ever to take place on board a radio ship occurred on Tuesday 20th September, on board the MV *Caroline*.

Disc jockey Mick Luvsit married Janet Teret, the sister of former Caroline DJ Ray Teret. It was a dull foggy day, which prevented the parents of the bride arriving in time for the ceremony, which was held in the main lounge just after the 6 pm news.

The Master of the MV *Caroline*, Captain Martin Gips, officiated at the ceremony, which was broadcast live. The bride was wearing a white trouser suit, with a long lace coat, which was trimmed with blue ribbon, and was bare foot. The groom was wearing a maroon suit, and they were joined by crew and DJs, with two boat loads of invited guests. At the end of the ceremony the Captain announced, 'I, Martin Gips, Captain of the Panamanian merchant vessel MV *Caroline*, in the name of the Republic and by the authority vested in me, by the laws of Panama, now pronounce you man and wife'.

The live broadcast came to an end with the playing of the record *Climb Every Mountain*, after which the party was taken ashore, to a reception in the Isle of Man. The couple eventually moved to Canada, where they set up home in Vancouver.

The good times came to an early end for 'Swinging Radio England, where the action is'. The station had not been very successful in attracting advertisers, or listeners. The brash American format was not popular, even though English DJs had joined ship, names such as Roger Day, Colin Nichol and the legendary Johnnie Walker.

Radio England closed on Friday 4th November, the station being sold to a Dutch group with an address in Amsterdam. The new station opened the next day, using the callsign 'Radio Dolfijn' (Dolphin). The station took over Radio England's studio, and broadcast an easy listening format from 6 am until midnight.

On Thursday 24th November Estuary Radio, the owners of Radio 390, appeared in a Canterbury Court. The prosecution stated that the Geneva Convention of the Sea, held in 1958, and ratified by the British Government in 1964, concluded that the Thames Estuary could be described as a Bay.

The territorial waters were extended from a line, drawn from North Foreland to Walton on the Naze, which meant that the Red Sands Fort was inside territorial waters. In spite of powerful arguments by the station's defence team, led by Sir Peter Rawlingson QC, Estuary Radio was found guilty.

The station was fined £100, the maximum allowed under the Wireless Telegraphy Act. The station Managing Director, and the company Secretary were both given an absolute discharge. The Post Office also made an application to have the transmitting equipment confiscated, but this was rejected.

Radio 390 gave notice of its intention to appeal against the decision and, so as not to jeopardize the appeal, it was decided to close the station. To the sound of the National Anthem, Radio 390 closed, just before midnight on Friday 25th November.

The owner of Radio Essex (BBMS), Roy Bates, appeared in Court on Wednesday 30th November, conducting his own defence. He was found guilty and fined £100. Once again the Post Office applied to have the equipment confiscated, but the judge refused this application. Mr Bates announced his intention to appeal, adding that BBMS would remain on the air.

November may have brought problems for the fort-based stations, but this did not stop changes being made on Caroline North. The station made its normal close at 8.30 pm, on Monday 31st October, but resumed transmissions two hours later.

At 10.30 pm, engineers started test transmissions on 257 metres (1169 kHz), using a 10 kilowatt transmitter. The test broadcast continued until just before 6 am, when normal programmes resumed on 199, using the second 10 kW transmitter. The tests lasted for six weeks, with Radio Caroline North moving to 259 on Sunday 18th December.

On Tuesday 13th December, Radio 390 had its appeal heard, by three judges, who voted two to one to uphold the earlier Court ruling. The Court ruled that the station could make another appeal, but Estuary Radio decided not to do so.

On Tuesday 20th December, the Government published its White Paper, detailing the future of British Broadcasting. The Paper stated that the BBC would operate an all-pop service, on the medium wave. The old BBC names of Home, Light and Third, would be renamed Radio's 1, 2, 3 and 4.

Radio 1 would provide the pop music on 247 metres (1215 kHz), in addition the BBC would set up nine local radio stations, on a one year trial. These stations would take about one year to set up, and they would broadcast on FM.

With the British Government totally opposed to Radio Caroline, or any other pirate coming ashore to broadcast legally, Ronan sounded out the Isle of Man. The island had its own Government, which was on very friendly terms with Radio Caroline, as the north ship had been advertising the island, free of charge.

In November, however, it was made clear that the impending legislation would cover the island, and the Channel Islands, which effectively blocked any prospect of Caroline coming ashore.

Things were not going to plan for BBMS (Radio Essex) either; having run out of money the station closed mid-afternoon on Christmas Day. Just six days later, on New Year's Eve, Radio 390 resumed broadcasting. The station owners announced that they had new evidence that put the Red Sands Fort in international waters.

1967

Top 20 for week commencing Friday 6th January, 1967

1	(1)	Green, Green Grass Of Home	Tom Jones
2	(2)	Morningtown Ride	Seekers
2	(3)	Sunshine Superman	Donovan
4	(-)	I'm A Believer	Monkees
5	(4)	Save Me	Dave Dee, Dozy, Beaky, Mick and Titch
6	(5)	Happy Jack	Who
7	(9)	In The Country	Cliff Richard and the Shadows
8	(13)	Anyway That You Want Me	Troggs
9	(6)	Dead End Street	Kinks
10	(7)	What Would I Be	Val Doonican
11	(18)	You Keep Me Hangin' On	Supremes
12	(16)	Pamela Pamela	Wayne Fontana
13	(19)	Sitting In The Park	Georgie Fame
14	(12)	Friday On My Mind	Easybeats
15	(11)	Good Vibrations	Beach Boys
16	(12)	What Becomes Of The Brokenhearted	Jimmy Ruffin
17	(32)	Night Of Fear	Move
18	(15)	Under New Management	Barron Knights
19	(23)	(I Know) I'm Losing You	Temptations
20	(10)	My Mind's Eye	Small Faces

For Whom the Bell Tolls

On Tuesday 17th January, Roy Bates had his appeal heard at Chelmsford Magistrates Court. His appeal was not upheld, the court ruling that the Knock John Fort was inside territorial waters. Mr Bates stated that his radio station would not be silent for long, he was moving all of the equipment to another fort which was definitely in international waters.

During January Mrs Calvert, who had taken over the running of Radio City after the death of her husband, became concerned that there were rumours of a raid being planned on the fort. She informed the police and went out to the Shivering Sands, to bolster the morale of the station workers.

On Thursday 9th February Mrs Calvert was in Court, facing charges for operating an illegal radio station, from a fort inside territorial waters. She was found guilty and fined £100, and the Court ruled that Radio City must close. In compliance with that order, Radio City closed that same evening, at midnight.

Disc jockey Tom Edwards closed the station, 'From Radio City, your host on the coast, God bless and thank you for being a marvellous audience. Goodnight and Goodbye'. The station closed to the sounds of the National Anthem.

The three stations that had broadcast from a fort had all been successfully prosecuted, and two of them, Radio City and Radio Essex, had closed down. The future for the third station, Radio 390, was also looking far from secure. In spite of this, the station agreed to pay royalties to the Performing Rights Society.

The station Managing Director, Mr Allbeury, had tried to persuade shareholders that if the station was to survive, they must vacate the fort and purchase a ship. He failed in his attempt, so on 10th February he resigned and formed his own company, Carstead Advertising Ltd.

Meanwhile, Britain Radio was experiencing problems, it was losing popularity to such an extent that the owners decided to close the station. 'Hallmark of Quality, Britain Radio' closed on Wednesday 22nd February.

The radio ship, *Olga Patricia*, had now lost both of its original stations. Radio England had been replaced by Radio Dolfijn, and on 23rd February a new station commenced broadcasts, Radio 355. The station used the same format as Radio 390, but in an English way, unlike Britain Radio, which was brash and Americanised. Ted Allbeury was now at the helm of a ship-based radio station.

On the same day that he resigned, Radio 390 found itself in court. Estuary Radio were facing 28 charges of broadcasting without a licence. On Thursday 23rd February the station was fined £200, and each of the six Directors of Estuary Radio were fined £60. The station's new manager stated that they would appeal, and that Radio 390 would remain on the air.

Olga Patricia was damaged in February by storm force winds, Radio Dolfijn and Radio 355 were put off the air. It was decided to take the ship to Holland, to allow repairs to the mast to be undertaken.

The ship was repaired in Amsterdam, and then returned to her usual anchorage. The ship's name had been changed to *Laissez Faire*, and Radio Dolfijn had changed its name. Radio 227 took over, using a top 40 format which replaced the light music format of Radio Dolfijn. The new station used modified Radio England jingles, and soon became quite popular.

The British Government, meanwhile, was setting about closing all of the stations. On Wednesday 15th February the Marine Offences Bill came before the House for its second reading. After a very stormy debate, it was passed with a majority of 87 votes.

The Conservatives were against the Bill, until the Government had implemented a broadcasting policy which would take into account the obvious needs of the millions of listeners. There had to be a suitable alternative to the pirates, who had at least 40 million listeners and they had to have choice and variety.

Mr Paul Bryan MP, Shadow Postmaster General, voiced the concerns of the opposition. He said that the Bill would kill the enjoyment of the listeners, and that the Conservatives were duty bound to protest on their behalf.

He went on to add that the Conservatives were in favour of local radio, on a far larger scale than had been proposed by the Government. They also wanted to see the introduction of commercial radio, which would end the monopoly enjoyed by the BBC for so long.

The debate was long and hard, with the opposition fighting to protect the interests of the listener and, no doubt, aware of the fact that it could be a good vote winning strategy. The Government won the day, but a Commons Select Committee was formed to further debate the proposals.

There were several amendments put forward, one Conservative tried to have television exempted. This proposal failed because of the prospect of having pirate TV broadcasts. There had already been the rumour that one would soon start broadcasting. Radio & TV Radex, was rumoured to be almost ready, with considerable American backing. There had also been the Radio & TV Noordsee project, which had been forcibly closed by the Dutch authorities in 1964.

It was no good closing pirate radio stations, if they were just replaced by a multitude of pirate TV stations. The Government could not take the chance, by leaving a loop hole which would soon get exploited by operators.

There was very nearly a reprieve for Radio Scotland. It was suggested that the station be allowed to continue broadcasting, because in large areas of Scotland it was the only station that could be heard. The amendment was defeated by just four votes.

The opposition also wanted more time, to allow a proper alternative to the Pirates. The opposition tried to have the introduction of the Bill delayed, for two years, after Royal Assent had been given, and then introduced only if both sides of the House agreed. Needless to say, this amendment also failed.

Far from getting a reprieve, City and County Commercial Radio (Scotland) Ltd, found itself in court. The company was charged with having broadcast, without a licence, from within territorial waters. The court ruled that the Firth of Clyde could be described as a Bay, as had been decided with the Thames Estuary.

Radio Scotland was found guilty and was fined £80, but the station owner was cleared of any charges. The station closed that evening, Tuesday 14th March, whilst its future was decided. It was agreed that the *Comet* would be towed back to its original anchorage, in the Firth of Forth.

Bad weather prevented the tow from taking place, and during the interim, plans were changed. The radio ship was towed to an anchorage off Ballywater, Northern Ireland. The new anchorage was in the North Channel, between County Down and the Mull of Galloway, Scotland.

The new location put the ship about 20 miles east of Belfast, but more than 100 miles south-west of Glasgow. In recognition of this position, the station commenced broadcasts on Saturday 8th April using the new callsign 'Radio Scotland and Ireland'.

Just three days before the station resumed transmissions, the Marine Offences Bill entered the Report Stage. This was the last stage before it was passed to the House of Lords. On Wednesday 5th April the Bill received a very stormy passage.

Once again a motion to exempt Scotland was defeated, as was an amendment which sought to protect the freedom of the Press. Under the new law it would be illegal to mention the stations, or advertise on the stations. This amendment was dismissed by Mr Short, the Postmaster General, who maintained that it was necessary in order to deal with those who would collaborate with the pirate stations.

The Bill was eventually passed, and prepared to go before the House of Lords, but at the same time the Isle of Man's House of Keys rejected the Bill. This was, of course, good news for Ronan who restarted negotiations with the Manx Government to bring Radio Caroline ashore. The decision to reject the Bill led the island's representatives on a collision course with the British Government, and feelings were to run very high.

On 2nd May the Government found itself defeated in the House of Lords. Lord Denham, an opposition Peer, proposed that the Bill be delayed, until the alternative BBC programmes had commenced. Lord Sorenson answered for the Government, stating that as the period between the demise of the offshore stations, and the start of the new BBC programming was only a month, or so, the Bill need not be delayed.

This proposal was put to the vote, and the amendment was carried, by a majority of 21 votes. The opposition were jubilant, but the taste of victory did not last long. Lord Sorenson stated that the Bill would become law one month and one day after the Royal Assent had been received.

Whilst this had been going on, Radio Scotland and Ireland was still having problems. The new station name was proving to be quite a mouthful, so it was changed to Radio 242. Reception in Scotland was very poor, and the Irish authorities were making it difficult to supply the ship.

Whilst Radio Scotland had been off the air, prior to moving to this location, it had lost in the region of £24,000 in advertising revenue. It was costing in excess of £1,200, per week, to keep the *Comet* at sea, but there was no point if the broadcasts could not be heard.

It was suggested that the *Comet* might be towed out into the Atlantic, but common sense prevailed. Instead she was towed around the north coast of Scotland, to an anchorage off Fife Ness. The new anchorage, off the northern shores of the Firth of Forth, put Radio Scotland just over 30 miles north-east of Edinburgh. The station resumed broadcasts on Monday 8th May.

On Saturday 1st July the Marine Offences Bill was finally passed by Parliament, and on Friday 14th July it received Royal Assent. The Postmaster General duly announced that, after a waiting period of one month and one day, the Bill would become law on Tuesday 15th August, 1967.

The death knell had finally been sounded for the pirate stations. The plans to evade the new legislation fell by the wayside, only Radio Caroline re-affirmed its intention to remain broadcasting; the hopes and plans of Radio London, Radio Scotland, and Radio 270 were dashed. They all announced that they would comply with the new legislation and close before the deadline, making their final day of broadcasting on 14th August.

Radio 227, which had been broadcasting from the *Laissez Faire* for just five months, closed suddenly at 6 pm on Friday 21st July. The last live programmes finished five hours earlier, the last hours being pre-recorded.

Radio Caroline

THE CAROLINE CLUB

— SOLE SELLING AGENTS —

PLANET PRODUCTIONS LIMITED · 6 CHESTERFIELD GARDENS · LONDON W.1 · HYDE PARK 9721

Overseas Cables & Telegrams: Palairwave London W1   Telex 261816

Dear Members,

Hallo again from the old Club but a new secretary - with more Caroline News.

As you know your former secretary, Kathie Jeffrey left Caroline just after Christmas and resumed her former career as a croupier in London. She sends her best wishes to everyone.

I myself have been with Caroline for almost two years but with the Club only since the New Year.

The D.J. scene has changed a little during the first part of 1967. Gordie Cruse has left the North ship after 7 months. His visit to England was originally planned to be quite brief - one of many stops on his solo working world tour - but the opportunity to join Caroline was one he couldn't bear to pass up, so he stayed with us rather longer than expected. He told me that he had been extremely happy here and that 7 months on an offshore radio station was an expereince he will never forget. I know the rest of the boys on the North ship were very sorry to see him go - as were all his faithful listeners. As this is being written I believe Gordie is in Honolulu. It might be years before he finally gets back home to Canada.

One of the South ship newsreaders John Aston left just recently. He is working in the North of England but I think he is hoping to find work abroad.

Mark Sloane, another ex South ship newsman, paid a visit to Caroline House not long ago, looking very tanned after spending three months with a radio station in the West Indies.

I am pleased to introduce three new names to you. Two to the South ship: Tom Edwards, an English D.J., and Ian McRae, an Australian to the News staff. Gordie Cruse has been replaced on the North ship by yet another Canadian, Jerry King.

I'm sure that you will all be pleased to welcome back former Caroline North and South D.J., Rick Dane, who is the compere of the latest Caroline game, Lucky Birthday Bonanza.

Unfortunately Ian McRae's biography was not completed in time for this letter, but the others you will find at the end.

Both Steve Young and Keith Hampshire paid visits to their respective homes in Canada on their separate weeks off recently. They were both very excited about seeing home again but, fortunately for us, were happy to get back to their 'public'!

Keith, especially, said that everyone he met at home knows all about Caroline and just wouldn't stop asking him questions about Caroline: what life on a radio ship was like, etc. He made guest appearances on three radio stations and one TV station and did a lot of talking about Caroline.

Dave Lee Travis has recently been to Germany to appear in one of their TV pop programmes. The producers of the show were recently in England and filmed Dave performing live for one of their shows and then invited him back to Germany for a live TV appearance. I understand that he was a roaring success. I know we have a lot of members in Germany. If any of you saw Dave, do write and let us know what you thought of the show.

Steve Young and Mike Ahern just returned from Holland where they appeared at a club with great success, as far as I could gather from the brief telephone conversation I had with Mike.

There was a very successful rally held in Trafalgar Square in support of Free Radio on Saturday 13th May. Nick Lane and Gerry King of Radio Caroline, together with Conservative M... Tom Ironmonger and several Young Conservative leaders, spoke to a crowd of over 20,000, collected many thousand signatures on a giant petition and marched to Downing Street to hand it in at number 10. I understand that there is to be another rally in the same cause on May 28. I hope that as many as possible Club members will be able to go along.

I would like to say a very big thank you on behalf of all Radio Caroline to all of you who have written either to your local M...'s or to the Prime Minister or the House of Lords to protest against the banning of the offshore stations. Your response to our appeals and your letters of encouragement, and knowing that we have your support makes it worth while to go on fighting.

As you have probably heard over the air, we have started a monthly lucky Club No. prize spot. Each month two club membership numbers, (one from South and one from North) will be selected at random, and the member with that number will be the lucky winner of a prize L.P.

I hope that YOU will be a winner.

Until next time, best wishes and keep listening.

JERRY KING - NORTH SHIP

was born on 2nd May 1941 in Ontario, Canada.   He stands 6' 2",
has blond hair and 'baby blue' eyes.

He joined Caroline in March 1967, Spending a couple of weeks
down South before migrating to the North ship permanently.
He has D.J.'d for 2½ years in Ontario and then for another
year in Bermuda.

His interests are sports, reading and the cinema.   He says
his ambition is to be a success and eventually own his own
radio station.

TOM EDWARDS - SOUTH SHIP

describes himself as being very patriotic, being in the habit
of wearing red, white and blue socks and underwear.   He was
born in Norwich on 20th March 1944 and still lives there today.
He is a good-looking six footer with dark brown hair and blue/
green eyes.

After leaving school he became a journalist, then became interested in radio.   He worked as compere/announcer with Anglia,
Southern and Border TV, then as D.J. with Radio City before
joining Caroline South on 27th February this year.

The end was just as swift for Radio 390, which closed one week later. In May the station owners, Estuary Radio, had lost a civil action initiated by the Post Office which wanted to stop the station from transmitting.

The station appealed against this decision, the case being heard on 28th July. The defence, led by Sir Peter Rawlinson QC, asked for the ruling to be quashed, but they failed to convince Lord Justice Sellers. The earlier ruling was upheld and Radio 390 was ordered to cease broadcasting.

Just after 5 pm that same day, Alan Price singing *The House That Jack Built* was the last record to be played on Radio 390. Edward Cole then read the following closure announcement:

> We very much regret that due to an injunction imposed in the High Court today, at the request of the Post Office, Radio 390 is now required to cease broadcasting.
>
> We should like to express our immense appreciation, to the millions of listeners, who have always supported us during the past two years, and through our many struggles to stay on the air.
>
> It is very disappointing to all of us, that we are not able to continue to provide you with the programmes that you enjoy, but perhaps one day we will be allowed to do so again. Until then, on behalf of Mr Lye (the station's managing director), our London Office, the relief staff and everybody here, I should like to say Goodbye.

Radio 355 was the next station to close, it had only been on the air for five months, but in that short time it had become very popular. Broadcasting the same easy listening format as Radio 390, it never overtook its principal rival, but it did have an audience of several million.

It had not always been plain sailing for the station; on Monday 3rd July, one of the Dutch seamen assaulted the captain of the *Laissez Faire* with a knife. An emergency message was broadcast to the Coastguard who informed the police. The police said it was not within their jurisdiction, so they informed the navy.

The radio ship sent another message saying that all of the persons on board had locked themselves into cabins, as the seaman was threatening them with a knife. The ship's engine had a fault, so the *Laissez Faire* could not sail into port. During the early hours of the next morning the tender arrived, and two Dutch seamen were taken ashore.

On Wednesday 2nd August, the following message was read to the listeners:

> Regrettably, we have to announce the closure of Radio 355, owing to the effects of the British Government's Marine Offences Bill, which becomes law in mid-August.
>
> Radio 355 will cease broadcasting at 12 o'clock midnight, this coming Saturday 5th August. Needles to say, all of us connected with 355 are very sad at the impending closure of the station. However, we do hope that you will enjoy the remaining programmes coming your way, on Radio 355.

The contract between the station owners, and the owners of the radio ship had ended, and it was decided that there was no point in prolonging the agony. The station closed down, just after midnight, on Sunday 6th August.

On that same day, a group of men boarded the Red Sands Fort, where technicians were removing the station equipment. The raiders stole some of the equipment, and then returned to their boat, heading for the shore. The men alerted the authorities, and the raiders were subsequently arrested.

The *Laissez Faire* remained at anchorage until 19th August when she sailed to Flushing (Vlissengen), in Holland. The ship was dry docked for repairs and to have her hull cleaned. On Friday 1st September the ship sailed from Holland, crossing the Atlantic to Miami. The crossing to Florida took three weeks, eventually arriving on 22nd September, having encountered extreme weather, which badly damaged the mast.   *B.V. Kon. Mij. de Schelde*

The Marine Offences legislation was now just days from implementation, and the British Government found itself embroiled in an acrimonious battle with the Isle of Man.

The Manx Government was furious that the Bill had been extended, to include its island, being a duly elected Parliament, older than the British, and yet having British laws forced upon it.

It fought its case hard, but in the end, the British Government had its way. Due to the protracted discussions, it was announced the Bill would take effect from Friday 1st September.

It was a bitter blow for the island, who were pro-Caroline but it also put the north ship in a strange predicament. Radio Caroline North would still be legal, two weeks after the south ship had become illegal.

Ronan had to abandon all plans to try and bring Radio Caroline ashore. If the station had any future, the ships would have to remain at sea. At this early stage, no one could know what the Government's action would be, but Ronan was determined to fight any sort of blockade.

Top 20 for week commencing Friday 10th August, 1967

1	(1)	*San Francisco (Be Sure To Wear Some Flowers In Your Hair)*	Scott Mackenzie
2	(2)	*All You Need Is Love*	Beatles
3	(4)	*I'll Never Fall In Love Again*	Tom Jones
4	(3)	*Death Of A Clown*	Dave Davies
5	(7)	*I Was Made To Love Her*	Stevie Wonder
6	(8)	*Up, Up And Away*	Johnny Mann Singers
7	(11)	*Just Loving You*	Anita Harris
8	(15)	*Even The Bad Times Are Good*	Tremeloes
9	(20)	*The House That Jack Built*	Alan Price Set
10	(5)	*It Must Be Him (Seul Sur Son Etoile)*	Vicki Carr
11	(6)	*She'd Rather Be With Me*	Turtles
12	(12)	*Creeque Alley*	Mamas and the Papas
13	(10)	*See Emily Play*	Pink Floyd
14	(9)	*Alternative Title*	Monkees
15	(16)	*You Only Live Twice/Jackson*	Nancy Sinatra/ Nancy Sinatra and Lee Hazelwood
16	(18)	*Gin House Blues*	Amen Corner
17	(14)	*Let's Pretend*	Lulu
18	(22)	*Tramp*	Otis Redding and Carla Thomas
19	(19)	*007*	Desmond Dekker and the Aces
20	(-)	*Itchycoo Park*	Small Faces

Caroline Continues

Offshore radio had come to Europe with the sounds of Radio Mercur in 1958. The distinctive sounds of free commercial radio were immensely popular with the listeners, but not Governments. The BBC radio monopoly was broken by Radio Caroline on 28th March, 1964, and just 12 days later over 7 million were listening to Caroline. Other stations, seeing the success, quickly followed, but

The Sealand State Corporation of the principality of Sealand, an independent state in international waters six miles off the Essex coast. With a P.O. box number in Felixstowe, this is a very grandiose address for Britain's nearest and newest neighbour. It issues its own stamps and passports, and is in the *Guinness Book of Records* as the smallest independent territory in the world. As befitting such notoriety Roy Bates is known as Prince Roy. It is all a long way from January 1966 when, the Rough Sands Fort (as it was then known) became a war zone. Radio Caroline had paid to have part of the platform cleared to provide a helicopter landing pad. Roy Bates, from Radio Essex, also wanted to use the tower. It was not long before fighting broke out. But an uneasy truce was declared. However, in April Radio Essex staff took over the fort which led to a resumption of fighting. During the evening of 27th June, 1967 Caroline staff were attacked with petrol bombs. It was also claimed that shots had been fired from the fort. Ronan O'Rahilly claimed that he had spent over £15,000 on the fort, which he planned to convert to a holiday hotel and health centre. Mr Bates claimed that he held out against eight attacks. The incident was discussed in Parliament and the Ministry of Defence and local police investigated. It was subsequently decided that the fort was outside territorial waters so no action could be taken.

Fotoflite

the situation was allowed to get out of hand, which forced the British Government to take firm and decisive action. Plans were made by several stations to remain on the air, after the Act became law. 'Save our station' campaigns were launched, but Radio Caroline decided to embark on a more positive plan so that they could continue broadcasting.

In January 1967 Caroline personnel boarded the Rough Sands Fort, in international waters off Felixstowe. They worked long and hard, and by the end of March they had cleared a large flat area on the top of the fort for use as a helipad. A contract was signed with a firm of aviation consultants, to provide helicopters to bring supplies and equipment out to the fort. It was obvious that Caroline meant business, and were determined to beat the law, but the Caroline Organisation were not the only people interested in the fort.

After Radio Essex had been prosecuted, and gone off the air, Roy Bates had announced that the station would move to another fort, which was definitely outside territorial waters. That tower was, you've guessed it, Rough Sands Fort, and he intended ferrying equipment to the fort from the Knock John Fort. Stories soon circulated of violent clashes between men from the rival stations, a truce was later announced and it was agreed that both stations would share the fort. Work resumed until April, when the two men working for Caroline had to go ashore as one needed medical attention. When the men left the fort Radio Essex claimed vacant possession, and Mr Bates declared that he would hold the fort against all comers.

The Caroline Organisation tried, unsuccessfully, to regain the fort but each time they were beaten off in fierce battles. Matters came to a head in June 1967, after a particularly nasty battle, during which Molotov cocktail bombs were used against the Caroline men. The news of the battle reached the press, and questions were asked in the House. Ronan wanted the police to take action. but as the fort was in international waters there was nothing that they could do.

After the many skirmishes Radio Caroline lost the battle for the appropriately named Rough Sands Fort. It was estimated that Caroline had spent in the region of £15,000 on the conversion. Mr Bates still has possession of the fort to this day, in fact he declared UDI, Unilateral Declaration of Independence , and renamed the fort the Independent Principality of Sealand. Sealand has its own passports, stamps and currency, the passports are legal in many countries, especially Germany.

It was rumoured that the Germans intended assisting to extend the fort to become an offshore tax haven; whether the British Government would have allowed this to happen is another story.

Having lost the fort, and with the Bill soon to become law, Radio Caroline looked to America and Canada for staff for the two radio ships, as it would soon be illegal for British citizens to work for the station. The British subjects already working for Caroline were asked if they wanted to continue doing so, even if it meant changing nationality or leaving the country. Several of the staff decided to leave, but Mr Philip Soloman, a major shareholder who had invested £200,000, and was a Director of Caroline changed his nationality, so that he could continue working with the station.

An office was opened in Holland, from where it was hoped to run the two ships. Agreement was reached with the Wijsmuller Company to continue running the tender service for both of the ships. A plan was also devised to broadcast a joint English and Dutch format from the south ship. Ronan toured many countries to obtain advertising, so as to finance the operation. DJs were recruited from America, Canada, and Australia, and some of the existing DJs said that they would remain with the station.

On 14th July, 1967 the announcement that had been long awaited was made in the House of Commons: the Marine Offences Act would become law on 15th August. Radio London, which had said it intended defying the Act, being supplied from the Continent, surprised listeners on 28th July when the following statement was broadcast:

> Here now is the announcement you have all been waiting for. With the passing of the Marine Offences Bill, Radio London regrets to inform you, that after nearly three years of broadcasting it will be forced to close down in mid-August.

For Radio London, Scotland and 270 the end was very near, but Caroline was forging ahead with its plans to continue broadcasting. Fake advertisements had been taped, so as to protect the real clients from prosecution. Two of Caroline's most popular DJs, Johnnie Walker and the 'Admiral' Robbie Dale, announced publicly that they intended staying with the station. They were to be joined by many other English staff, all of them prepared to fight for free radio, even though they could face prosecution and become criminals if they returned home. Ronan stated that if any of his staff were prosecuted he would fight their case at the Court of Human Rights at Strasbourg.

As well as all the plans that Caroline had drawn up, the Isle of Man, in defending its right to govern its own island, came out on Ronan's side. The Manx Government vetoed the British Government's right to extend the Marine Offences Act to include the island. The Manx men felt that the Labour Government had no right to force its intentions, by overruling the island's own Government.

Many of House of Keys members voted in favour of further cutting of ties with Britain. Ronan went back to the island to watch the proceedings. He re-asserted that even if the Act was extended to include the island, Caroline North was remaining. The ship was to be serviced from the Republic of Ireland, and from Holland.

Eventually, the British Government got its own way, by drawing up an Order in Council, which was given Royal Assent, allowing the Act to take effect from Friday 1st September. The fate of the pirates had been sealed, and with the exception of Radio Caroline, all of the stations closed before the Act became law.

Monday 14th August dawned, a dull and windy day. A very sad day for the millions of listeners. It was one of those days, like when President Kennedy was assassinated, when you can remember exactly where you were, and what you were doing.

Off the east coast of Britain, four radio ships wallowed in the moderate swell, just 12 hours later, only one of them would still be broadcasting. Radio London was the first to say an emotional goodbye.

At 2 pm they commenced 'Their Final Hour', the show was hosted by Ed Stewart (now with Radio 2 FM), with Paul Kaye and Keith Skues. Taped messages were played, from DJs past and present, and some of the top artists of the day.

The MV *Galaxy* was home to Radio London from 1964 until 1967. The first test transmission was broadcast in November 1964, with regular programmes from 23rd December. The final broadcast was on 14th August, 1967. She stayed at anchor until Saturday 19th August, when she sailed to Hamburg, arriving two days later.   *Coastal Cards*

The farewell messages were interspersed with meaningful records, and some of the most popular jingles and adverts. Most of the goodbye messages ran along similar lines, thanking collegues and listeners, but Keith Skues added some points of interest to his farewell.

> 15th August is indeed a black, a sad day, in offshore radio history. During the past three years the pace and interest in radio has more then trebled, and the sale of radios has quadrupled. Offshore radio has been directly responsible.
> Over the past three years a large number of pop stars have been born, and a number of new record companies launched. Moreover you, the listener at home, have been well satisfied with the sounds eminating from your radio sets.

Records played during that final hour included, *It's All Over Now*, *The Last Time* and *Heroes and Villains*. The hour was very well produced, and very emotional. It was as Keith Skues had said, a very sad day.

The DJs who bid the station goodbye included Tony Blackburn, Chuck Blair, Dave Cash, Chris Denning, Pete Drummond, Kenny Everett, Duncan Johnson, Paul Kaye, John Peel, Mark Roman, Keith Skues, Ed Stewart, Tommy Vance and Tony Windsor.

Stars included, Madeline Bell, Beach Boys, Cat Stevens, Cliff Richard, Dusty Springfield, Jonathan King, Lulu, Mick Jagger, Ringo Starr, and the Walker Brothers.

The last advert on 266 was for 'Consulate, cool as a mountain stream'. After the final farewell message Paul Kaye, who had been the station newsreader, and had been with the station since before it went on air, introduced the Managing Director of Radio London. Mr Philip Birch made the following emotional speech.

It was just three years ago, this month that the idea for Radio London was born. Four months after that time Radio London was on the air, and four months after that, National Opinion Polls showed that it had millions of listeners - now it is to end.

During the past three years I feel that Radio London has done very little harm, but an awful lot of good. During that three years it has helped organisations such as The Institute for the Blind, Oxfam, The Cancer Fund, and the Lifeboat Service, to raise funds for their worthwhile causes. It saved the life of an airman, who bailed out over the North Sea, and was picked up by Radio London's tender.

In closing, Radio London, would like to give very special thanks to Lord Denham, who fought our case, in the House of Lords, and Lord Arran for all his help. To the Shadow Postmaster General, Paul Bryan, to Ian Gilmore, and the other MPs who stood up in the House of Commons, and fought our case.

I would also like to give my personal thanks to all of the staff at 17 Curzon Street, to all of the DJs, to Captain Budega and his crew. To the 1,027 advertisers, who supported Radio London in the last three years, and used Radio London to help sell their products.

But most of all I would like to thank you, one of the 12 million listeners in Holland, Belgium, Germany, and the other countries on the continent, for all of the support that you have given Radio London during the last three years.

If during that time Radio London has brought a little warmth, a little friendliness, a little happiness into your life, then its all been worthwhile. As one listener put it, the world will get by without Big L, but I'm not sure it will be a better place. Thank you.

The Beatles followed singing *A Day In The Life*. At the top of the hour Paul Kaye, who had been the first voice to be heard on Radio London, closed the station by saying: 'Big L time is 3 o'clock, and Radio London is now closing down'. The very last sound on 266 was the station theme tune, 'Big Lil', 98 seconds later Radio London was just a memory.

The MV *Galaxy* was silent, never again would she swing to the sound of pirate radio. The ship rusted away for several years in the German port of Kiel, where the vessel sank at its mooring in 1979, and was scrapped in 1986.

It was not long before many of the ex-Radio London DJs were heard again, this time working for the BBC. The 'Big L' had been such a successful venture, with advertising handled by Radlon (Sales) Ltd, that when the station closed it showed a profit of over £100,000.

The next to go was Yorkshire's finest, Radio 270, which very nearly missed the deadline. The station had been off the air from Friday 4th August, due to technical problems. The ship had left its anchorage, only returning on Sunday 13th August, to a new location off Bridlington.

'This is Radio 270, broadcasting on 1115 kilocycles, in the medium wave band. The time is 1½ minutes before midnight, and we are now closing down.' The station had become very popular in the North East, with over 4 million listeners, it did not make a profit, but it did manage to break even.

The *Oceaan VII* sailed into Whitby, the next day, where she was offered for sale. The radio staff soon dispersed, some later appearing on other pirate stations, the one who became the most well known was Paul Burnett, who worked for Radio Luxembourg and Radio 1.

Radio Scotland closed down at midnight, to the sound of a bagpipe lament. This station had become very popular, but it was left with a loss of £100,000. This had been incurred by the long periods spent off the air, and the cost of the towing operations from one anchorage to another. Some of the DJs went on to work for Radio Caroline, but the most well known was Stuart Henry, who went on to work for Radio 1 and Radio Luxembourg.

Caroline, broadcasting from two ships, was all that was left of the pirate stations. Caroline North was still legal, but Caroline South was not. Having opened offices in Holland, Canada, and America both ships operated with a new callsign, 'Radio Caroline International'. During the afternoon of 14th August the last legal tender arrived alongside the *Mi Amigo*, ready to take the staff to Felixstowe. With the moderate swell, and strong winds, it was not a pleasant trip, but not as bad as could be expected when the trip had to be made to Holland.

Disc jockey Tom Edwards, who went on to work for the BBC, was presenting his last show when the tender arrived. Four DJs came aboard, Johnnie Walker, Robbie Dale (The Admiral), Spangles Muldoon and Ross Brown. Going ashore were Tom Edwards, Roger Day, Gerry Burke, Kilroy, and Keith Hampshire. Roger Day told me:

> The last tender ride was a strange affair, knowing that it would be the last time, the next time would be from Holland, as criminals (supposedly). I arrived at Liverpool Street on the train before the Radio London DJs, and the crowd had to be seen to be believed. As I was quite a new face nobody bothered me. The DJs came home to a welcome usually reserved for superstars, which in their own way they were.

Portrait of Johnnie Walker.
Author's Collection

Portrait of Roger 'Twiggy' Day.
Author's Collection

When Radio London had closed down, Radio Caroline observed one minute of silence, as a mark of respect for the demise of their main rival. For the rest of the day the tension mounted, Caroline now had in excess of 20 million listeners.

At 9 pm Johnnie Walker commenced his last legal show. He had been told by Radio Luxembourg that he would never be a good DJ. His first opening had been with Radio England, joining Radio Caroline in October 1966. Radio Luxembourg had got it wrong, he went on to be one of the most popular DJs on Caroline, with his own fan club.

As the midnight hour approached, the DJs became more excited, a feeling shared by the millions of listeners waiting expectantly ashore. The last record of the legal service was *Puppet on A String* by Sandie Shaw, which was followed by an advert for Consulate cigarettes.

It was midnight, and the deadline for closure had been reached, but Caroline was not closing down, they were fighting on. Johnnie Walker announced, 'This is Radio Caroline, it now twelve midnight'. This was followed by the anthem *We Shall Overcome*, which was accompanied by some very enthusiastic, but off-key accompaniment by the DJs.

Johnnie then played the station theme tune, *Caroline*, by the Fortunes, which had been banned after Radio Caroline had adopted it. Johnnie then made this historical proclamation:

Radio Caroline would like to extend its thanks to Mr Harold Wilson, and his Labour Government for at last, after 3 years of broadcasting recognising the station's legality. Its right to be broadcasting to Britain and the Continent. Its right to give the music and service to the people of Europe, which we have been doing since Easter Sunday 1964.

And we in our turn recognise your right, as our listener, to have the freedom and choice in your radio entertainment, and of course that Radio Caroline belongs to you. It is your station, even though it costs you nothing. And as we enter this new phase in our broadcasting history, you naturally have our assurance that we intend to stay on the air. Because we belong to you, and we love you. Caroline Continues.

The very first record, on the new international service, from Radio Caroline South was *All You Need Is Love* by the Beatles. A record which had become Caroline's anthem.

Meanwhile, on shore, motorists began flashing their headlights toward the ship. Many people indulged in late night parties to celebrate the continuing sounds of free radio, Radio Caroline International.

There are a lot of people along the coast tonight, who are flashing their headlights at us, its very nice to see you. You have made us more happy, and I couldn't think that it was possible, but you have made us more happy then we already were.

Caroline South was now illegal, but Caroline North, anchored off the Isle of Man, still had 15 days before it became illegal. During the evening of Thursday 31st August the last legal tender made the journey from the radio ship to Ramsey. Amongst those leaving was Dave Lee Travis, who went to work for Radio 1, and Tony Prince who went to Radio Luxumbourg.

At midnight Don Allan announced, 'This is the northern voice of Radio Caroline International on 259 metres'. The DJs now had to face the long trip to Dundalk, in the Republic Of Ireland.

The DJs and crew of the *Mi Amigo* also faced a long tender ride to and from Holland, which could take 18 hours, or more,depending an the weather. The journey was not popular with the DJs, but it did not deter them from returning.

Roger Day always referred to the ordeal as 'that dreadful ride', he went on to tell me:

> The long tender rides were tedious, 18 hours from Ijmuiden and 12 from Flushing. The best thing to do was sleep, so on the night before I was due on board, or to come ashore, I stayed up so that I was really tired.
> The worst trip was when we were half way across, a force 10 gale blew up, and that trip took 22 hours! Fortunately I never got seasick, but I was always very glad to get to the *Mi Amigo*, which was always a very homely place.
> Morale on board was always quite good, except when the tender had to go to the North ship, to supply its oil and water. This meant that we did not get a tender for at least two weeks. Water was rationed, and we did get very down.

Programming continued with its familiar format, and DJs Roger Day, Johnnie Walker, Robbie Dale and Ross Brown were joined by Spangles Muldoon, Bud Balou, Stevie Merrick, and Andy Archer. These and other DJs and staff all faced prosecution if they were caught, but that did not deter them.

In spite of the new legislation by the British Government, the tender supply service proved very successful, and new records and tapes were available. A tremendous amount of revenue from advertising was lost but over the following months Caroline was able to maintain her happy routine.

When the BBC opened Radio 1, in September 1967, many people tuned to 247 metres to see what the new station was like, but they soon returned to 259. The new station was using some ex-pirate DJs, with jingles, some of which had been inspired by the pirates but it was just not the same.

It was not an all-pop format and, being a national service, it had to cater for all tastes. It was more powerful, with the potential for more listeners, but those who had heard the pirates, were not impressed by the new pretender.

Radio 1 had been opened by Tony Blackburn (and his barking dog, Arnold), and the first record had been *Flowers in the Rain*, by the Move, but listeners preferred Radio Caroline. The fact that the station had taken on the Government and won, was one good reason. The British love the underdog. The best reason for listening to Radio Caroline, was that it played the music you wanted to hear.

With programmes such as the US Hot 100, and the news service, Caroline News Beat, nothing seemed to have changed. The whole concept of Radio Caroline was to bring happiness, and to continue the sounds of free commercial radio.

The Summer of 1967 was enlivened by her broadcasts. One hot day DJ Bud Balou was presenting his show, when he was showered with cold water by his colleagues. It was this kind of attitude, fun loving, which so endeared the station to its listeners.

Considering the size of the two ships, with their cramped living and working conditions, there were few personality problems. The happiness was infectious, and contributed to Caroline's continued success. Throughout the Summer, almost everywhere you went, Caroline could be heard, on the beaches, in the towns, from cars, and public transport.

One of the most distinctive sounds that came from Radio Caroline, and is probably remembered by many, was Johnnie Walker's very emotional 'Let no man ever forget'. The story (dream more like) was played many times, after the introduction of the Marine Offences Act. It represented the hopes, and aspirations, of not just the staff, but also the millions of devoted listeners.

This is the story of man's fight for freedom. The beginning is in the past, the middle is now, the end is in the future. It is the story of sadness and of triumph.

August 14th, as disc jockeys Robbie Dale, Johnnie Walker and Ross Brown leave Liverpool Street London, spurred on towards the sea, by the hundreds of cheering people. See them now as they stand an the tender, there are tears in their eyes as their families, their homes and their loved ones are left behind.

3 o'clock on this Monday afternoon and on 266, *Big Lil* is heard for the last time, Caroline is alone. These three men prepare for midnight, for in a few hours time they are to challenge the might, and the power, of the British Government, they will become criminals.

Midnight approaches, it is August 15th, Johnnie Walker announces that Caroline belongs to you, that she loves you, and she will continue. The Beatles sing *All You Need Is Love*. Even the men sound happy, but underneath they are sad, for they now know that they have reached the point of no return. They are not sad for long, for they are joined by other men, who also gave up so much to fight for freedom.

The seas are rough and cruel, life is hard, but as each day passes the moment of triumph draws nearer. The British people rally round, they send food, they send comfort, and they send their love. All you need is love, and love overcomes.

The British Government relents, Caroline raises her anchor and heads for England. See her now majestically, and proudly, sailing up the river towards the capital, that has welcomed so many victors in British history. But none as victorious as these men.

They stand on the deck, waving to the millions of people that line the Thames. This time the tears flooding from their eyes are tears of happiness, The insurmountable odds have been surmounted. They reunite with their families, with their friends, with their loved ones.

We near the end of our story. London's skyline has a new landmark, Caroline's aerial, at last beaming out its love and music to a free, and peaceful nation. We have overcome, the battle is over, free radio becomes a way of life, but never taken for granted. For no man will ever forget Monday August 14th, 1967.

In spite of the drastic drop in clients, Radio Caroline had enough advertising booked to enable the station to continue broadcasting for at least six months. Ronan was fairly optimistic about the future, he was certain that he could obtain new clients. With offices in the USA, Canada and Holland, there should be enough companies willing to use Caroline. It was admitted that a payola scheme was in operation. Caroline's Top 50 was based on the bestseller's lists published by the music press. Other records could be added to Caroline's playlist at a cost of £100 per week, up to a maximum of two weeks. Although unpopular with the DJs who had to play these 'payola' records, there was no shortage of suppliers prepared to pay to have their music played.

A contract had been signed for a series of religious broadcasts, which proved very lucrative. The morale on the south ship remained very high, but it was a different story on Caroline North.

One DJ thought that it was the unfriendliest station that he had worked on. He described it as being soulless, there was no team spirit, it was just a group of individuals doing their own thing. Everyone on the north ship seemed to sense that it was just a matter of time before the station closed.

1968

Top 20 for week commencing Friday 29th February, 1968

1	(1)	*Cinderella Rockafella*	Esther and Abi Ofarim
2	(3)	*Legend Of Xanadu*	Dave Dee, Dozy, Beaky, Mick and Titch
3	(2)	*The Mighty Quinn*	Manfred Mann
4	(6)	*Fire Brigade*	Move
5	(14)	*Rosie*	Don Partridge
6	(15)	*Jennifer Juniper*	Donovan
7	(7)	*Pictures Of Matchstick Men*	Status Quo
8	(4)	*Bend Me Shape Me*	Amen Corner
9	(5)	*She Wears My Ring*	Solomon King
10	(11)	*Green Tambourine*	Lemon Pipers
11	(8)	*Words*	Bee Gees
12	(36)	*Delilah*	Tom Jones
13	(10)	*Darlin'*	Beach Boys
14	(21)	*(Sittin' On) The Dock Of The Bay*	Otis Redding
15	(12)	*Gimme Little Sign*	Brenton Wood
16	(10)	*Suddenly You Love Me*	Tremeloes
17	(9)	*Everlasting Love*	Love Affair
18	(13)	*Am I That Easy To Forget*	Engelbert Humperdinck
19	(19)	*Back On My Feet Again*	Foundations
20	(34)	*Me The Peaceful Heart*	Lulu

Hijack!

As predicted in Johnnie Walker's story, times did get much harder. As early as September 1967, Caroline South had ceased broadcasting for 24 hours every day. In spite of the early optimism, when contracts expired it proved very difficult to get new advertisers.

Some of the top stars were secretly giving money to Caroline, to help keep the station on the air. To the average listener it seemed that Radio Caroline International was taking on the British Government and winning.

Although money was getting hard to come by, the quality of the broadcasts did not suffer. The New Year arrived. On the south ship, the staff were preparing to celebrate Caroline's fourth birthday. Behind the scenes, however, trouble was brewing which led to a dramatic climax that shocked Radio Caroline, and the millions of listeners.

The Wijsmuller brothers, who owned and ran the tender service, to both ships, were in disagreement with each other and Radio Caroline over debts. Ronan agreed that he did owe the company money, but that it was part of their normal business procedure. No one could have foreseen what would happen next.

One of the brothers decided to take the law into his own hands, and he told his brother exactly what he intended to do. Thinking that it was just hot talk he did not inform Radio Caroline, which was not prepared for what happened next.

It was not just hot talk, the brother dispatched two tugs, the *Titan* and the *Utrecht* which made their way to the ships, with orders to tow them into a Dutch port. One way or another he wanted the financial problem resolved!

The tug *Utrecht* was used to tow the MV *Caroline* from the Isle of Man to Holland so that the outstanding debts could be cleared. The tow took one week, it was the end for the MV *Caroline* and Radio Caroline North.   E. *Houwerzijl*

The *Utrecht* made the long voyage to the MV *Caroline*, arriving at around 2 am on the morning of Sunday 3rd March, 1968. Radio Caroline North had closed for the night at 10 pm on Saturday 2nd, and the off duty staff had either gone to bed or were watching TV.

The crew of the tug got onto the ship and told the staff that they had orders to cut the anchor chains and tow the ship to Holland. Cutting the anchor chains took longer than the tug crew had envisaged, and it was not until late in the afternoon, that they were able to commence the tow.

Meanwhile, the *Titan* had gone alongside the *Mi Amigo*, during the early hours of Sunday morning. Roger Day had risen, and was preparing for his early morning show. The duty engineer had already opened the station by broadcasting continual music from 5 am until Roger took over at 5.30 am.

Crew from the *Titan* boarded the ship, and told the engineer that he could not broadcast any messages. Realising the enormity of the situation, he did try to broadcast, but the microphone was taken from him, and the studio was locked.

Roger Day takes up the story:

> I had woken at 5 am as usual, to do my early morning show, and almost immediately I heard a boat come alongside. I went upstairs to investigate, and saw that it was the *Titan*, nothing unusual about that as any Wijsmuller vessel would call, if they were in the area.
>
> One of the Dutch seamen joked that they were going to tow us to Japan! I just laughed and got on with shaving, and getting ready for my show.
>
> I was in the studio, at 5.25 am, cueing up my first record, when our Captain, and the tug Captain came in. He said that we had one hour to clear up the studio, as we were being towed to Holland for repairs. They immediately switched off the transmitter, so that we could make no further broadcasts.

I asked why, and could I make an announcement to say how long we would be off. They said 'No', so they towed us, and we cleared the studio. We contacted our land agent, who was most surprised. It was a very sad trip, with many tears.

I think that we all knew that it was the end. When we docked, the next day, we were told that they would contact us to tell us when to report back. We are still waiting! The agent was there to meet us with our pay, I even left some of my belongings on board.

We almost came back on Radio 270's ship, three weeks later, but some fool told the press, and that was that. That last day was very sad, we all knew that it was the end, but nobody dared to mention it.

That Sunday morning had been very misty, in the southern North Sea, so nobody from shore saw the *Mi Amigo* being towed away. The first person to see the radio ship leaving, was the duty watchman onboard a Trinity House lightship, who contacted the authorities to let them know.

The *Mi Amigo* arrived in Amsterdam the next day, but the MV Caroline faced a long slow journey, which was to last a week. The *Utrecht* towed her down the Irish Sea, along the English Channel, and across the North Sea. The ship was towed through the canal to Amsterdam, by a smaller tug.

One of the DJs said that the ship had left its anchorage on Sunday evening, and that the voyage had been quite friendly. Some of the Dutch crew remained on board the radio ship playing cards and eating with the Caroline staff. The sea had been quite rough, but the journey had been quite uneventful, to the point of being boring!

When they arrived in Holland the staff were told, like those from the *Mi Amigo*, that they would be told when to report back. Having been paid they went their separate ways, it was generally accepted that this was the end.

Millions of listeners were amazed, when they switched on their radios, on the morning of Monday 3rd March, only to find silence. They had no way of knowing that the ships had been silenced, and were being towed to Holland.

There had been some mention that the ships were in need of repair, so it was generally assumed that a breakdown was the reason for the silence. As 259 remained silent, the news of the ships leaving their anchorage was reported by the Press.

Some of the reports stated that Radio Caroline had finally fallen victim to the effects of the Marine Offences Act. Other reports stated that the ships would return, after essential works had been completed. Even the Wijsmullers confirmed that the reason for the ships being taken to Holland was for repairs.

The disappointment of the listeners turned to optimism that they would soon have their favourite station back. Ronan, however, knew the truth, it was a bitter blow for him. There was some pleasure in the fact that it had not come to an end because of the new legislation. He was, however completely shattered, and later stated that he had been on the verge of a nervous breakdown.

The two radio ships were moved to the Old Timber Harbour, where they were berthed side by side, but facing in opposite directions, so as to avoid damage to the aerial masts. Writs were attached to the masts preventing the ships from sailing, until the debts had been cleared. To get the MV *Caroline* back would have cost in the region of £60,000.

This was the first time that the two ships had been together, since Friday 3rd July, 1964. That had been the occasion of the merger between Radio Caroline

The MV *Caroline's* last sea voyage, the pirate silenced by a piratical deed. Sailing through the English Channel, being towed by the *Utrecht*. *Sky Fotos*

and Radio Atlanta, and Radio Caroline had been entering a new era of total optimism. Strangely enough, as we have already seen, that merger came about because Project Atlanta had owed the Wijsmullers money.

It was the first time that the MV *Caroline* had been in port for four years, and it was just two years since the *Mi Amigo* had been repaired after running aground at Frinton. On that occasion, Ronan had been pleased that the *Titan* had towed the *Mi Amigo* to safety.

Both of the radio ships needed insurance, if they were to keep their Panamanian registration. The insurance was up for renewal, the ship had to be seaworthy to obtain that certificate. This just gave credence to the reason for repairs to be carried out, whilst the ships were in port.

It was estimated that for every month that Radio Caroline was off the air, it would cost around £5,000. The normal running costs of the whole operation, including wages for the staff of 60, was in excess of £20,000 per month.

Ronan, however, was reported on Sunday 31st March as saying, 'Radio Caroline will soon resume broadcasts. If the GPO are congratulating themselves on beating us, they are a bit premature. Advertisers still want to deal with us. and young disc jockies are keen to have the chance to broadcast with us.'

When asked about the financial problems Ronan replied, 'Money is the least of my problems. I have been able to raise cash at times of greater crisis, than this.'

As it became clear that Radio Caroline's silence was going to last longer then had been expected, the mystery surrounding the station's future once again made the news.

A spokesman for the shipping office that had arranged the refit for both ships said:

Both ships have been completely overhauled, and with one or two minor repairs, they could put to sea at any minute. They are laying [sic] completely idle, and we have received no orders, as to what to do with them.

Having promised that Radio Caroline would soon be back on the air, and both ships ready for sea, why did they remain in port? It appears that the reason was financial; it was cheaper to start with another ship, than to pay for the *Caroline* and the *Mi Amigo*. If he could get Caroline back on the air, the revenue from advertising would pay for the ships.

Ronan travelled to Whitby, in early April, to try and negotiate for the use of the *Oceaan VII*, which had been used by Radio 270. The ship was being offered for sale, complete with transmitting equipment, for £12,500.

Built in 1939, at the Capelle yard, of A. Vuijk & Zonen, the *Oceaan VII* was 179 tons, and 118 feet in length. The converted trawler was a lot smaller then either the *Caroline* or the *Mi Amigo*, but she did have a 10kW RCA transmitter, fed to a 154 foot radio mast, and she was ready to put to sea.

It was planned to anchor the ship off Frinton, near where the *Mi Amigo* had been anchored, and that broadcasts would commence on Sunday 14th April. It was arranged that DJs 'Daffy' Don Allen, Andy Archer, Freddie Beare, Roger 'Twiggy' Day, Jim Gordon and Roger Scott, would man the station.

Unfortunately,the story of Radio Caroline's imminent return was leaked to the Press, which resulted in the owners of the radio ship being threatened with prosecution. The deal fell through, and the *Oceaan VII* was decommissioned as a radio ship, with the aerial and the transmitting equipment removed. The ship

A view of the MV *Caroline* near Zaandam as she transits the canal to Amsterdam on Saturday 9th March, 1968.

E. Houwerzijl

was put on the market again, with an asking price of £12,000; there were no offers, so the ship was scrapped.

Radio Caroline closed its office in Holland, lack of potential advertising was blamed. Ronan had visited leading advertising agencies, but they were not interested. Having met with no success, Ronan left Holland, and was reported as having gone into retreat.

Once again it was time for speculation, one theory put forward was that Ronan would be invited to run Manx Radio on the Isle of Man. Another theory was that he would become more involved with the film industry. This had more substance, as Ronan had been a director of the company that had made the film *Girl On A Motorcycle* starring Marianne Faithful.

It was not until Friday 1st November that anything else was heard about the future of Radio Caroline. The Free Radio Association of Great Britain announced that Caroline would soon be back on the air. The Association secretary added, 'American firms, with British subsidiaries, have decided to advertise on the new Caroline, so there should be no problems in that respect. Nothing can stop us now, we have the ship and the DJs.'

The ship they were planning to use was the MV *Galaxy*, which had been the home for Radio London. The *Galaxy* had sailed to Hamburg, on Saturday 19th August, 1967, where it had been completely overhauled and repainted white. The work had been completed in October 1968, but nothing further was heard about this proposed return, so the *Galaxy* remained in the German port and Radio Caroline remained silent.

The two radio ships rotted away in the Old Timber harbour in the port of Amsterdam for four years. This 1971 view shows the silent ships and allows a comparison in size between the *Caroline* and the *Mi Amigo*.   *Ron van den Bos*

Chapter Three

The Dutch Era,
1970-1974

1970

Top 20 for week commencing Sunday 4th January, 1970

1	(1)	*Two Little Boys*	Rolf Harris
2	(2)	*Ruby Don't Take Your Love To Town*	Kenny Rogers and the First Edition
3	(5)	*Melting Pot*	Blue Mink
4	(9)	*Tracy*	Cufflinks
5	(7)	*All I Have To Do Is Dream*	Bobby Gentry and Glen Campbell
6	(3)	*Sugar Sugar*	Archies
7	(4)	*Suspicious Minds*	Elvis Presley
8	(12)	*Good Old Rock'n'Roll*	Dave Clark Five
9	(6)	*Yester Me, Yester You, Yesterday*	Stevie Wonder
10	(16)	*The Liquidator*	Harry J. All Stars
11	(11)	*The Onion Song*	Marvin Gaye and Tammi Terrell
12	(13)	*Durham Town (The Leavin')*	Roger Whittaker
13	(10)	*Without Love*	Tom Jones
14	(8)	*Winter World Of Love*	Englebert Humperdinck
15	(14)	*(Call Me) Number One*	Tremeloes
16	(30)	*Reflections Of My Life*	Marmalade
17	(17)	*But You Love Me Daddy*	Jim Reeves
18	(21)	*Something/Come Together*	Beatles
19	(-)	*Comin' Home*	Delaney and Bonnie and Friends
20	(29)	*If I Thought You'd Ever Change Your Mind*	Cilla Black

The Unbelievable has happened

The British offshore radio era ended, with the closure of Radio Caroline, in March 1968. For most of the country, it was no longer possible to listen to pirate radio being broadcast from a ship. But for some, living in the South East, they could tune into Radio Veronica, which was anchored of the Dutch coast.

Radio Veronica commenced broadcasting from a converted German lightship, *Borkum Riff*, which had anchored off the resort of Katwijk ann Zee in 1960. Regular broadcasts commenced on 6th May, on 185 metres, but this caused interference to other stations. In retaliation the Dutch Government authorised the jamming of Veronica.

The station moved to 182 metres, but this caused even more extensive interference; as a result the station closed down on 13th May. Just two days later broadcasts resumed, on 192 metres (1562 kHz), using a 1kW transmitter.

Radio Veronica had survived for eight years, and apart from that initial skirmish with the authorities, the station had been left alone. The popularity of its broadcasts soon established Radio Veronica as Holland's favourite radio station.

The owners had taken great care to give *Veronica* respectability, and because of this, the Dutch Government tolerated the broadcasts. With plenty of advertising contracts, the station was making a profit, estimated at £1 million. With this revenue the owners purchased a new radio ship.

In November 1964, the *Norderney*, a converted trawler, replaced the ageing *Borkum Riff*. The new ship was anchored off the coast of Scheveningen and was fitted with all of the latest equipment. The Gentlemen of Veronica, as the owners were affectionately known, were justly proud of their new ship.

Two years later, in Germany, the MV *Galaxy* had just completed a major refit. The ship had been purchased for £10,000, and it was planned that the ship would commence broadcasts on 1st November, 1968, from an anchorage near Cuxhaven. Broadcasting on 266 metres the station would be on the air from 5 am until 1 am, with light music during the day and pop music at night.

The *Galaxy* did not leave port, as the work had not been completed. In the meantime the German Government announced that they would introduce a Marine Offences Act, from 2nd July, 1969. As a result backing for the project was withdrawn and the *Galaxy* did not commence broadcasts.

Two Swiss radio engineers, who had worked on the project decided to try and get their own station on the air. Erwin Meister and Edwin Bollier purchased the 347 ton Norwegian coaster *Bjarkoy*, just before Easter 1969. The 124 ft vessel was renamed *MEBO*, derived from the first two letters of their surnames. And, coincidentally, the initials of the Marine etc. Broadcasting(Offences) Act.

The two set about the conversion with alacrity (perhaps they should have used screwdrivers!), because they suddenly decided that the ship was not big enough. They purchased the 630 ton *Silvretta*, which they renamed *MEBO II*.

The 186 ft ship had been built in Holland, in 1948, at the Slikkerveer yard of De Groot & Vliet. The ship was prepared for its new role at the same yard that she had been built in.

No expense was spared during the conversion; the cabins, the two studios and the transmitters were the best that money could buy. The ship had equipment to broadcast on medium wave, short wave and FM. The main transmitter was the only one of its kind, with an output of 105 kilowatts the most powerful ever fitted to a pirate radio station. It also had two 10.5kW short wave transmitters, and one 1.2kW FM transmitter.

The *MEBO II* left the yard on 22nd January, 1970, heading out into the cold North Sea. The multi-coloured ship anchored off the Dutch resort of Noordwijk. Radio North Sea International (RNI) began test transmissions at 10.30 pm the next evening on 6210kHz in the 49 metre band, and 102mHz FM. These broadcasts comprised continuous music, interspersed with English and German announcements.

Broadcasts in the medium wave, 186 metres (1610kHz), commenced on the 11th February with Roger 'Twiggy' Day making the announcements. The station officially opened at 6 pm on 28th February, 1970. Programming comprised German language from 6 am until 8 am and 6 pm until 8pm, with English from 8 am until 6 pm and 8 pm until midnight.

Three weeks after RNI opened, the owners had a surprise in store, they decided to move the *MEBO II* to the English side of the North Sea. During the

The brightly painted *MEBO II* at anchor. The psychedelic paint job was to represent an explosion of music from the sea. Events were to happen which made this choice prophetic.

afternoon of 23rd March, the radio ship raised anchor, and headed for the English coastline, broadcasting as they went. The people of Holland were thanked for their co-operation, 'And to the people of Great Britain, we can only say, we are on our way'.

The ship anchored in a position of 51 degrees 42.5 minutes north, 01 degrees 17 minutes east, off Clacton, at 9 am on 24th March. RNI ran into problems straight away, with medium wave transmissions causing interference to other maritime broadcasts.

Coastguards at Walton on the Naze complained that they were unable to contact any of the Trinity House lightships, 'All we can hear, between 6 am and 1 am, is pop music'. The Coastguard used 183 metres to contact the lightships, whilst RNI was on 186 metres.

The power of transmissions, from Radio Northsea, caused local interference right down to 180 metres. As a result of the interference contact between the Coastguard, and the lightships, was restricted to those hours when RNI was off the air.

This situation could not be tolerated; one Coastguard officer stated, 'They do not help any, we could do without them!' A spokesman for RNI, DJ Carl Mitchell, replied, 'We do not want it to be said that we are risking the life of anybody. I would assume that if it's true our owners will take this into account, and maybe change our wavelength.'

Complaints were made to RNI's Zurich office, and on Friday 27th March, having apologised to all of the services involved, Radio Northsea went off the air. Having made adjustments, broadcasts resumed on Friday 10th April, on 190 metres (1578 kHz).

Just five days later, on 15th April, the Ministry of Posts and Telecommunications broadcast a jamming signal, authorised by John Stonehouse MP. It was announced that this, almost unprecedented action, was being done at the request of Italy and Norway.

That evening RNI went off the air, to make further adjustments. Tests were broadcast on 217 metres (1385 kHz) and on 244 metres (1230 kHz), commencing on Friday 1st May. The lower frequency was not suitable, so further tests were made on 244 metres, from Wednesday 13th May.

Normal programming, using the new frequency, commenced on 16th May, but five days later jamming recommenced, this time it was claimed to have been at the request of Czechoslovakia. The jamming signal, which was broadcast from a Naval radio station at Rochester, caused a high pitched whistle, which made it unpleasant to listen to RNI.

The station hit back, by reading the following statement, which had been issued by the Directors of RNI:

Radio Northsea moved to the frequency of 1230 kilocycles, 244 metres, because this frequency does not cause any interference to emergency broadcasts, or legally authorised stations.

However, the British Government has accused us of interfering with other stations, although no proof can be found of this, and certainly no complaint has been received by our offices in Zurich.

We would remind the British Government, that all frequency infringement allegations, must be investigated by the Intertelecommunications Union, in Geneva. That is the body that controls all European frequencies, and prevents nations having to handle complaints with other nations personally.

This would have been the legal method of investigating the alleged interference, rather than the chosen illegal jamming of Radio Northsea.

The cost of which, the British taxpayer has to provide. No free western country has ever jammed a free broadcasting station, even in times of war.

Radio Northsea trusts that the legal right that we have to broadcast, without interference to you, will soon be restored. Radio Northsea International intends to stay on the air.

From Thursday 28th May RNI tried to dodge the jamming signal, by alternating its frequency, every few minutes. However, where RNI went the jamming signal quickly followed. It was only the medium wave transmissions that were affected.

In spite of the jamming (or maybe because of it) the station gained in popularity, wherever the station went, so did the listeners who were prepared to put up with the unpleasant jamming signal. Within a few weeks, some of Radio Northsea's DJs were highly placed in a national top 40 list of DJs.

For those devoted listeners that had stayed loyal to a station that liked to surprise, there was a shock announcement on Saturday 13th June. 'You are currently tuned to 244 metres 1230 kilocycles, in the medium wave band, and on FM channel 43,100 megacycles. Please standby for an important news development'.

radio nordsee international

the ship broadcasting 6½ miles off Clacton on 244 meters has been "jammed" by the G.P.O. for the past two months.

"Jamming" is a practice only exercised so far by communist government's dictatorships—*and in the case of R.N.I.—By the Labour Government.*

Radio Nordsee International is a *legal* station operating in International waters *and therefore not under British jurisdiction.*

Therefore, the "jamming" of R.N.I. by the G.P.O. is *illegal*, according to the International Radio Regulations signed in Geneva in 1959.

This "jamming" can only be called a **dictatorial** action by the Labour Government.

if you disagree

With these tactics, if you want to be free to tune into the radio station of your choice, if you agree with us that the "jamming" of R.N.I. could be the beginning of the end of freedom in Britain then you

Vote against the illegal "jamming" of R.N.I. by the Labour Government.

Make sure that the candidate you vote for is willing to bring

free radio back to britain!

'Good evening, this is Carl Mitchell welcoming you to the new sound of Radio Caroline International'. This was followed by *Caroline*, by the Fortunes.
'Good evening, this is Andy Archer, the unbelievable has happened, this is the return of Radio Caroline International'. For the first time in 2 years, 103 days, Caroline was back on the air.

It was quite a shock for the listeners, even many of RNI's DJs had previously been working for Radio Caroline. The only original sound that could not be found was Caroline's bell, so a recording was made of the *MEBO II's* bell.

The owners of Radio Northsea International had come to an agreement with Ronan O'Rahilly to use the Radio Caroline callsign, and the station jingles. It was hoped that by using the name of Britain's pioneering commercial station, that it would invoke more support for the anti-Labour campaign that the station was about to embark on.

It was the first time that an offshore radio station had embarked on such a political campaign, its only motive was to see the ousting of Harold Wilson's Labour Government. The owners of Radio Northsea International were so determined to beat the Government that they announced that if Labour were returned, they would close the station.

A General Election was to be held on Thursday 18th June ,1970, it was to be the first at which 18-year-olds could use their vote, and it was to this section that Radio Caroline was appealing. During the week preceding the election, Caroline broadcast constant anti-Labour propaganda.

The campaign had its own theme tune, 'Who do you think you are kidding Mr Wilson, if you think Free Radio's down', which was sung to the theme tune to the *Dad's Army* TV programme.

There were constant appeals for helpers, in the fight for free radio such as, 'Be a Caroline girl', or 'Phone these three numbers, do it today, and help Caroline in her fight for freedom'. The decision to rename the station was certainly paying off, thousands of people responded.

A rally was held in Trafalgar Square, on Sunday 14th June, which was followed by a march to Downing Street. Ronan and Simon Dee were there, and there were posters depicting Mr Wilson as Chairman Mao.

With each day that passed, the campaign stepped up a gear, listeners were reminded that it had been the Labour Government which had banned the offshore stations in 1967 and had authorised the jamming of RNI/Caroline. To vote for the Conservatives, who believed in local commercial radio, was a vote for Caroline, 'Join in the fight for free radio, your weapon, the Vote'.

In retaliating and in attempt at self preservation, the Government ordered the strength of the jamming signal to be increased. The transmitter, at Droitwich was put into use, this had a power of one megawatt. The intention was to blot Caroline out, completely, but it was too late!

Paul Bryan, Conservative spokesman on broadcasting, stated that if his party were to win the election, stations like Radio Caroline and RNI would be allowed to broadcast legally, from land.

The Conservatives duly won the 1970 General Election, no one can say how much Radio Caroline/RNI influenced the vote, but many believe that it was a contributing factor. Many first time voters were prepared to use their vote for the Conservatives, who they thought would make Radio Caroline legal.

In spite of their enthusiasm for commercial radio, the Conservatives did not stop the jamming of Radio Caroline, although the lower power transmitter was put back into operation.

Radio Caroline closed, as normal, in the early hours of Saturday 20th June. However, when broadcasts resumed the station had reverted to the callsign Radio Northsea International. Many felt that Caroline had been used, duped into making the propaganda broadcasts, so that if there was any come back they would take the blame, not RNI.

Caroline may have been down, but she was not out. Rumour spread that Radio Caroline was planning to broadcast television programmes! Ronan stated that he had chartered a Super Constellation aircraft, which was in Spain. It had been equipped with extra fuel tanks and could stay airborne for about 26 hours.

The home for this new project was to be (the former) Yugoslavia, which had given its approval, in return for free adverts for its tourism industry on the new service.

It was planned the aircraft would transmit programmes, including colour, for eight hours per night, from 6 pm until 2am. It was planned that programmes would be recorded in London, and the tapes broadcast from the aircraft. It was envisaged that, at least, 75 per cent of the UK and parts of the near Continent would be able to receive the broadcasts.

Advertising was not going to be a problem, as American firms with European outlets had already booked airtime; it was claimed that the station had in excess of 1 million US dollars sponsorship. Ronan was interviewed by an Irish newspaper, in which he stated that they would broadcast anything that people wanted, with programmes coming from around the world. It was envisaged that Simon Dee would host a chat show.

The project took about two years to get underway, and it was announced that the new service would commence on 1st July, 1970, just 11 days after Radio Caroline stopped broadcasting from the *MEBO II*.

That was all that was heard about the project, no one seems to know for sure whether the stories were true, or just an elaborate hoax. There have never been any reports of anyone seeing Caroline TV. Was it true, or not? The British Government was taking no chances, it placed full page warnings in newspapers, informing would be backers and advertisers that they would be prosecuted.

Meanwhile, on 3rd July, the new Minister for Posts & Telecommunications met with representatives from RNI. Mr Chataway would not give any indication as to when, or if, the jamming would cease. RNI then made further adjustments, from 244 to 217 and back to 244, but still the jamming followed them.

To make matters worse, Norway had commenced jamming RNI's 49 metre short wave broadcasts. The owners decided that it was pointless to remain at anchor off the English coast, so the decision was made to leave.

On 23rd July the *MEBO II* raised anchor, and headed out into the North Sea. Listeners were told that the ship was moving to an anchorage off the African coast, but that they would still be able to hear the station on 6210kHz, in the 49 metre band.

In fact, the ship did not go to Africa, the very next day it anchored just 4½ miles off the Dutch resort of Scheveningen. It may only have been a short sea voyage, but the *MEBO II* managed to sail straight into stormy waters, metaphorically speaking.

The British jamming signal was turned off, but that was not the end of the problems for RNI. Broadcasts on 244 caused interference to the Dutch radio station, Hilversum 3, so once again RNI went off the air, to make adjustments, at 1.45 pm on 30th July.

Test transmissions commenced on 3rd August, on 217 metres, but this frequency was not suitable. After further adjustments broadcasts resumed, at 8 am on 24th August, using 220 metres (1367kHz). After all of the problems that the station had encountered (and caused) it seemed, at long last, that the station might just settle down.

It did not last long, just five days in fact! RNI was nothing, in those early days, if not consistent. On Saturday 29th August, at 1.25 pm, two vessels came close to the *MEBO II*, they were the tug *Huskie*, and the launch *Viking*.

The *Viking* came alongside the radio ship, and Mr Kees Manders asked for, and was given permission, to get on board the radio ship. Mr Manders was a well known night club owner, and at one time was going to be a Director of RNI. He had planned to broadcast a Dutch service, from the ship, but for various reasons the plans did not proceed.

It seems that he was now feeling aggrieved, claiming that MEBO Ltd owed him money, and that they were in breach of contract. He tried to persuade the captain, with a cash inducement, to take the ship into port. Mr Manders had already served a writ on the *MEBO I*, which had been arrested in Scheveningen.

The captain refused the offer, and told Mr Manders to get off the ship. A very angry Mr Manders did as he had been told, but he informed the captain that he would cut the anchor chain, and tow the ship into port.

Whilst this exchange was taking place, the DJs made urgent appeals for listeners to contact the Zurich office, or the Grand Hotel, at Scheveningen. As the tension mounted, the appeals became more urgent, and the studio doors were locked to prevent any unauthorised interruption to broadcasts.

Off duty DJs and the ship's crew stood by, to repel boarders, all kinds of odds and ends being thrown at the attackers, who made four attempts to seize the *MEBO II*.

Having failed to get onto the ship they tried to stop broadcasts, by using a high pressure water cannon, directed at the radio mast. To avoid possible damage, FM and short wave transmissions were suspended, but medium wave transmissions continued with urgent appeals for help.

Disc jockey Carl Mitchell warned the attackers that they risked electrocution, if they did not stop spraying the mast. This warning was heeded, and the water cannon was turned off. They then turned their attention to the anchor chain, trying to cut it, so that they could tow the ship away.

It was then that those on the radio ship noticed that there was a woman and child on one of the ships, in an attempt to stop RNI from defending itself. Disc jockey Spangles Muldoon angrily warned the attackers that they would use fire bombs, if they did not pull away.

By this time the constant appeals for assistance had worked, several vessels were proceeding to the radio ship, even Radio Veronica had sent a launch. Amongst these craft was the tender *Eurotrip*, with Erwin Meister and programme director Larry Tremaine on board.

On seeing the arrival of reinforcements, the attackers withdrew, warning that they would be back. Later that evening the Dutch Royal Navy frigate *Van Nes* (F805) arrived, and spent the night as a guard ship to the embattled radio ship.

Larry Tremaine went on air to explain details of the attack, and went on to assure listeners that there had never been an agreement between RNI and Mr Manders. He also thanked all of those who had responded to the calls for help, and for 'Lighting up the switch board at the Grand Hotel'.

He then added this warning, to possible attackers, that although the *MEBO II* was not around to cause injury, or death, at sea the ship would be protected at all costs. No one was going to take the *MEBO II* away. That appeared to be the end of the problem, at least for the time being.

The very next day regular broadcasts commenced from another radio ship. *King David* was anchored off Noordwijk, and was home to Capital Radio. This new station broadcast on 270 metres, using much of the equipment that had been used by Radio 270 when it had broadcast from off the English coast.

The station had been formed in 1969, but had not been able to commence broadcasts, due to technical problems. They had purchased the 359 ton coaster *Zeevaart*, which was converted at Zaandam. The ship was fitted with a revolutionary circular aerial, which had a circumference of 67 metres.

Capital Radio started test transmissions on 25th April, 1970, but after just a few hours the aerial collapsed, so the ship returned to port for repairs. Further tests commenced from 14th June, but still the aerial had problems. However, the broadcasts made with a 1kW transmitter were reasonably received in Holland, Belgium, and parts of the south-east of England.

Owned by International Broadcasters Society, the station's problems were still not over, just nine days later it was forced off the air with aerial problems. It was decided to take the ship back into port, but the crew could not raise the anchors. The only option was to cut the chains, the first gave no problems, but the second chain suddenly ran out, crushing the leg of one of the crew.

The man was seriously injured, requiring immediate medical assistance. An Air Sea Rescue helicopter responded to the calls for help. In spite of the strong winds and rough sea which was buffeting the radio ship, a doctor was lowered. The injured crew man was made comfortable and then winched up to the helicopter which flew him to hospital, where his leg had to be amputated.

The radio ship's tender assisted the *King David* into port, where the ship entered dry dock for repairs to the hull, and to the ring antenna which had collapsed. Whilst in port it was discovered that a fuel tap had been opened, flooding the engine room with diesel. The owners of Radio Veronica were convinced that the highly publicised events surrounding RNI would force the Dutch Government to legislate against the pirates. The last thing anyone wanted was yet another pirate radio station taking to the air. Whilst sabotage could not be proved Capital Radio were concerned that they might be sucked into the dispute.

Meanwhile, it seemed that Radio Northsea was, at last, not causing any problems. Broadcasts were being made of a World Service, which started on on 22nd September and continued the next day. In fact the station was running very low in funds due to the lack of advertising. A shock announcement was read, by disc jockey Spangles Muldoon, on 23rd September.

Radio Northsea International voluntarily closes down tomorrow, at 11 o'clock, due to the pressure in the Dutch Government to close down the offshore stations. Our directors, in Zurich, feel that it would be better for the people of Holland for us to suspend broadcasting, so that the Dutch Government will not attempt to close Radio Veronica, so dearly loved by the people of Holland for the past ten years.

RNI's final hour was presented by Alan West and Andy Archer, and at 11 am on Wednesday 24th September, 1970, the station closed down. The station had only been broadcasting for seven months, but in that time Radio Northsea had become the most controversial station in the history of offshore radio.

The *MEBO II* was offered for sale, with an asking price of £800,000, and it was reported that the ship had been sold to an African country. The deal did not proceed, so the radio ship remained at its anchorage, but did not resume broadcasting.

In the meantime repairs to the *King David* had been completed, and the ship was ready to return to sea. The owners were taking no chances; on board the ship were several firearms, they were prepared to protect their ship, if needs be. As the ship left harbour part of the aerial collapsed, yet again, so they had to return to port!

After two days the ship put to sea, and on 10th October, Capital Radio returned to the air, with a light music format. It looked as though the station had come through the worst of its problems, the broadcasts were proving very popular, and mail for the station was increasing.

One month later the North Sea was ravaged by gales, which gave the three radio ships a pounding. At 2 am on the morning of Monday 10th November the *King David's* new anchor chain snapped, leaving the ship adrift. The crew made frantic efforts to lower the emergency anchor, but their efforts were delayed when it was found that a securing pin had been hammered into position.

It took over half an hour to release the anchor, but any elation the crew may have felt was short lived; due to the severe weather the anchor was not heavy enough to stop their drift.

The crew were unable to start the ship's engine as there was no engineer on board, the previous one having left the ship just before it had sailed in October. Shortly after 5 am on that stormy morning the ill-fated *King David* ran aground, on the beach at Noordwijk. The disc jockeys, and most of the crew were able to get onto the lifeboat that had responded to the calls for assistance. Only the captain and an electrician remained on board the ship.

The Wijsmuller company were appointed to try and salvage the ship. After some initial delays, the *King David* was dragged off the beach by the tug *Hector* at 3 pm on 13th November. The ship was towed into port, where the hull was checked.

The Wijsmuller company told the owners of the *King David* that they would not let the ship leave port, until the salvage fee had been paid in full. The salvage operation was costed at £15,000 and a further £5,000 was needed for repairs before the ship could resume broadcasting.

The station owners pleaded with the salvage company to allow the *King David* to leave port and resume broadcasting. They assured them that advertising revenue would more than cover their expenses, but the salvage company would not allow this.

Presumably the salvage company was concerned that if the *King David* regained international waters, it would not get paid for its services. Capital Radio was unable to raise the necessary cash, and so the station perished. At the end of May 1971 the company was declared bankrupt, and the *King David* was sold for scrap.

The story of Capital Radio is a sad one, and one that highlights the dangers of operating a floating radio station. Many questions were asked about the incidents surrounding the station, but most of them remain unanswered. There were certainly some inexplicable events, which were thought to have been the result of sabotage, but there was no real proof. Was it merely coincidence, or was there something more sinister?

Whatever the real reasons may have been, one cannot help but wonder how many of the problems encountered by Capital Radio could have been avoided. Had the ship been fitted with an orthodox aerial, instead of the unstable ring antenna, broadcasts would not have been so regularly interrupted.

The owners had sought expert advice, and it had been claimed that the aerial would be far more efficient. Like all new ideas, the system had its teething problems, not least its tendency to collapse. The system was just not suited to a small radio ship, which was constantly buffeted by wind and sea. The system incurred a lot of expense, not only in repairs, but in loss of advertising revenue.

The stories of sabotage may have been unfounded, but when they were considered within the context of the problems between Radio Veronica and Radio Northsea, it gave the stories more credence. It was made known that the real reason for the closure of RNI had been lack of cash. Radio Veronica had then paid £100,000 to keep Radio Northsea off the air.

With RNI and Capital Radio off the air, representatives from both stations had a meeting. Capital Radio wanted to lease the *MEBO II*, but they were informed that the ship had been sold and would be moving to the Mediterranean. They subsequently revealed that that Radio Veronica had paid £100,000 to silence RNI.

The situation in Holland, at the time, was similar to those conditions experienced in Britain during the 1964-67 offshore radio era. The Dutch Government had only a small majority, and it did not want to risk its already precarious position by closing Radio Veronica.

The owners of Veronica were concerned that the broadcasts by Radio Northsea International would force the Government's hand to take action. RNI had already caused problems with interference to British, Dutch and Norwegian broadcasts. It had interfered in the British General Election, and the attempted hijack had all resulted in unwanted publicity. This highly controversial pirate had to be silenced!

MEBO Ltd tried to repay the £100,000, they even took a case loaded with notes to the Radio Veronica office, but the latter refused to take the money. Throughout the month of December 1970 MEBO Ltd tried several times to get Veronica to take the money, but on every occasion they refused it.

1971

Top 20 for week commencing Sunday 3rd January, 1971

1	(2)	*Grandad*	Clive Dunn
2	(1)	*I Hear You Knockin'*	Dave Edmunds
3	(3)	*When I'm Dead And Gone*	McGuinness Flint
4	(10)	*Ride A White Swan*	T. Rex
5	(5)	*I'll Be There*	Jackson Five
6	(6)	*Cracklin' Rose*	Neil Diamond
7	(11)	*Blame It On The Pony Express*	Johnny Johnson and his Bandwagon
8	(8)	*Nothing Rhymed*	Gilbert O'Sullivan
9	(4)	*It's Only Make Believe*	Glen Campbell
10	(7)	*Home Lovin' Man*	Andy Williams
11	(12)	*You've Got Me Dangling On A String*	Chairman Of The Board
12	(20)	*Apeman*	Kinks
13	(13)	*Lady Barbara*	Peter Noone and Herman Hermits
14	(9)	*My Prayer*	Gerry Monroe
15	(17)	*Broken Hearted*	Ken Dodd
16	(14)	*Indian Reservation*	Don Farndon
17	(15)	*I've Lost You*	Elvis Presley
18	(31)	*Black Skinned Blue Eye Boys*	Equals
19	(16)	*Julie Do Ya Love Me?*	White Plains
20	(19)	*Voodoo Chile*	Jimi Hendrix Experience

Pirates at War

The owners of RNI decided that they would have to try a different approach. On Tuesday 5th January, a launch went out to the *MEBO II*, which was being manned by a crew paid for by Radio Veronica. The captain of the silent radio ship was told that he had to go ashore and phone the Veronica office as there was an important message for him.

When the captain got ashore he found that he had been duped. He returned to the radio ship, where it was found that Edwin Bollier, who was still the legal owner, had retaken control of the ship.

Mr Bollier had gone to the ship, in a second launch, with an engineer and they boarded the *MEBO II* as soon as the captain had gone. It was reported that they had taken firearms with them, to defend the ship, but in the event fire extinguishers were used to fight off one attempt to retake the ship.

Later in the day, another boat went out to the *MEBO II*; on board were the owners and some staff from Radio Veronica. They tried to persuade Mr Bollier to relinquish control of the ship, but he refused to accede to their demands. He apparently backed up his words with threats to use the firearms!

On Thursday 7th January, the anchor of the *MEBO II* was raised and two tugs towed the radio ship to a new position, off the coast of Belgium, near Knokke. It was claimed that whilst Radio Veronica had been in control of the ship some damage had been done to equipment, which had to be repaired before transmissions could resume.

The idea behind the moving of the radio ship was to try and avoid even more friction with Radio Veronica. Part of the earlier requirements was that the *MEBO II* would not broadcast off the Dutch coast, and that they did not broadcast a Dutch language service.

Test transmissions commenced on Thursday 28th January, from the *MEBO II*, but the station was given no identification. However, this anchorage proved too exposed, so the decision was made to move the ship to an anchorage off the Dutch coast.

Over the following weekend, the radio ship was moved, dropping anchor off Scheveningen and within sight of Radio Veronica's ship. Tests transmissions were broadcast over the following two weeks, but once again the station was not identified, although it was obvious where the broadcasts eminated.

As from Sunday 14th February, the station resumed using the Radio Northsea International callsign during the test programmes. It was not until 3 pm on Saturday 20th February that the station officially reopened, with an all-English format. However, just two weeks later, on Sunday 7th March, a Dutch language service was broadcast from 9 am until 4 pm.

Having Radio Northsea back on 220 metres was pleasing millions of listeners, on the Continent and in this Country. The Directors of Radio Veronica, however, were far from pleased with the developments. They had paid a substantial sum to prevent RNI from broadcasting, but the station was not only back on the air, it was also providing a Dutch service in direct competition with themselves.

In early March 1971, a writ was issued against the owners of RNI claiming that Meister and Bollier were in breach of contract. It also asked the Court to order RNI to cease all broadcasts, and for the *MEBO II* to enter a Dutch port. Once in harbour, Radio Veronica wanted the ship to be arrested until they were paid their £100,000.

The writ also claimed that MEBO Ltd was in breach of contract, for tricking the radio ship out of Veronica's control. With the benefit of hindsight, this really was a crazy course of action.

The whole idea of keeping Radio Northsea off the air was to stop the Dutch Government from introducing legislation which would also close Radio Veronica. The subsequent Court battle was putting the pirates back in the spotlight, and showing a very detrimental side to their operations.

On Wednesday 10th March the case was heard in a court in Rotterdam and the result was made known on 25th March. The court ruled that as MEBO Ltd had offered to repay the money, it was not in breach of contract and as such RNI could continue to broadcast.

Over the following months, RNI continued to gain in popularity. Millions were tuning to 220, although the Dutch service was not as well liked as Radio Veronica. There was, however, some disappointment in this Country at the loss of the all-English format, but at least there was another offshore station.

With regular broadcasts, the station was attracting advertisers; it really did seem that this controversial station had finally settled down, but it was not destined to last for long! Behind the scenes plans were being formulated that would shock the people of Britain and Holland, and which would give new meaning to the RNI jingle: 'It's blast off time on sunny radio, we're going into orbit'.

Tune in & TURN ON

Radio NorthSea International 220 m.

During the evening of Saturday 15th May, whilst the English service was on the air, an explosion ripped through the engine room of the *MEBO II*. Off duty personnel got out on deck, just in time to see a rubber dinghy making off into the distance.

The fire, which had started in the engine room, started an inferno which rapidly engulfed the whole stern section of the ship. As the fire raged, DJ Alan West broadcast a mayday message, which detailed the attack and subsequent damage to the radio ship, and repeatedly gave their position.

> SOS, SOS, this is Radio Northsea International. The *MEBO II*, anchored 4½ miles from the coast of Scheveningen Holland, by the radio ship *Norderney* Veronica. We need help immediately, we may have to abandon ship soon.
> The fire that started in the engine room has now reached the bridge. Mayday, Mayday, our position is 52 degrees 11 minutes north, 04 degrees 16 minutes east. The fire was caused by a bomb thrown on board from a small motor launch.

Off duty personnel were meanwhile tackling the blaze, which was rapidly spreading, and in danger of getting out of control. It was not long before the fire had spread to the crew quarters and the bridge. Alan West kept broadcasting appeals for assistance, and played the station's theme tune, *Man of Action*, so that there could be no doubt as to where the broadcasts were coming from.

A full scale rescue operation was mounted, the *MEBO II's* tender, *Eurotrip*, was one of the first ships on the scene. After an hour since the fire started, transmissions ceased. All personnel, except the captain and two engineers, had abandoned ship and been taken to the safety of the *Eurotrip*.

Shortly afterwards a Dutch fire fighting tug, arrived on the scene, training its high pressure water cannons onto the flames. Other ships, including a Dutch Royal Navy frigate, were soon assisting in bringing the fire under control.

The *MEBO II* had all the repairs carried out whilst she remained at anchor in International Waters. The owners feared that if the ship were to enter port it may be seized, so as to keep the station quiet. This view shows the replacement wooden bridge.

The fire was extinguished by 2.30 am, and shortly after that it was deemed safe for personnel to return to the ship. The fire had gutted the stern section, including the engine room, bridge and some of the crews' quarters. Incredibly no one was injured, and no damage was caused to the transmitter equipment or the studios. The damage, which was all repaired whilst at sea, cost in the region of £28,000 to repair.

Thanks to the information broadcast from the *MEBO II*, the police found the rubber dinghy, and the remains of three wet suits, on the beach near Scheveningen. Within a few hours the three attackers had been detained for questioning.

Within two days, police enquiries led them to Radio Veronica's office, where they arrested one of the Directors and the advertising manager. The five men appeared in court in The Hague on 20th May, just five days after the incident.

The people of Holland were truly shocked to hear that Radio Veronica had paid three men £10,000 to get the station off the air and the ship into Dutch waters, where it could be seized.

Radio Veronica admitted that it had wanted to get the *MEBO II* into territorial waters, so that it could have served a writ on the vessel and reclaim their £100,000. It did, however, deny conspiring to endanger life.

The five men were all found guilty of organising and participating in the attack on the *MEBO II*. It was tantamount to piracy on the high sea, which could result in 12 years' imprisonment. In the event they were sentenced to one year in prison, on Tuesday 21st September.

Meanwhile the attack had, once again, put the pirate ships in the spotlight. The Dutch Prime Minister announced, on Thursday 27th May, that his Government would soon take action to silence the radio ships. He stated that the recent events were not the prime reason, although such action was totally unacceptable; there were continuing reports of interference to broadcasts in Britain and Norway.

In June 1966, Radio City had been boarded and temporarily silenced and its owner shot dead. In January 1967, Radio Caroline personnel had fire bombs thrown at them when they tried to retake the Rough Sands Fort. History was repeating itself, again, hostilities between rival stations had developed into open warfare!

It was this sinister side of the pirate stations that had forced the British Government to take action, and it was similar tactics that was forcing the hand of the Dutch Government.

This unwelcome, and regrettable, aspect had focused attention on the darker side of the pirates detracting from the pleasure that they gave to countless millions. It was these nefarious antics that made the continued presence unacceptable. Radio Veronica had truly shot itself in the foot!

The war between the two stations had come to an explosive end, what followed was an uneasy truce. The publicity resulting from the attack led to an increase in listeners to RNI, where spirits were very high. Veronica tried to redeem itself, by paying for the repairs to the *MEBO II*, but the stigma of their actions was not so easy to overcome.

The rest of the year was spent quietly and uncontroversially by RNI, but on the morning of Monday 22nd November the *MEBO II* lost her anchor and started drifting. Throughout the following day the ship was held in position by a tug, and it was not until the 24th that a new anchor was fitted. RNI had to suspend broadcasts, for a time, as the radio ship had entered territorial waters, but they resumed on Wednesday 24th.

1972

Top 20 for week commencing Sunday 2nd January, 1972

1	(4)	I'd Like To Teach The World To Sing	New Seekers
2	(1)	Ernie (The Fastest Milkman In The West)	Benny Hill
3	(2)	Jeepster	T. Rex
4	(6)	Softly Whispering I Love You	Congregation
5	(9)	Soley Soley	Middle of the Road
6	(5)	Theme From 'Shaft'	Isaac Hayes
7	(3)	Something Tells Me (Something Is Gonna Happen Tonight)	Cilla Black
8	(13)	Sleepy Shores	Johnny Pearson Orchestra
9	(8)	No Matter How I Try	Gilbert O'Sullivan
10	(16)	I Just Can't Help Believing	Elvis Presley
11	(7)	Tokoloshe Man	John Kongos
12	(18)	Mother Of Mine	Neil Reid
13	(12)	Morning	Val Doonican
14	(15)	It Must Be Love	Labi Siffre
15	(17)	Fireball	Deep Purple
16	(14)	Coz I Luv You	Slade
17	(21)	Kara Kara	New World
18	(20)	Is This The Way To Amarillo	Tony Christie
19	(10)	Gypsies Tramps And Thieves	Cher
20	(22)	Sing A Song Of Freedom	Cliff Richard

The First Lady Returns

Whilst all the hostilities had been taking place between RNI and Radio Veronica, the two Radio Caroline ships lay rusting in the port of Amsterdam. The ships were in a very bad state, after four years of neglect and vandalism. Paint was flaking off, exposing large areas of rust, windows had been smashed, and equipment and fittings stolen.

On Monday 29th May, 1972, the two radio ships were offered for sale, by public auction. The MV *Caroline* was sold for £3,117 to Frank Rijsdijk Holland N.V., Hendrick Ido-Ambacht and was scrapped shortly after.

The *Mi Amigo* was sold to the Hoffman Shipping Agency for £2,400 (20,000 guilders). At first, it was assumed that the *Mi Amigo* would also go for scrap, but it was subsequently announced that she would not. In fact, the Dutch Free Radio Association, with financial assistance from Gerrard van Dam, had acquired the ship.

Radio Caroline had been silent for four years since March 1968, the victim of piracy. The two ships were berthed, side by side, quietly rusting and being vandalised. There was a triumphant return for the *Mi Amigo*, but the cutters' torch awaited the MV *Caroline*.

Ron van den Bos

The radio ship was moved to a berth at Zaandam, where the clean up operation began. It was announced that the *Mi Amigo* was destined to be used as a pirate radio museum, the accommodation was to be refurbished and the studios restored to full working order.

There are differing stories, as to what happened next. I have no way of knowing which account is correct, so will leave the reader to decide. The Dutch enthusiasts who had purchased the *Mi Amigo* were led by Mr van Dam, who had borrowed the money to purchase and refurbish the ship. Apparently they were tricked into letting Ronan take over the project, and they were left feeling very bitter towards him.

The other version of events claims that Ronan returned to Holland when he heard that the ship had been released, to see if he could get involved. His dream was to see the *Mi Amigo*, back at sea, broadcasting the sounds of Radio Caroline again. An agreement was reached, which allowed the ship to resume broadcasting.

Whichever account is true, and only those involved know which is the correct account, the refurbishment programme continued. A 50 kilowatt transmitter, which had been removed from the MV *Caroline*, was taken to the *Mi Amigo*. This transmitter had been purchased whilst the ship had been anchored off the Isle of Man, but had never been installed because of the 1968 hijack.

A last look at the MV *Caroline*. Built in 1930, the 702 ton *Fredericia* was a product of the Danish ship builders, Frederickshaven's V&F A/S. Built as a passenger ferry, she was named after a Danish queen. She had a length of 188 ft, with a 30 ft beam and was capable of 14 knots. In preparation for her role as a radio ship she was given 300 tons of concrete ballast, and her mast was 160 ft high.

"What we are doing is 100% legal. We are more legal in this position than many European broadcasting stations. For instance Radio Luxembourg is the most powerful pirate in Europe, today. It broadcasts on a frequency that it is not allocated and therefore under the European Broadcasting Union, it is a pirate. We are not pirates because, in strict legal terms, we did not sign any 1948 Copenhagen Plan. We did not agree not to broadcast, and it is quite legal to in International Waters, so we are doing nothing illegal".   Ronan O'Rahilly, January 1973.

Ron van den Bos

The *Mi Amigo* was equipped with a new TV lounge and bar, and the hull was painted yellow. Most of the equipment was overhauled, and where needed replaced, if money would allow.

The ship was placed into the ownership of Vagabond Films, a company based in Liechtenstein, which effectively gave Ronan control of the project. A new company, Bell Commercial Radio of Amsterdam, was set up to help organise financial backing.

At the beginning of September, it was announced that the *Mi Amigo* was to be moved to England. It was claimed that as Radio Caroline had been broadcasting, principally to the UK, the museum would attract more visitors, and backing.

The *Mi Amigo* was towed from her berth, on Saturday 2nd September, and out into the North Sea, but she did not continue to England. During the early hours of the next morning, the ship was anchored four miles off the coast of Scheveningen, near the *MEBO II*. The museum story had just been a ruse, so that officialdom would not try to prevent the ship from leaving port.

Anchored in international waters, the preparations could continue, without fear of the ship being impounded. During the evening of Friday 29th September, 1972, a test transmission was broadcast on 253 metres (1187 kHz). At 12.30 pm the next day further broadcasts were made of non-stop music, but the station was not identified.

On that same date, 30th September, Radio Veronica changed frequency, from 192 to 536 metres, in an attempt to improve night time reception. Shortly after Veronica had vacated 192, Radio Northsea International began test transmissions on the frequency. 'Good afternoon ladies and gentlemen, this is the start of test transmissions from RNI 2, we are broadcasting on 192 metres.'

These broadcasts were made in English, and they continued until 7 pm, and resumed the next morning at 6 am. The transmitter was switched off at midday, and apart from some short tests at the beginning of October, nothing further was heard from RNI 2.

It later became apparent that these tests were designed to show potential advertisers how versatile the station was. Versatile they may have been. Trouble free they were not! The English service from RNI did not commence on Tuesday 24th October. The Dutch programme director had decided that as the programmes made no money, he would close them down.

The English staff were sacked, their programmes being replaced by continuous music. The station owners had not been informed prior to this action, and they were furious. All of the staff were given their jobs back, but it was not until Friday 3rd November that English programmes resumed.

Test transmissions from the *Mi Amigo* continued throughout October but it was not until Thursday 9th November that a voice was heard, when DJ Spangles Muldoon tested the microphone. Any elation they may have felt was to be short-lived.

On Monday 13th November the *Mi Amigo*, *MEBO II*, and the *Norderney* took a severe beating from storm force winds, which reached force 11, with gusts to 75 miles per hour. At the height of the storm the *Mi Amigo's* anchor chain snapped and the ship drifted for three miles, before the crew could lower two emergency anchors.

But there was still worse to come, as the ship wallowed in the heavy swell, the 168 ft aerial collapsed. The aluminium mast, which had been designed on the Isle of Wight, had withstood the worst that the elements had to offer since 1963, but this was one storm too many.

The wounded radio ship was towed back to a new anchorage, just 500 yards from the *MEBO II*. Over the weekend of 18th-19th November a new, and heavier, anchor and chain were fitted to the ship. Within days, work started on rigging a temporary aerial, which allowed test broadcasts to be made on Thursday 30th November.

The transmissions were made on 259 metres (1187 kHz), using a 10 kilowatt transmitter. Reception reports were requested, with PO Box 2448, The Hague, Holland, given as the contact address. From 1st December, the DJs decided to present the programmes, but they did not identify themselves, or the name of the station.

These tests were intermittent, whilst tuning and adjustments were made. During the evening of 17th December, transmissions on 259 ceased, and the frequency was changed to 197 metres (1520kHz).

On Monday 18th December, the station was identified as Radio 199, with programming in English and Dutch. The programmes were mixed, rather then the usual format of Dutch during the day with English at night.

A new office was opened in The Hague, which also had a recording studio. Advertisers would phone the office, the commercials were then prepared in the studio and then radioed to the *Mi Amigo*. Within minutes the advert could be broadcast, from Radio Caroline.

Just before Christmas, the Caroline team decided on a change of strategy, which led to a surprise for Radio 199 listeners. When broadcasts commenced, at 6 am on Friday 22nd December, the station name had been changed to Radio Caroline.

The station broadcast for 24 hours per day, over the Christmas period, maintaining the same format of mixed language programmes. 'Serving the European Continent, from the North Sea, this is the new Radio Caroline.' After all of the trials and tribulations, Caroline was back. 'From a point at sea, to the circles of your mind, this is the new Radio Caroline.'

The euphoria of the return was soon to disappear. Behind the scenes trouble was brewing, which led to scuffles on board the *Mi Amigo* on Wednesday 27th December. Some of the Dutch crew were angry that they had not been paid; during the early hours of 28th December the fuel line to the lighting generator was cut, plunging the ship into darkness.

Members of the crew decided to leave the *Mi Amigo* and go ashore in search of their wages; only the captain, three DJs and a radio engineer were left on the ship. Later that day a tender took an engineer out to the *Mi Amigo*, and the fuel line was repaired, allowing Caroline to resume broadcasts.

Meanwhile the Dutch crew had still not had any money, and when they heard that the station was back on the air they were furious. A tender was hired, and they went back to the radio ship where fighting broke out again. Just before 4 pm, disc jockey Andy Archer announced that the station was going off the air because of the fighting.

An agreement, of sorts, was reached with the disgruntled crew, which allowed broadcasting to resume after a break of two hours. The crew had been told that if the station was on the air it could earn money, from advertising, which would help to pay them.

The outbreak of violence was shown on Dutch TV, including footage of the captain brandishing a rifle. The crew had used the firearms to get onto the ship, but had then thrown them into the sea. Apparently they then carried lumps of wood, to deter any counter attacks.

Ronan flew to Holland, on Friday 29th, and went out to the ship that evening to see if he could help settle the dispute.

Radio Caroline went off the air, at 3 am on Saturday 30th December, when it was announced that the station would return within a few days on a new frequency of 259 metres (1187 kHz). As soon as the station went off the air, the crew cut the anchor chain.

The radio ship was towed to Ijmuiden by a vessel owned by the same company that tendered Radio Northsea. The *Mi Amigo* was then taken to Amsterdam, where she was berthed near the central station. For the second time in four years, the *Mi Amigo* had been silenced as a result of piracy.

Radio Caroline stated that what was first thought to be a salary dispute turned out to be a traitor problem! Caroline had a traitor amongst her own crew. They named Captain Van der Kamp, and claimed that he had been paid by another radio station to make sure that the *Mi Amigo* was taken into any Dutch harbour.

Gerrard van Dam, who had been on board at the time, went on to say.

> At 3 o'clock, we ended programmes, a small boat came alongside with Captain Van der Kamp and about eight other former crew members. They had come to collect the money that they were owed.
>
> They got on board the *Mi Amigo*, everything had been organised, [including a] tug boat from the company that supplied Radio Northsea. They sawed the anchor chain off, and towed the ship into harbour.

Ronan was furious, he came out on another tender to try and stop it. He tried to deliver the money to the crew members, but it was too late!

When the vessel arrived in harbour a lawyer representing the crew came aboard. He asked for 7,000 guilder, otherwise the ship would be officially seized. Gerrard arranged with the lawyer that he would produce the money before Monday morning. The lawyer agreed, and decided that the radio ship did not need to be chained up. On the Sunday afternoon, Gerrard's mother paid for a tug to tow the *Mi Amigo* back out to sea. The ship was underway when someone informed the crew that the ship was leaving.

The ship was stopped, and then towed into the harbour of Ijmuiden, where she was boarded by officials. They decided that the ship was not seaworthy because of a small hole in the stern. Gerrard claimed that Ronan had decided not to have it repaired, because of the cost.

Gerrard was very angry at this situation, claiming that passing the ship over to Ronan O'Rahilly was a big mistake. Right from the start Ronan had promised there would be money, the trouble was that there never was any!

Because of the leak, the ship was not allowed to proceed, and it was seized on behalf of the crew who were still owed their money. A court injunction was issued in favour of the crew, which prevented the ship from sailing until the crew had been paid the £4,000 that they were claiming.

Ronan, and other members of the Caroline team, visited prominent business people in The Hague to see if they could get any financial support. Incredibly, after just a few hours, they had raised over £8,000. Most of the money came from the owner of a chain of clothing stores, who had been pleased by the response to his adverts, aired on Radio Caroline.

1973

Top 20 for week commencing Sunday 7th January, 1973

1	(1)	*Long Haired Lover From Liverpool*	Little Jimmy Osmond
2	(4)	*Jean Genie*	David Bowie
3	(2)	*Solid Gold Easy Action*	T. Rex
4	(3)	*Crazy Horses*	Osmonds
5	(10)	*Hi Hi Hi/C Moon*	Wings
6	(15)	*Ball Park Incident*	Wizzard
7	(20)	*You're So Vain*	Carly Simon
8	(11)	*Big Seven*	Judge Dread
9	(9)	*Gudbuy T'Jane*	Slade
10	(13)	*Always On My Mind*	Elvis Presley
11	(8)	*Shotgun Wedding*	Roy C
12	(12)	*Ben*	Michael Jackson
13	(9)	*Nights In White Satin*	Moody Blues
14	(7)	*My Ding-A-Ling*	Chuck Berry
15	(6)	*Happy Xmas (War Is Over)*	John and Yoko and the Plastic Ono Band with the Harlem Community Choir
16	(-)	*Blockbuster*	Sweet
17	(16)	*Why*	Donny Osmond
18	(14)	*Help Me Make It Through The Night*	Gladys Knight and the Pips
19	(22)	*Desperate Dan*	Lieutenant Pigeon
20	(17)	*Crocodile Rock*	Elton John

Caroline to the rescue

On Monday 1st January, 1973, Radio Caroline regained control of the *Mi Amigo*. Arrangements were made for two tugs to tow the ship back to her anchorage, the voyage commencing the next morning at 7.30 am. The radio ship was anchored near the *MEBO II*, and *Veronica*, from where broadcasts restarted at 3 pm, on Tuesday 2nd January.

The format was changed, from alternate English/Dutch, to Dutch from 6 am until 6 pm, with English programmes during the evening. With his station back on the air, Ronan agreed to an interview on Dutch TV. This is what he had to say:

Q. Does this mean that the problems are now solved?
A. Well, yes, it's now running as a radio station. Caroline had a few difficulties, to say
    the least, and those difficulties were beyond our control. Nobody had any
    permission to move the ship. It was brought in on the basis of seaworthiness, but
    there was no problem with seaworthiness.
Q. But that's not for you to decide, it's up to the captain of the ship.
A. But the problem was that he was not the captain of the ship. He claimed to be the
    captain, but I had left the ship that night, and when I left Peter Chicago was the
    acting captain. Captain Van der Kamp was not on the ship then. Captain Van der
    Kamp came onto the radio ship at 3 o'clock in the morning, without my consent,
    but that is a matter that is now in the hands of the lawyers. It's very complicated,
    involving international law. I have informed the Dutch navy, and the police, and
    the matter is being dealt with, in the only way it can be dealt with, through the
    process of law.
Q. Was it financial problems that bought this situation about?
A. Well I dispute that, completely. As far as I am concerned the cost of the operation,
    to tow the ship to Ijmuiden, and then Amsterdam, is a very expensive operation.
Q. Who paid for it?
A. I would love to know who paid for it. All I know so far, is the name of the tender
    company that did the job.
Q. That company is under contract to Radio Northsea!
A. Well, I know that they are under contract to Radio Northsea, but I can't say
    anything. Everyone has their own conclusion, a lot of people have said different
    things. I can't draw any conclusions, or make any statement about who really is
    behind what happened, last week.
Q. Maybe it would be interesting for people, from another pirate station, to kill the
    third one?
A. Well of course it is, obviously always a possibility, that the other stations . . . I mean,
    they tried to buy me off, on two occasions. They came and offered me money to
    take it away.
Q. How much?
A. Well, I mean, the offers were, you know, are not something I want to get into here,
    like the actual amount. But, the fact is, they tried to buy us off and we said no. We
    are not for sale.

Meanwhile, out on the *Mi Amigo*, a fire broke out in the engine room, just
before midnight on Thursday 18th January. Repairs were being made, using
welding equipment. A spark ignited some rags, as a precaution an emergency
message, requesting assistance, was broadcast. In the event, the staff
extinguished the blaze which caused little damage.

This, however, was not the end of the problems faced by Radio Caroline
during January 1973. Technical faults led to several breakdowns, and output
was still reduced. A new aerial had been ordered, but in the meantime the
makeshift system could not be used on full power, the output being restricted
to about 7 or 8 kilowatts. Whilst the station struggled to maintain broadcasts,
the result of her pioneering transmissions was taking shape.

It was almost nine years since Radio Caroline had made her historic first
broadcast, and now, with the help of the Conservative Government, legal
commercial radio was just starting in Britain.

The Independent Television Authority (ITA) had been formed in 1954, with
responsibility for commercial television. Following on from all of the debates

Above: The converted trawler *Norderney* which was the home of Radio Veronica from 1966. The 475 ton radio ship lost its anchor on Monday 2nd April, 1973 and ran aground near Scheveningen at 11.30 pm. It was eventually salvaged nine days later.

Author's Collection

Right: Radio Veronica had made its first test transmission on 16th December, 1959, not from a radio ship but from a hotel in Amsterdam. The station purchased the *Borkum Riff*, and started broadcasting from the sea in May 1960. In 1966. They converted the *Norderney*, which then replaced the original ship. Transmissions came to an end at 6 pm on 31st August, 1974, but the ship remained at anchor until 11th August, 1975, when it was towed into Amsterdam. The *Norderney* was then moved to Zaandam, 17 days later, where she was converted for use as a TV studio.

that had arisen due to offshore radio, the Government extended the powers of the ITA. The company was renamed, in 1971, to become the Independent Broadcasting Authority (IBA) with a mandate to set up a network of local commercial radio stations.

On Monday 15th January, 1973, the IBA commenced test transmissions from its first radio station. The new station was called Capital Radio, which broadcast on 539 metres, effectively blotting out Radio Veronica, in the South East, which broadcast on 538 metres.

Whilst these tests were being carried out, the First Lady of Music, Radio Caroline, was facing all kinds of problems to remain on the air. There was a minor panic, on Friday 23rd February, when those on the *Mi Amigo* thought that the ship was adrift. It was subsequently ascertained that it was the *MEBO II* that was adrift, but in the meantime the *Mi Amigo* staff had been firing red flares. The *Mi Amigo* staff could not afford to take any chances, because the ship's engine was not working. The mistake was realised when a fix was taken on Radio Veronica's ship.

When the *MEBO II* realised its predicament, it announced that the station was going off the air, as it was concerned that it might enter territorial waters. The red flares, fired from the *Mi Amigo*, had been sighted, and the emergency services were on alert. A tug was sent to assist the *MEBO II*, which by this time was just a few hundred yards from the beach.

The next day, the radio ship was towed back to its anchorage, and a new anchor and chain was fitted. Radio Northsea International resumed broadcasts, but these were of low power whilst the main transmitter was serviced. Just three days later, it was Radio Caroline that was in trouble.

On Monday 26th February, a major generator breakdown forced the station off the air. This was a serious fault, which resulted in Radio Caroline being off the air for several weeks whilst engineers tried to repair the fault. Some test transmissions were broadcast during March, but for most of the month the station remained silent.

Hurricane force winds swept across the North Sea on Monday 2nd April, which left a trail of havoc, and devastation, across Holland. One person was killed and several were injured. Out in the North Sea, the three radio ships took a severe beating.

Radio Northsea International was forced off the air, at 5 pm, when flooding caused an electrical fault on the generator. Damage was also caused to the FM aerial, which resulted in FM broadcasts being suspended for three weeks. Medium wave transmissions, on low power, resumed the next afternoon.

Radio Caroline was still off the air, as she had been for over a month, the *Mi Amigo* riding out the storm with few additional problems. Radio Veronica managed to maintain her broadcasts, but at 8.45 pm the anchor chain snapped.

The 475 ton *Norderney* began drifting towards the coast; with its engine not working, the staff were in dire peril. Normal programmes were suspended, whilst emergency broadcasts were made. Such was the ferocity of the storm, the local lifeboat had a very difficult, and dangerous, operation to take the crew off.

After 1½ hours, all of the personnel had been taken off the stricken radio ship which continued to drift towards the shore. The *Norderney* ran aground, near Scheveningen, at 11.30 pm that evening. The stranded radio ship spent all of the next day on the beach, whilst a salvage operation was mounted by the Dutch company Smit Tak.

The *Norderney* was firmly on the beach, and it was obvious that she would not be refloated quickly. At low water the ship was left high and dry, so that people could walk all the way around her. Earth-moving equipment was used to dig out a deep channel in the beach, but still the ship refused to be moved.

Meanwhile, Ronan who was in Britain, phoned the offices of Radio Veronica, offering the services of the *Mi Amigo* until such time that the *Norderney* could resume broadcasts. Although the offer was much appreciated, the Radio Veronica Directors were very sceptical because Radio Caroline had been off the air since 26th February.

This was, however, an important time for Radio Veronica (and the other pirate stations), as the Dutch Government was about to undertake a review of the broadcasting situation. Radio Veronica had been urging its listeners to attend a special rally, to show support for the station.

Now that Veronica was off the air, the Directors were concerned that the rally would lose support. The salvage operation was going to cost a lot of money, and advertising revenue was being lost. The Directors were faced with three options:

1.   Take up an offer from RNI, and broadcast from the *MEBO II*.
2.   Broadcast from the *Mi Amigo*, at cost price.
3.   Remain silent, and risk losing support for the rally.

They decided to take up Ronan's offer, as long as he could guarantee that broadcasts could commence before the rally.

Engineers, on the *Mi Amigo*, had to work long and hard, but they eventually coaxed the generator into life. At 9 am on Wednesday 11th April, test transmissions commenced, on 253 metres (1187 kHz). Using a 10 kilowatt transmitter, regular broadcasts of Radio Veronica began three hours later.

Throughout the broadcasts, much mention was made of the rally, so as to get maximum support. One week later, on 18th April, members of the Dutch Parliament held discussions with representatives from Radio Veronica, and the Dutch music industry, as to the future of the station. Also included in these discussions were representatives for the artists and many listeners to Radio Veronica.

At the same time, thanks in part to the broadcasts from the *Mi Amigo*, hundreds of thousands of listeners attended the rally. They were there to protest against the Bill, before the Dutch Parliament, to ratify the Strasbourg Treaty and close the offshore radio stations. Many of the protesters took their radios, to listen to Radio Veronica which was playing special messages.

This was a very memorable day for Radio Veronica; at 4 am the *Norderney* had been towed off the beach, after its 16 day sojourn. Within the hour the radio ship was back at its anchorage and test transmissions started almost immediately, and by 10 am regular broadcasts commenced.

The *Mi Amigo* broadcast details of the return of the *Norderney*, and then relayed programmes which were being broadcast by Radio Veronica on 538 metres. At 6 am on 20th April the *Mi Amigo* fell silent, her assistance no longer required.

The *Mi Amigo* remained silent, after Veronica had departed, but those involved with Radio Caroline were far from inactive. A new mast, designed by DJ Chris Cary, had arrived on the quay at Scheveningen. It had been ordered in December 1972, but due to lack of cash they could not afford to pay for it.

Thanks to the money earned by broadcasting Radio Veronica the aerial was eventually paid for, but the professional erectors refused to build the mast whilst the ship remained at sea. Sections were taken to the *Mi Amigo*, and erected by the DJs and staff of the radio ship.

Whilst the aerial was being constructed, a second studio was being equipped, on board the *Mi Amigo*, and the transmitters were being overhauled. During the evening of 13th May, 1973, test transmissions were made on 389 metres (773kHz) using a 10 kilowatt transmitter. The 50 kilowatt transmitter was tested on the 15th May, on 1187kHz, and just two days later both transmitters were in use, and both frequencies. This was the first time that two different frequencies had been used, simultaneously, from the *Mi Amigo*. During the test transmissions the output from both studios were switched from one transmitter to the other, or simulcast from both.

On 31st May transmissions on 389 (773kHz) were identified as Radio Caroline One, whilst those on 1187kHz were known as Radio Caroline Two. On 4th June Caroline International commenced programming on 773, using the 10 kilowatt transmitter, a Dutch service being broadcast on 1187kHz. Dutch programming was from 6 am until 7 pm, whilst the English programmes ran from 6 am until 2 am on 773, and 7 pm until 6 am on 1187.

Generator breakdowns forced the two stations off the air on 23rd and 24th June, and both stations left the air during the evening of 26th June. It was not until 15th July that transmissions resumed, but only using the 259 transmitter.

During the 12 days that the station was off the air, the final two sections of the aerial were erected. These sections had been added by Radio Caroline staff, which took the mast to its full height, of 180 feet. The staff were paid an extra £100 for completing the task.

Whilst they were sorting out the problems on the *Mi Amigo*, Radio Veronica were taking steps to try and survive. On Wednesday 20th June, 1973, they formed a new company, Veronica Broadcasting Foundation, which then applied for a licence to broadcast legally on a new frequency.

The first debate by the Dutch Government was held on 26th and 27th June, and they rejected Veronica's application by a small majority. It was felt that Holland would not be able to obtain a new frequency, and that it would not be fair to other broadcasters if they did allocate it to Veronica.

It was also decided not to allow the station to have air time on the state-owned Hilversum network. Almost any organisation could qualify to broadcast on Hilversum, provided that it could prove that it had at least 100,000 members. The more members, the more airtime it was allowed.

On 28th June, the Dutch Second Chamber passed a Bill which would ratify the Strasbourg Treaty, and outlaw the pirate radio stations. In spite of the obvious popularity of Radio Veronica, and the success of the support rally in April, the Bill was passed with a majority of 61. The Bill then had to be prepared to go before the First Chamber, in a similar procedure to our own House of Commons and House of Lords.

CAROLINE CONTINUES !

259m and 389m

SHOW YOUR SUPPORT <u>NOW</u> BEFORE IT'S TOO LATE

COME TO THE BIG

OFFSHORE RADIO RALLY

AND MARCH TO DUTCH EMBASSY

THIS COULD BE YOUR LAST CHANCE TO HELP 'FREE RADIO'

SPEAKERS CORNER, HYDE PARK
3.00pm SUNDAY 19th AUGUST

SUPPORT CAROLINE/R.N.I./VERONICA

JOINTLY ORGANISED BY BRITAIN'S LEADING FREE RADIO GROUPS.
FOR FURTHER DETAILS/ MORE OF THESE LEAFLETS/ OFFERS OF
HELP — SEND S.A.E. TO:
"RALLY"B.M. — F.R.C., LONDON WC1V 6XX.

It was a very sad day for Radio Veronica which had been broadcasting since 1960, and was to have no part in the future of broadcasting. Many felt that the open warfare between Veronica and RNI was responsible for the hardening of opinion against Holland's most popular station. RNI had got involved in British politics by broadcasting anti-Labour propaganda, and transmissions from the *MEBO II* had caused interference to legitimate stations.

Meanwhile, Radio Caroline had been concluding a deal with a businessman from Belgium, Adriaan van Lanschoot, who would hire facilities on the *Mi Amigo*. It was a three month contract for the use of one of the transmitters for 13 hours each day, at a weekly rate of £2,000. The name for the new station was to be Radio Atlantis, which would broadcast in Flemish on 385 metres.

This agreement would help Caroline solve some of her financial problems, which had led to her tender service being suspended, at the beginning of July 1973, until all outstanding debts had been cleared. The ship's crew had to go ashore to obtain the supplies, however, following discussions, presumably about the new source of income, the tender service was reinstated.

Test transmissions, from the *Mi Amigo*, commenced at midday on Sunday 15th July, which continued until 7 pm. Radio Atlantis commenced regular broadcasts the next day, from 6 am until 7 pm, initially on 259 metres. All of the programme were pre- recorded ashore, and then taken out to the ship.

The new service soon proved popular with listeners in Belgium, but not with the authorities, who threatened legal action against any advertisers, or suppliers. It will be remembered that the Belgian Government had outlawed such broadcasts, in December 1962, after Radio Antwerpen had commenced broadcasts.

After Radio Atlantis had closed for the night, at 7 pm, on 21st and 22nd July non-stop music was broadcast. At 9 pm, on Tuesday 24th July, a new station took to the air, from the *Mi Amigo*. Radio Seagull broadcast each evening, until 6 am, when Radio Atlantis resumed transmissions.

Ronan had been looking into the possibility of broadcasting an all-album format, as artists were putting more effort into the production of albums. No radio stations were, at that time, catering for this section of the market. Radio Caroline had experimented with a progressive album format, but many listeners felt that they could not relate to Radio Caroline using the format.

Radio Seagull derived its name from the book *Jonathan Livingstone Seagull*, which expressed freedom. It was felt that the new name would give Caroline freedom to experiment with musical content, using heavy rock, jazz, even classical tracks.

The station was not an immediate success with the listeners, who turned off in their droves. Some felt that the programmes were poorly produced, and of low quality, even dedicated Caroline followers struggled with the new format. Radio Atlantis, on the other hand, had the opposite effect rapidly gaining popularity in Belgium and Holland.

Like all new ideas, it took a while for Radio Seagull to establish itself. Even as ex-Caroline DJs such as Andy Archer, Bob Noakes, Norman Barrington-Smythe, Tony Allen and Peter Chicago struggled with their new found freedom, the Dutch Government was doing its best to curtail that freedom. Protest rallies were arranged, on both sides of the North Sea, the largest being on 19th August, 1973.

October 1973, with the *Mi Amigo* looking much the worse for wear. The remains of the second aerial can be seen, in this poor quality view, which had collapsed on 30th September. The temporary mast, however, also collapsed.

The owner of Radio Atlantis was a very successful businessman, and with his financial support, and revenue from advertising, a regular tender service had been arranged. Food and water, fuel, tapes and records were regularly being taken out to the ship. As the weeks passed the two stations, working together, continued to gain in popularity, but disaster was soon to strike.

Strong winds swept the North Sea, forcing the two stations off the air. Radio Seagull came to an abrupt end at 3 am on Sunday 30th September. The silent *Mi Amigo* rode out the storm, but at exactly 1.41 pm the aerial mast collapsed into the sea, leaving just a 26 ft section.

The staff, directed by engineer Peter Chicago, managed to rig a temporary aerial, comprising four wires, supported from the aerial's remains and the ship's mast by the bridge. Test transmissions were broadcast on 4th October, but these were of very poor quality. These broadcasts continued until 9.30 am on Thursday 18th October, when this temporary aerial collapsed.

Adriaan van Lanschoot decided that it was time to leave the *Mi Amigo*, although he apparently denied this to Ronan. However, events soon gave the rumour credence; on Wednesday 31st October he purchased an ex-Icelandic trawler, which was to have been used by Radio Condor.

Radio Condor had purchased the 403 ton vessel that year, from which they were planning to broadcast religious programmes. The ship had been purchased cheaply because the engine had been destroyed by fire.

The ship was towed to an anchorage off the Dutch coast, on Monday 30th July, but on 10th August the anchor chain snapped and the ship had to be towed back into port. It was subsequently sold for scrap, but was re-purchased by the owner of Radio Condor, who then sold it to Adriaan van Lanschoot, for £8,000.

History has a habit of repeating itself; now Radio Atlantis found itself in a race with Radio Mi Amigo, which had hired the facilities on the *Mi Amigo*. Ronan had completed a deal with another Belgium businessman, Sylvain Tack. Mr Tack owned several sweet factories and a music publishing company. He was planning a new station which would broadcast to Belgium and Holland, in direct competition with Radio Atlantis and Radio Veronica. The *Mi Amigo* needed a new aerial, and Radio Atlantis had to get its own ship ready; it developed into a race, just like it had with Radio Caroline and Radio Atlanta.

Radio Mi Amigo had already made some broadcasts from the ship that had given the station its name. A short programme had been broadcast on 6th and 7th October using the callsign 'Station 385', and again on 13th and 14th, but then the aerial collapse ended all further broadcasts, albeit temporarily.

Radio Atlantis had to convert the ship for its own use, and they hired a transmitter, which had last been used by Radio & TV Noordzee, during 1964. It was part of the agreement that the recording company could use the transmitter, at night, to broadcast Dutch programmes. Radio Atlantis would broadcast, in Flemish, during the day.

The ship set sail at the beginning of November, and test transmissions commenced almost immediately. However, on Tuesday 6th November the *Jeanine* parted company with her anchor and started drifting. The four persons on board abandoned the ship, which was still without a working engine.

A Wijsmuller tug, *Titan,* got a line onto the ship, which was just one mile from the shore, and towed it to the German port of Cuxhaven. Whilst in port, the ship was fitted with a new, and heavier, anchor and chain. Other work, totalling over 80,000 guilders was carried out, but there was some bad news for the station.

On Wednesday 28th November, 1973, the body of the station's radio engineer was found in the harbour. It is thought that he slipped, whilst boarding the ship, and drowned in the very cold water.

It was not until 22nd December that the *Jeanine* was towed from the port, and taken to an anchorage off the Belgium coast, near Knokke. Test transmissions started on Sunday 23rd December, on 269 metres (1115 kHz). Radio Atlantis may have beaten Radio Mi Amigo on the air, but the station was to be plagued by technical problems.

The testing continued over the Christmas period, but night time reception was very poor. All programming had been in English until Sunday 30th December, when a Flemish service commenced. The next day the transmitter broke down, forcing the station off the air.

Meanwhile, back on the *Mi Amigo,* a new mast was being erected. It had actually been ordered by Radio Atlantis, but as the station now had its own ship, Mr van Lanschoot did not want to purchase it. The company that had built the mast offered it to Ronan at cost price, a deal that was too good to be missed.

The mast was taken out to the *Mi Amigo,* that same day, and work on its construction started right away; by Friday 23rd November all but four sections had been completed. Professional erectors completed the task in December, taking the yellow-painted aerial to its full height of 165 feet on Monday 24th December.

Test transmissions commenced that same afternoon with special programmes being transmitted from 9 am on Christmas Day, which continued until 1 am on Boxing Day. Radio Mi Amigo commenced test transmissions on Friday 28th December, which lasted for 15 hours.

1974

Top 20 for week commencing Sunday 6th January, 1974

1	(1)	*Merry Xmas Everybody*	Slade
2	(2)	*You Won't Find Another Fool Like Me*	New Seekers
3	(7)	*The Show Must Go On*	Leo Sayer
4	(4)	*I Wish It Could Be Christmas Every Day*	Wizzard
5	(5)	*My Coo-Ca-Choo*	Alvin Stardust
6	(14)	*Dance With The Devil*	Cozy Powell
7	(3)	*I Love You Love Me*	Gary Glitter
8	(16)	*Pool Hall Richard/I Wish It Would Rain*	Faces
9	(26)	*Radar Love*	Golden Earring
10	(8)	*Lamplight*	David Essex
11	(13)	*Love On A Mountain Top*	Robert Knight
12	(11)	*Forever*	Roy Wood
13	(9)	*Roll Away The Stone*	Mott The Hoople
14	(6)	*Paper Roses*	Marie Osmond
15	(10)	*Street Life*	Roxy Music
16	(17)	*Gaudete*	Steeleye Span
17	(12)	*Why Oh Why Oh Why*	Gilbert O'Sullivan
18	(15)	*Truck On (Tyke)*	T. Rex
19	(22)	*Vado Via*	Drupi
20	(18)	*When I Fall In Love*	Donny Osmond

Farewell to the Dutch Pirates

Radio Mi Amigo officially opened, at 12 noon, on Tuesday 1st January, 1974. However, the excitement was quickly forgotten, after just one hour the generator failed, forcing the station off the air. It was not until 6 am on 2nd January that programmes recommenced.

Adverts were carried by the station, a loophole in the Belgian law helping the station. The commercials were preceded by the jingle 'Mi Amigo information', details of the product or service then being read from a magazine.

Due to the loophole, this was no longer classified as an advert, but an information service, and therefore did not constitute an infringement of the law. In this way, Radio Mi Amigo's clients were protected from prosecution.

Radio Mi Amigo broadcast daily from 6 am until 9 pm, at which time the transmitter was switched off for maintenance. However, transmissions from the radio ship went to 24 hours per day, when Radio Seagull returned at 9 pm on Monday 7th January, 1974.

Over the following weeks there were problems with the 10 kilowatt transmitter, which resulted in both stations going off the air at times. On 6th February the 50 kilowatt transmitter (ex-MV *Caroline*) was put into operation, which gave excellent reception in most of Europe and Britain.

On Saturday 23rd February, 1974, Radio Caroline commenced broadcasts at 9 pm. The Radio Seagull callsign was dropped without explanation, although the same style of format was retained.

Meanwhile, Radio Atlantis was still encountering problems, a test broadcast being made on 5th January which continued through the night. Regular broadcasts commenced on Monday 7th January (the same day that Radio Seagull had returned) but there were constant interruptions, as engineers made adjustments.

Radio Atlantis was forced off the air, by a generator failure, for the last two weeks of January. Programming returned on Sunday 2nd February, on 269 metres (1115 kHz), but the next day a test was broadcast on 201 metres (1439 kHz) in an attempt to improve reception.

On 4th February broadcasts returned to 269 metres. Programmes were mainly in English, with just an occasional Flemish programme. On 3rd March the station changed frequency to 225 metres (1331 kHz), as they struggled to improve reception.

Their problems were far from over: on Wednesday 20th March, 1974, Radio Atlantis was jammed by a signal broadcast from Italy. On 4th April Atlantis changed frequency yet again, but 227 metres was a poor choice as there was another station using that frequency. The station moved back to 225 metres, where the Italian jamming signal was waiting for them.

On Wednesday 17th April the station moved further along the dial, re-appearing on 312 metres (962 kHz). Transmissions became more regular, with Flemish during the day, and English from 6 pm until 7 am.

During January 1974, the Dutch Government debated the future of the pirate stations. At that time there were three ships broadcasting off the Dutch coast: the *Mi Amigo*, *MEBO II* and the *Norderney*. Radio Atlantis was broadcasting from just down the coast, off Belgium.

On Wednesday 20th January, the Dutch First Chamber voted in favour of ratifying the Strasbourg Treaty with a majority of 37 votes. The Minister for Culture, Henri van Doorn, had received another application from Radio Veronica asking to broadcast legally. Although the decision had been taken to close the stations, no date was set for its implementation so as to give more time to consider Veronica's latest application.

Having had an earlier request, made in 1973, turned down, Veronica had formed the Veronica Broadcasting Organisation to give support to the Veronica Foundation. An application was presented requesting airtime on the Hilversum network, as they now had well over 100,000 members.

The Dutch Government started moving the goal posts, by introducing new criteria to qualify, which Radio Veronica had a hard time complying with. It seemed that the station was no longer welcome, after 14 years as the nation's favourite.

VERONICA STAYS (IF YOU WANT IT TO !)

IF you want it to, fill in this card with your name, address and
signature and send it to Radio Veronica (5p stamp) at,
ANTWOORDKAART, MACHITIGING nr.123, HILVERSUM, HOLLAND.

NAME ....   SIGNATURE ....

ADDRESS ....

....   THANK YOU!

....

ENGLAND

Not only has Radio Veronica besmirched its reputation, by paying for the boming of RNI in 1970, it had not been the nation's favourite radio station since 1971, when Hilversum 3 took the number one slot. It would have to try harder to survive.

The decision by the Dutch Government to close the stations was the main reason for dropping the Radio Seagull callsign. This was an act of defiance by Radio Caroline; Radio Seagull had been gaining in popularity, but it would not have inspired the same level of support as Caroline.

Radio Seagull had been plagued by technical problems, not least the collapse of the aerial, resulting in the station being off air from October 1973 until January 1974. In fact, from opening to closing 24th July, 1973 until 23rd February, 1974, Radio Seagull had spent just 48 days on the air!

Radio Caroline and Radio Mi Amigo had no intention of complying with the impending Dutch legislation, in fact both were actively taking steps to beat the law. During April the lower sections of the radio aerial were strengthened, and on 1st June Radio Caroline closed its office in The Hague, moving into the Radio Mi Amigo property at Breda in southern Holland.

Radio Atlantis, meanwhile, had installed new equipment in the ship's studio, and was busy improving the quality of its broadcasts. At the beginning of June 1974 storms lashed the North Sea, the three ships off the Dutch coast experiencing no real problems, but that was not the case for Radio Atlantis.

The radio mast collapsed, which, combined with transmitter faults, forced the station off the air. During the night the ship parted from its anchor, and started drifting. The ship was driven north by the wind for a distance of about 20 miles, eventually going aground on a sand bank off the Dutch coast.

The *Jeanine* was towed back to its anchorage, where transmissions resumed on Sunday 9th June, three days after the mast had collapsed. A new anchor and chain were fitted to the ship, and the aerial repaired. The quality of the transmissions increased, giving the station a good-sized following, in Belgium and Holland and parts of the south east of Britain.

At the end of June they stopped transmitting adverts, because the Belgian authorities were threatening to prosecute companies whose adverts were broadcast.

During July Radio Atlantis made a low powered test transmission on short wave, this was a one off, and no furthe tests were made. At the time is was costing £1,500 to keep the station on the air.

On Monday 12th August the Dutch Government announced that the Marine Offences Act would become law on Sunday 1st September, 1974. The Minister for Culture stated that he expected Radio Northsea International and Radio Veronica to close by that date, but there was no mention of Radio Caroline/Mi Amigo or Radio Atlantis.

In an attempt to beat the new law, Radio Mi Amigo moved from Holland and opened an office and studio in Spain. The new office was situated in the Mediterranean resort of Playa de Aro, Gerona.

Radio Atlantis announced that the Flemish service was to end, on Sunday 25th August, and that the station would adopt an all-English format. It was to see if enough advertising could be obtained to keep the station on the air, as they were planning on defying the law and were proposing moving the office to Spain.

The owners of Radio Northsea International announced that the station would close down, before the deadline. The English service would go first, at midnight Friday 30th August, the Dutch service would close 24 hours later.

It was stated that the *MEBO II*, after conversion and repairs, would sail to a new anchorage in the Bay of Genoa, off the Italian coast. The new station would broadcast in Italian during the day, with English programmes during the night, using many of the DJs from RNI.

This new station was to be called Radio Nova International, taking its name from the Nova Hotel in Zurich, which was owned by RNI joint owner, Edwin Bollier. It was anticipated that the new RNI would broadcast a World service, on 6205 kHz in the 49 metre short wave band, which would be audible in the UK.

Radio Veronica announced that it would close, before the new law took effect, as it did not want to jeopardise its case for being allowed to broadcast legally from land. Closure was set for 6 pm on 31st August.

On Saturday 17th August, at 3 pm, Radio Atlantis announced that due to the effects of the Dutch Marine Offences Act the station would close on 31st August at 7 pm. The Flemish service ended at 2 pm on Sunday 25th August, and was replaced by an all-English format.

Listeners on both sides of the North Sea were stunned, once again the offshore radio stations were being forced to close. Time for the Dutch pirate radio era was fast running out, and all too soon the grim day arrived.

At 8 pm, on Friday 30th August, Radio Northsea International began its last four hours of the English service. Special one hour programmes were presented by 'Daffy' Don Allan, Robin Banks and Brian McKenzie.

The final hour was given over to the DJs to make their closing messages, and Don Allen with Brian McKenzie relived the station's stormy and very eventful life. The very last record to be played was *Peace*, by Peter, and then Brian McKenzie announced: 'Timex time in central Europe is now exactly midnight, and the International service of Radio Northsea is closing down'. This was followed by the station's theme tune, *Man of Action* by Les Read. Then there was a short silence, but before listeners could dry their eyes the Dutch services took over.

Saturday 31st August, 1974 will be remembered as, yet another, very sad day in the history of offshore radio. From that very first broadcast, from Radio Mercur in July 1958, pirate radio ships had broadcast thousands of hours of pleasure, to countless millions of listeners, causing very little harm. To use an overworked cliché, it really was the end of (yet another) era, the like of which will probably never be seen again.

In what amounted to a carbon copy of 14th August, 1967, the stations bade their final farewells. The first to go was Radio Veronica; for over 14 years she had been loved by the people of Holland, but she took with her the responsibility for the bombing of Radio Northsea.

From 5pm the last live programme was broadcast from the *Norderney*. After the 5.30 pm news a taped message was broadcast, throughout that last programme a clock could be heard ticking, counting out the dying minutes. The last words to be broadcast were: 'This is the end of Veronica. It is a pity for you, for Veronica, and especially democracy in Holland'. The Dutch National Anthem was played, followed by a Veronica jingle, which was switched off before it had finished.

One hour after Veronica had gone, Radio Atlantis closed down. The last two days had been spent broadcasting, 24 hours per day, in English. The final hour was the Goodbye Party, and at exactly 7.05 pm Radio Atlantis closed down.

Radio Northsea's Dutch service was the last station to go, the final hour commencing at 7 pm. It had been intended to close at midnight, but at the last minute the decision was made to close at 8 pm. During that last hour, all of the staff, both Dutch and English, said their goodbyes. At 8 pm *Man of Action* was played, followed by a jingle depicting Radio Northsea sinking beneath the waves.

The Dutch era will long be remembered for its hijacks, fire bombs, sabotage, driftings and aerial collapses. It will also be associated with the return of Radio Caroline, after four years of silence.

It should also be remembered for providing listeners with the music and pleasure that they were seeking. The era had lasted four years, generating a great deal of happiness, and it will be remembered with much affection.

Chapter Four

The Fight For Survival,
1974-1980

1974

Top 20 for week commencing Sunday 25th August, 1974

1	(19)	*Love Me For A Reason*	Osmonds
2	(1)	*When Will I See You Again*	Three Degrees
3	(2)	*You Make Me Feel Brand New*	Stylistics
4	(5)	*I'm Leaving It All Up To You*	Donny and Marie Osmond
5	(3)	*Summerlove Sensation*	Bay City Rollers
6	(4)	*What Becomes Of The Broken Hearted*	Jimmy Ruffin
7	(15)	*Y Viva Espana*	Sylvia
8	(12)	*Mr Soft*	Cockney Rebel
9	(29)	*Kung Fu Fighting*	Carl Douglas
10	(13)	*Honey Honey*	Sweet Dreams
11	(7)	*Rock The Boat*	Hues Corporation
12	(20)	*Na Na Na*	Cozy Powell
13	(9)	*I Shot The Sheriff*	Eric Clapton
14	(17)	*Hello Summertime*	Bobby Goldsboro
15	(8)	*Rocket*	Mud
16	(6)	*Rock Your Baby*	George McCrae
17	(10)	*Just For You*	Glitter Band
18	(26)	*Annie's Song*	John Denver
19	(22)	*Rock'n'Roll Lady*	Showaddywaddy
20	(11)	*It's Only Rock And Roll*	The Rolling Stones

Alone Again!

The Dutch offshore radio era may have come to an end, but what happened
to Radio Caroline? Ronan had no intention of closing the station, why should
he, when he had been through so much to get her and keep her broadcasting?

At 4 pm on Thursday 29th August, the MV *Mi Amigo* raised anchor and,
using her own engine, sailed away from the Dutch coast. A tug accompanied
the radio ship throughout her epic voyage, carrying a new anchor and chain.

The 200 hp engine drove the *Mi Amigo* slowly across the North Sea, until 24
hours later, when she anchored in a new position 20 miles off Frinton on Sea.
The *Mi Amigo* was anchored in the Knock Deep Channel, at 3 pm on 30th
August, in position 51 degrees 41.5 minutes north, 01 degrees 35 minutes east.

Much research had gone into choosing the new anchorage, between two
sandbanks, which would shelter her from the worst of the North Sea storms,
except those which came from the north-east.

Transmissions were maintained, throughout the voyage, although no
mention was made that the ship was underway. During the evening of the 29th,
broadcasts did stop for two hours, it being announced that this was due to a
labour dispute!

On 29th August, 1974 the *Mi Amigo* left the Dutch coast and sailed across the North Sea, anchoring 20 miles off Frinton on Sea the next day. Caroline had come home.

John Wilson

During the evening of Saturday 31st August, whilst the stations off the Dutch coast were closing, Radio Caroline was fighting on. At midnight, DJ Tony Allen repeated history by playing *Caroline* by the Fortunes, followed by *All You Need Is Love* by the Beatles, just as Johnnie Walker had done seven years previously, on 14th August, 1967.

When Radio Caroline had commenced broadcasts 10 years earlier, she was anchored alone in the North Sea. She was joined by others, but they had gone. In 1972 she had joined a small group of radio ships, now these had gone, once again Caroline was alone. In fact she was more isolated than she had ever been; she was one of a kind, and further from the coast than any other radio ship had been.

Not only was she alone, she had been outlawed by all of the countries whose coastline bordered the North Sea. There could be no running for shelter from the storm-lashed waters that were effectively her prison. She may have been free, in International waters, but she dared not go inside territorial waters, so her freedom was at a high price, not only for her but for those who served on her.

Meanwhile, on 1st September, the Radio Atlantis ship was towed into the port of Vlissingen where, two days later, it was arrested. It had been seized on behalf of the owner of the radio transmitter, who claimed that he was owed money for rental.

Rumours soon spread that the station was going to resume broadcasts, but from a structure rather than a ship. In mid-September a work party was landed on the disused Gunfleet lighthouse, which was just over five miles off the Essex coast.

Over the following weeks the lighthouse was prepared for its new role as the home for Radio Dolphin, which was due to commence broadcasting in English on Christmas Day. However, on Thursday 19th December the lighthouse was visited by Police and Trinity House officers. Trinity House still owned the structure: the interlopers complied with the request to leave and nothing further was heard of Radio Dolphin.

On Monday 9th September, 1974 the *MEBO II* entered dry dock, in the port of Slikkerveer, for overhaul prior to leaving for the Italian coast. The ship's hull was cleaned of marine crustaceans and the transmitters were serviced. The height of the aerial was increased, by 15 feet, and new short and medium wave aerials were fitted.

The refit, which was reported to have cost in excess of £400,000, also included new studios and a new record library. There had been two studios, but these were replaced by three smaller ones.

As this work was progressing, the *MEBO I* had been painted white, and renamed *Angela*. On Wednesday 9th October it was reported that the *MEBO II* was ready to leave port, but that she was not sailing to Italy, she was instead going to anchor off the Kent coast.

Whoever leaked that report did RNI no favours, during the evening the ship was seized by the Dutch authorities. Edwin Bollier attended a hearing on 11th November, where it was claimed that the ship had contravened the law by having transmitting equipment on board.

On 24th December the court ruled that the ship had to remain, and the transmitters had to be removed. RNI appealed and a further hearing was scheduled for 3rd March, 1975. It was then ruled that the ship could leave, provided that she was gone within two months and did not broadcast from European waters for two years. The owners had to pay a bond, of about £40,000, which would be forfeit if they broke the agreement.

Meanwhile, Radio Caroline was back in the news, for assisting in the rescue of a launch crew. The vessel had tied up to the *Mi Amigo*, as the crew had become seasick in the choppy conditions. Following requests for assistance from Radio Caroline, the lifeboat from Walton on Naze escorted the launch into port.

The *Mi Amigo* was supplied from Spain, with stores, fuel and water, but this proved difficult and expensive, the journey taking at least three days. Disc jockeys, and other staff, had to run the gauntlet, by joining the ship from small launches which sailed from secluded locations either in this Country, or from the Continent.

The Home Office announced that they would be keeping a close watch on the radio ship, and its activities. With this in mind the whole operation of getting staff, and stores, to the ship was cloaked in secrecy.

DJs used a series of code numbers to let their colleagues, on shore, know of any developments or requirements. Trinity House and the Coastguard were asked to keep a look out for the supply boats, and police launches patrolled river estuaries to intercept suspect vessels.

To provide the continuing sound of Radio Caroline, all of the personnel had to face considerable risks from the elements and the authorities. From this point the story of Caroline includes some of the arrests, and subsequent prosecutions, made against Caroline staff, their suppliers and some of the listeners.

In June 1974 Radio Mi Amigo moved its operation to Spain, where they later shared an address at RADO, Playa de Aro, Gerona, with Radio Caroline. Spain was a safe refuge because the country had not been invited to sign the Strasbourg Treaty, and as neither of the stations broadcast to the Country, it was hoped that Spanish officials would show little, if any, interest in their operations.

The official interest in this Country did not take long before it claimed its first victims. On Tuesday 29th October, Caroline personnel left Burnham on Crouch in a small launch to make the journey to the *Mi Amigo*. On arrival, the launch went alongside the radio ship, stores were delivered and personnel exchanged.

Whilst this was taking place a fishing vessel, which had been nearby, moved in closer and photographers could be seen on the deck. The whole operation was photographed from the fishing vessel which had been in the vicinity of the *Mi Amigo* for some time. No one on the radio ship had taken notice of the vessel, why should they, fishing vessels passed every day?

When the exchange had been completed, the launch returned to the coast, where it was met by a police launch which escorted the tender from when it entered territorial waters into port. All of the occupants of the tender were searched and their details were taken.

Radio Mi Amigo's Spanish premises at Playa de Aro, with an ex-Trinity House colleague and his family posing for the camera.   *Pete Halil*

Another tender was intercepted, on Tuesday 26th November, as it returned from the *Mi Amigo*. This time it was revealed that a helicopter had been used to monitor the illegal supply run.

On the same day, a man from Holland on Sea was charged with operating an illegal ship-to-shore radio link to the *Mi Amigo*. The man was subsequently fined £100, and all of his radio equipment was seized.

Daunted, but not deterred Radio Caroline continued to gain wide support, not just from the listeners, but also from recording companies and artists. Each evening the station opened with the following ID, 'Live from the North Sea, this is Radio Caroline, Europe's first and only album station'.

The all-album format was giving airtime to artists that would not otherwise have been heard. The format was proving extremely popular, one opinion poll revealing that over 3 million listeners were tuning into Radio Caroline at some time during the week.

During its heyday Radio Caroline had in excess of 20 million listeners, but that had been helped by the fact that they had two ships. The number of listeners had dropped significantly, but the station was catering for a completely different audience, opening up an unexplored niche in the market. Recording companies were well pleased, because the station was generating a lot of album sales, which in turn pleased the artists.

1975

Top 20 for week commencing Sunday 3rd August, 1975

1	(2)	Barbados	Typically Tropical
2	(1)	Give A Little Love	Bay City Rollers
3	(12)	I Can't Give You Anything (But My Love)	Stylistics
4	(6)	If You Think You Know How To Love Me	Smokie
5	(5)	Jive Talkin'	Bee Gees
6	(8)	It's In His Kiss	Linda Lewis
7	(7)	Sealed With A Kiss	Bryan Hyland
8	(16)	Delilah	Sensational Alex Harvey Band
9	(10)	Je t'Aime	Judge Dread
10	(3)	Tears On My Pillow	Johnny Nash
11	(17)	I Write The Songs/Get It Up For Love	David Cassidy
12	(22)	Sherry	Adrian Baker
13	(28)	It's Been So Long	George McCrae
14	(29)	The Last Farewell	Roger Whittaker
15	(19)	New York City	T. Rex
16	(21)	Blanket On The Ground	Billy Jo Spears
17	(11)	Rollin' Stone	David Essex
18	(23)	Dolly My Love	Moments
19	(15)	Action	Sweet
20	(4)	Misty	Ray Stevens

Loving Awareness

Radio Caroline, and her sister station Radio Mi Amigo, welcomed in the New Year. Little did they realise what the year was to hold for them, for this was the year that the British Government decided to get tough with the thorn in its side.

Official interest, in the supply and manning of the station, increased dramatically, both at home and on the Continent. When asked how much the operations against the *Mi Amigo* was costing, the Home Office spokesperson replied:

> Since this only forms part of our general expenditure on the prevention of illicit radio transmissions, and harmful interference, it cannot be separately identified. It has to be understood that it is the need to ensure a planned, and regulated, use of the radio frequency spectrum, and not a deliberate act of perversity on our part, which makes it necessary for us to take this action, against such illicit broadcasting stations.

The Home Office official was also asked, 'You mention harmful interference, have you any cases of interference caused, specifically by Radio Caroline?' 'Radio Caroline has been causing interference to various university broadcasting stations, in this Country, which operate legally on the same frequency.'

In May it was reported that the Government had been approached by officials from Holland and Belgium, which wanted the Government to take positive action against the two stations that were broadcasting from the *Mi Amigo*. Both countries were annoyed by the continuing sounds of Free Radio; they had stopped the broadcasts from around their shores, now they wanted Britain to do the same.

Many felt that the depth of feeling against the radio ship was as a result of Radio Caroline's involvement with Radio Northsea International. RNI had embarked on the highly controversial political involvement during the run up to the 1970 General Election, but had used the callsign Radio Caroline for its campaign.

If a pirate station could be used for broadcasting propaganda once, what was to stop it from happening again? The fact that the ship had continued to broadcast for so long, after the introduction of legislation to silence her, could only be a minor source of embarrassment. Unless one does take into account the aspect of propaganda, or uncontrolled freedom of speech.

The Governments of Europe could not control Caroline's broadcasts, and it was felt that she had blackened her name, and done irreparable damage, which made her continued existence so totally unacceptable. All that Radio Caroline, and Radio Mi Amigo, wanted to do was continue to broadcast. There was absolutely nothing to gain, but everything to lose, if they did try to broadcast political propaganda.

Having said that, Radio Caroline, and later Radio Mi Amigo, did transmit a kind of propaganda, but it was not of a political nature, although it was seen, by some to be very controversial.

The *Mi Amigo*, the 'Love Ship', broadcasting Love and Peace live from the North Sea. Loving Awareness is a way of life. *John Wilson*

In the beginning there was darkness, and the Spirit of DA reared its head. In habitual pattern, preying on the minds of men, oppressing him. And then one man turned to himself and said, in a voice free from fear, Let there be LA!

I think I am - therefore I am - I think! And for him DA vanished, and the light of everlasting LA began to spread, from his point of view, on to the world.

And his fellow man took notice, some mocked the man saying, 'Thou art a fool, look what thou hast hast given up. Thou art surely the all time sucker!'

And the man smiled, for he knew that he had given up nothing but had, in fact, gained the world. And gradually it became less difficult for the man to relate to the Spirit of LA continuously. And more men took notice of him, and saw that LA was good, and asked, 'What made him different?'

And the man said, 'You make me different from yourself, for verily we are all the same. Know thyself, and fear not, for there is nothing to fear, but fear itself. Above all, do unto others as you would do unto yourself. And the Spirit of LA will forever guide your life'. And the people saw that it was good, and became one, with the man.

This was the concept of Loving Awareness (LA), it was an experiment formulated by Ronan, in the early 1970s, but it really reached its zenith by the mid/late 1970s.

Ronan had followed the teachings of Martin Luther King, and of Gandhi, and he wanted to try and stimulate people into thinking about love. It is a basic force, which most people have inside them, an energy, they just need help to find those feelings. It is easier to think Loving Awareness, then to adopt a policy of Defensive Awareness (DA).

In some respects the LA concept became more controversial than Ronan could have imagined. Some of the DJs were too embarrassed to mention it, whilst they were on the air. Listeners either loved it, or hated it, there seemed to be no middle ground.

There were some letters from listeners who thought that it was a good idea, a positive idea. But many more wrote to say that they were turned off by the whole thing, it was not up to Radio Caroline to preach, and that they would tune to another station if it did not stop.

When the concept began, it was left to the DJs whether they wanted to take part, or not. If they did join in, they were allowed to speak freely, to voice their own feelings. The initial response was very poor, but slowly the word spread, and limited amounts of money were put into the project.

New jingles were produced which soon became a regular feature of Caroline's broadcast, jingles such as:

Loving Awareness is free. Loving Awareness is a simple concept. Just treat people in a loving way, and in return they will give you all the love in the world. LA the only way.

There are many decisions we have to make these days, in our lives, but surely one of the easiest is to choose Loving Awareness. Go on, give it a go.

Call it a dream a fantasy not to be believed, but call it hope. The newly completed LA States offers you, and your loved ones, paradise on earth, and promises to change your life styles to what it was meant to be.

At LA State you will be blessed with harmony and peace of mind, never before available, in any other living environment, and you will realise that its all just a question of attitudes. Conveniently located to all life's necessities, LA States is closer then you imagine, centred right in the heart of downtown humanity. For further information on the harmonious LA State, enquire.

Radio Caroline's propaganda was Love, which should have been a harmless concept. Ronan was surprised that it could provoke such a diverse and at times hostile reaction. Ronan said of LA,

> In the great lake of life LA is just a tiny pebble, in the middle of that lake. But it is a pebble, and it does hit the lake, and it is bound to cause ripples. When those ripples hit the shore, and if they hit the shore, at what point and how, will depend on many factors. The main factor is, how receptive the person is, who receives that message.
>
> I think that if millions of people could live that idea, not for any religious reason, but because they felt better in their own head for being there, that is the basis feeling of it. That is the best way to sell it, that you feel better if you live in your head, in that sort of place, positive and optimistic.

There you go man,
Keep as cool as you can.
Face piles of trials with smiles,
it riles them to believe that you perceive.

During 1976 a four man group called Loving Awareness started to record songs of special significance. It had been hoped that they would be allowed to call themselves The Beetles, as they were following an example that had been set by the 'Fab Four'. Permission was not obtained for the name change, and the group had only very limited success.

Loving Awareness was an experiment that was not a major success. However, in the face of adversity, Radio Caroline became synonymous with love. Mi Amigo means my friend. The Beatles' *All You Need Is Love*, was the station anthem.

Each evening Radio Caroline started its programmes by playing the jingle.

Sail away on an ocean of love.
Twenty four hours a day,
Caroline and Mi Amigo,
sailing away on the Love Ship.
And we would like you to join us,
it's easy, just climb aboard the Love Ship.
and sail away.
Caroline and Mi Amigo,
sailing on an ocean of love,
with you.

The Raid

August 1975 was quite an eventful month for Radio Caroline. On Friday 1st, a Berlin service was introduced. The programme was broadcast during the early hours of the morning. The first three programmes were recorded at the American Forces Network (AFN) studio, Berlin.

This new service proved very popular and soon increased to three, one hour programmes per week. New studios were constructed to make the recordings, which continued until Monday 29th December, 1975 when the service ended without explanation.

On Sunday 24th August test transmissions were broadcast on 389 metres. Power was low, and the testing was intermittent, as Caroline tried to reinstate an all day English service. Meanwhile, both Caroline and Mi Amigo continued to broadcast on 259.

Simulcasting, the term used to describe more than one transmission being made from one aerial, had been achieved for a short time, back in June 1973, prior to Radio Atlantis commencing broadcasts. It was planned to have Radio Mi Amigo on 259, using the 50 kilowatt transmitter, whilst Caroline used 389, with a 10 kilowatt transmitter. The 389 frequency was not, however, successful and the tests ended in mid-October.

On Sunday 14th September broadcasts were interrupted, at 4.40 pm; the crew of the *Mi Amigo* had seen a yacht get into difficulties. The yacht had fired a distress flare, as sea conditions worsened. The appeals for help resulted in a helicopter being scrambled from RAF Manston in Kent. Whilst this rescue was underway, a second yacht got into difficulties and had to be given assistance.

Just four days later Caroline was back in the news, but on a far less auspicious occasion. Two DJs appeared at Southend court, on Thursday 18th, this case having arisen from the boarding of a tender as it returned from the *Mi Amigo* in November 1974.

The two DJs were both found guilty of taking part in illegal broadcasts, and were fined £150 each. The owner of the launch was fined £35, for taking persons to and from the pirate radio ship.

At another court case, on Thursday 9th October, another DJ was charged with making illegal broadcasts, but as he pleaded not guilty his case was transferred to the Crown Court.

On Tuesday 16th September a fishing vessel which had visited the *Mi Amigo* was intercepted by Dutch authorities as it entered port. Two men were arrested, but released after questioning. On board the tender they found a part from a diesel engine, and several programme tapes. It was later revealed that an aircraft had been used to track the vessel.

Storm force winds lashed the *Mi Amigo* on Saturday 8th November, the 470 ton radio ship was snatching violently at its anchor chain. The wind was coming from the north-east, the only direction from which the ship was not protected.

Just after 6 pm, Radio Caroline DJ Simon Barrett announced that the *Mi Amigo* had lost its anchor and was drifting. The drama had started two hours earlier when the crew thought that they were drifting, but there was no reliable navigation equipment on the ship to confirm their fears.

The *Mi Amigo* lost her anchor on Saturday 8th November and drifted across the Thames Estuary. Broadcasts recommenced five days later, but on 14th November the ship was raided by Home Office officials. It was not until 26th November that the ship was moved to International waters and transmissions restarted.   *Sky Fotos*

Contact was made with a passing vessel, and the Coastguard was alerted. Radio Caroline, having announced that they were adrift, made constant appeals to the listeners not to contact the Coastguard, as they were already aware of the situation. The Coastguard was able to take bearings of the *Mi Amigo*, and passed the information to the captain, so that he could keep a plot of their drift. Whilst the drama was continuing music continued to be broadcast, but just after 7 pm the situation worsened as the ship had run onto a sandbank. The ship's engine was put to full astern, but it was to be 50 minutes until the ship was refloated. The Coastguard kept in contact with the ship, advising the captain of its position.

Even with the ship's engine running, it was not powerful enough to halt the drift, but the Captain was able to get the ship onto a south-westerly heading, toward the Tongue lightship. After four hours it was realised that the *Mi Amigo* was nearing territorial waters, and the decision was made to suspend broadcasts.

On my way back home, by the New Riders of the Purple Sage, which includes the line, 'Flying to the sun, Sweet Caroline', was played and then the transmitter was switched off, just after 10 pm.

Just after 1 am, on Sunday 9th November, the crew managed to lower one of the emergency anchors, which was then followed by a second anchor. The ship was now about eight miles off Margate, having drifted right across the Thames Estuary.

Once at anchor the worst of the danger was over, but there was still a problem. The ship was very near to the South Edinburgh No. 3 navigation buoy. Whilst the ship was swinging around the anchors, it did strike a glancing blow to the buoy, but no serious damage resulted. Trinity House sent one of its ships to see if the radio ship had fouled the anchor chain of the buoy, but it had not.

The seven people on board the *Mi Amigo* maintained a 24 hour watch from the bridge, as they were not certain would happen next. Later in the next day a Port of London Authority vessel made contact with the *Mi Amigo*. They wanted to know when the ship would be moved, as it was near the shipping lanes.

Two tugs arrived, and stood by the radio ship overnight. Over the following days several different tugs were exchanged, as they kept watch on the *Mi Amigo*. In spite of having the tugs in the vicinity, the captain decided to wait at the temporary anchorage, until a Caroline-organised ship arrived, with a new anchor and chain.

The decision to wait was very fortuitous, when they heard a broadcast from Radio Orwell, a local commercial radio station. The report stated that the tugs had been instructed not to tow the *Mi Amigo* seawards. It was not until Wednesday 12th, that a tender arrived, in the shape of a large and powerful vessel. Not only did the tender bring a new anchor and chain, it also had stores, provisions and water, as the ship was running low on most items.

The supply vessel made several attempts to tow the *Mi Amigo* back to its Knock Deep anchorage, but to no avail. During one attempt damage was caused to the radio ship, and part of the ship's side rail was ripped off. During another attempt the tender fouled its own propellers, with the rope they had intended using for towing the ship. Then, as a last attempt, the new anchor chain was passed from the tender and the end was secured to the aerial mast, which could have resulted in all kinds of problems if the aerial had collapsed.

With the *Mi Amigo's* own engine assisting, the two ships began to move, but they had not gone far when the tow parted. The anchor, which had been secured to the tender fell overboard, resulting in the *Mi Amigo* being anchored, with the aerial as the securing point. At this point it was decided to leave the ship, before any further damage was caused, it was estimated that the ship had moved about one mile.

Whatever the actual distance, those on board thought that they were now back into International waters, and that they could resume broadcasting. At 9.30 am on Thursday 13th November transmissions commenced, using taped continuous music. Radio Mi Amigo started broadcasting later that morning. and Caroline returned at 6 pm.

During the afternoon two vessels, one of which was a tug, arrived in the vicinity of the *Mi Amigo*. Having circled the radio ship, they anchored nearby. One of the ships contacted North Foreland Radio, telling them that under instructions from the Home Office, they were to accept no further calls from the *Mi Amigo*.

Those on board began to fear the worst, but much to their relief both of the vessels left. Any feeling of elation felt on the *Mi Amigo* did not last for long. During the afternoon of the 14th, at 3 pm, a police launch came alongside the *Mi Amigo*; on board were some officials from the Home Office.

The officials got onto the *Mi Amigo*, and within minutes Radio Mi Amigo was forced to close, the last voice to be heard saying, 'No don't cut that', as the microphone lead was cut.

The raid lasted for about two hours, during which time details and photographs were taken of all those on board. The transmitter crystal was removed, to prevent any further broadcasts. The ship's captain, an engineer and two DJs were arrested and taken ashore, landing at Southend pier.

The men were detained overnight, appearing the next morning in the local Magistrates Court. The captain was charged with being the master of a ship used for making illegal broadcasts from within territorial waters. The engineer was charged with maintaining equipment used for making illegal broadcasts, and the DJs were charged with having made the broadcasts. They were all freed on bail, and had their passports confiscated.

On 17th November, three days after the raid had taken place, the *Mi Amigo* broadcast a request for medical assistance on marine VHF. Margate lifeboat responded to the call, and took two very seasick men from the radio ship. They were landed at Ramsgate, where they were interviewed by police and Immigration officers.

It was not until 26th November that the *Mi Amigo* returned to her proper anchorage, with transmissions of Radio Mi Amigo resuming that afternoon, Radio Caroline returned to the air at 6 pm. The broadcasts closed down at midnight, and had been made on low power.

Both stations continued broadcasting on low power, but on Monday 1st December Caroline's programmes came to an abrupt end, at 10.30 pm. The top section of the mast had broken off. However, transmissions did resume the next day, but once again they were on low power.

On 11th December the four man who had been arrested during the raid appeared in Southend Magistrates court. Three of them pleaded guilty, but the engineer decided to plead not guilty. The captain was fined £150, one DJ was fined £75, whilst the other was fined £250. The case against the engineer was adjourned until 23rd February, 1976.

The Magistrate also ruled that if the *Mi Amigo* should ever re-enter British territorial waters, the police were authorised to seize it. Following their appearance in court, the DJs decided never to return to the *Mi Amigo*.

1976

Top 20 for week commencing Sunday 4th January, 1976

1	(1)	Bohemian Rhapsody	Queen
2	(3)	The Trail of the Lonesome Pine	Laurel and Hardy
3	(2)	I Believe In Father Christmas	Greg Lake
4	(18)	Glass Of Champagne	Sailor
5	(5)	Lets Twist Again/The Twist	Chubby Checker
6	(13)	Wide Eyed And Legless	Andy Fairweather Low
7	(17)	Art For Art's Sake	10 cc
8	(9)	Golden Years	David Bowie
9	(4)	It's Gonna Be A Cold Cold Christmas	Dana
10	(12)	Can I Take You Home Little Girl	Drifters
11	(6)	Happy To Be On An Island In The Sun	Demis Roussos
12	(29)	Mamma Mia	Abba
13	(16)	If I Could	David Essex
14	(7)	You Sexy Thing	Hot Chocolate
15	(15)	Money Honey	Bay City Rollers
16	(14)	Christmas In Dreadland/Come Outside	Judge Dread
17	(8)	Na Na Is The Saddest Word	The Stylistics
18	(29)	King Of The Cops	Billy Howard
19	(27)	First Impressions	Impressions
20	(11)	Show Me You're A Woman	Mud

Trying Times

If the Caroline organisation had thought 1975 bad, 1976 was waiting with its fair share of problems. It was Radio Caroline's 12th birthday, and a lot of people were to find themselves in trouble for working on, or for advertising, the station.

The first job of the New Year, was to repair the aerial mast, and replace the broken sections. The work was carried out on Thursday 8th January, which allowed output to be restored to 50 kilowatts.

On Tuesday 17th February the trial began, which in its own way, was to become quite infamous. Everyone who worked for Radio Caroline knew that they faced the risk of arrest, and possible prosecution, if they were caught. This case proved they they were not the only ones who faced that risk!

Liverpool Magistrates Court was the setting for the hearing, which found three men facing Caroline-related charges. Two of these men owned and ran a mobile disco, which they called The Radio Caroline Roadshow. They faced charges of:

Having a door plaque, on which was inscribed, Radio Caroline Liverpool HQ, and, Official Caroline Club.
Advertising Radio Caroline on the Roadshow posters.
Displaying a window sticker which proclaimed, Sound of the Nation, Radio Caroline, tune to 259 metres.

They were also charged with having similar stickers on three road vehicles, and for promoting a radio station, whose activities were illegal. This last charge came as a result of a statement on a Roadshow poster which included the line, 'and is run in conjunction with the ship'.

The third man was a hotel owner, who had booked the Roadshow, for a disco at his hotel. To advertise the disco, he had displayed Radio Caroline Roadshow posters at his hotel. These posters were deemed to be illegal.

It was alleged that the posters were calculated to promote, directly or indirectly, the interests of a business considered illegal. This first hearing was adjourned until April, as the two Roadshow men insisted that all of the prosecution witnesses should be in the court.

Just six days later, Monday 23rd February, another court was dealing with a Radio Caroline offence. The engineer, who had pleaded not guilty at his first hearing, had changed his plea to guilty. The Home Office, during the November 1975 raid, had seized log books with his signature in them, alongside various notes and entries. He was found guilty and fined a total of £150.

The Liverpool three found themselves back in court, on Monday 26th April. The proceedings dragged on for over a week, with witnesses from the Home Office and the Post Office. It was revealed that two men had been employed, at taxpayers' expense, to monitor Radio Mi Amigo programmes, even though they could not understand what was being said or what language was being used!

At the end of the proceedings, the Magistrates took half an hour to reach their verdict. The three men were all found guilty, the hotel owner was fined £75, but sentence on the other two was deferred, pending further reports.

On 21st May the two men returned to the court for sentencing. Both were given 90 days imprisonment, suspended for two years, and were fined costs of £500 each. Both men lodged appeals, which were heard on 25th October.

One of the men, who had a previous conviction for making illegal broadcasts, had his earlier punishment reaffirmed. The second man had his suspended sentence quashed, to be replaced by a £100 fine, in addition to the earlier £500 fine.

Whilst the Liverpool case had been proceeding, other court cases had taken place. On 26th April a Caroline DJ appeared at Southend Crown Court, charged with making illegal broadcasts. The DJ had been found on a tender intercepted by the police in November 1974.

At his first hearing, in September 1975, he had pleaded not guilty; under the terms of the Marine Offences Act, a person can only be charged with one offence. The prosecution had to prove that the DJ had made live broadcasts, because if he had not, under the section of the Act with which he had been charged, he could not be guilty.

The prosecution had in their possession several tapes of the DJ, but as the case continued, it became clear that they could not prove that they were recordings of a live broadcast.

Council for the defence asked that the case be stopped due to the lack of evidence, and on the grounds that some of the evidence had not been recorded by the police. It was claimed that this evidence was unreliable, as it was only remembered, and not documented. The judge agreed and instructed the jury to return a not guilty verdict.

The British courts were not alone in prosecuting people involved with offshore radio. On 12th May a trial was being held in Holland, against the owner and skipper of a tender and the skipper of the radio ship *Mi Amigo*. This case had arisen when the two men had been apprehended when they returned from giving assistance to the radio ship, after it had run aground in November 1975.

The tender had taken a new anchor and chain to the *Mi Amigo*, but the men claimed that as the British authorities had removed the crystal from the transmitter the *Mi Amigo* was technically not a radio ship. They claimed that all they had done was go to a ship which was in an emergency situation. The fact that that ship had an extremely large mast did not mean that it could make illegal broadcasts.

The Public Prosecutor was not impressed by this argument, as it was well known that one of the men had, on several occasions, acted as the captain of the *Mi Amigo*. In fact he had been in charge of the ship when it returned to its anchorage off the Dutch coast, after the Dutch crew had led a mutiny in December 1972.

Both men were found guilty, and on 25th May they were sentenced. The captain of the *Mi Amigo* was fined £200, and received six weeks' suspended imprisonment. The other man was fined £400 with a suspended eight weeks' imprisonment. This was the first case to be made under the Dutch Marine Offences law.

One month later, Amsterdam's Public Prosecutor was back in action against *Mi Amigo* personnel. On this occasion seven men were facing charges arising from the drifting of the *Mi Amigo* in November 1975. Only three of the seven actually appeared in the court. The three were all found guilty, two were fined £1,600 with two months' suspended imprisonment. The third man, a crew member, was fined £200, with three weeks' probation.

On 14th September Amsterdam was the setting for yet another case. A Radio Mi Amigo announcer was fined £400, with six weeks' suspended imprisonment, in his absence. Another man, from the Hague, was found guilty of ferrying personnel to and from the *Mi Amigo*. He was fined £900 with six weeks' suspended imprisonment.

On 29th September, the courts in Belgium took up the fight against Radio Caroline and Radio Mi Amigo, and those who advertised on the station. On this occasion no less then 41 people were facing charges. Four of the accused, including Radio Mi Amigo's owner, Mr Sylvain Tack, were not present in court.

Mr Tack was facing three charges,

1. Operating an illegal radio station.
2. Threatening a Dutch film crew, which he denied.
3. Extortion against another company (name deliberately withheld)

which he also denied.

Amongst the others in court, were some of the companies that had been advertising on Radio Mi Amigo. Mr Tack's brother, who was also in court, was facing charges for being in charge of the Belgian end of the station's operations.

It was not until 12th November, 1976 that the court made known its verdicts. Mr Tack was found guilty on all three charges, he was sentenced to 19 months in prison, with a staggering fine of £65,466. His brother was sentenced to seven months in prison, with a fine of £32,733. Neither of the men attended the court, as they had moved to Spain. As there is no extradition treaty between Belgium and Spain, neither had paid the fine, nor served the sentence.

Fifteen others, including those from advertisers, were each fined £982 with one month's imprisonment suspended. Eighteen others were fined £1,039 with three months' imprisonment.

On The Move - Again!

Having followed some of the courts cases, we can now go back to March 1976, and rejoin events on board the Mi Amigo. On the last day of the month, Radio Caroline commenced test transmissions, on her old frequency of 199 metres, using a 10 kilowatt transmitter.

These tests were carried out whilst Radio Mi Amigo was broadcasting on 259, causing interference to the signals so the tests were suspended whilst engineers tried to rectify the fault. The tests resumed on 5th April, but on another frequency.

It was decided to use Radio Veronica's old frequency of 192 metres (1562kHz), but once again there was break through from Radio Mi Amigo. The tests continued intermittently, with non stop music, and then during the evenings Caroline's programmes, from 259, were relayed.

At 6 am on 15th May Radio Caroline commenced its new all-day service on 192. The very first record to be played was All You Need is Love, by the Beatles. For the second time the engineers had succeeded in achieving simulcasting, and on a very limited budget.

Caroline was on low power to begin with, but it was later increased to 10kW, whilst Radio Mi Amigo had use of the 50kW transmitter. Caroline was broadcasting 24 hours per day on 192, and from 6 pm until 5 am the programmes were also relayed on 259. Radio Mi Amigo was broadcasting from 5 am until 5 pm.

Caroline's 24 hour format only lasted for one week. As from 21st May the station closed at midnight, but then close down took place at 8 pm. With the advent of the all-day English service Caroline introduced some new features, which included traffic and weather reports 'For the 192 listening area'.

To accommodate the new two-station service, it was necessary to construct a second studio. The new studio was used by Radio Caroline services from 16th April, whilst Radio Mi Amigo had use of the original studio.

Over the following months, with only a few minor incidents, the all-day English service continued to gain popularity, as did Radio Mi Amigo's broadcasts on 259. September started quietly, as had previous months. Rough seas had come and gone, it was the way of life on board the radio ship.

It was not to last long, on Friday 10th September, 1976 the North Sea was, once again, lashed by gale force winds. These winds whipped the sea into a short steep swell, and spindrift filled the air. The wind howled through the aerial mast and its rigging like an express train.

The *Mi Amigo* was taking quite a pounding as she swung around her anchor, but this was not a new experience for the men on board. As the storm continued to rage, the swell got heavier, with torrents of water cascading across the heaving deck. Even the heavy fender tyres were being flung onto the deck. All hatches and port holes were firmly shut and the crew tried to make the best of an uncomfortable situation.

For one of Radio Mi Amigo's announcers that stormy day got off to a bad start. A large wave crashed across the deck with such force that one of the portholes was smashed allowing the sea to flood in. The announcer was soaked, as was all of the equipment, forcing the station off the air. Radio Caroline's broadcasts continued, but they consisted of taped music, as it was too rough to use the record turntables.

The transmitter was protesting at the accumulation of salt on the insulators, and at the excessive movements of the ship. There were several breaks in transmissions, one lasting for 20 minutes. At 11 am Radio Caroline closed, and vacated the studio, so that Radio Mi Amigo could resume broadcasting, using both frequencies.

It was a very trying and tiring day with items that had not been secured, including staff, being thrown around. Some of the off duty staff took to their beds, to avoid the worst of the punishment. As things worsened sea water flooded into the engine room, studio, transmitter room, cabins, even the main food locker did not escape. As bad as this was, there was worse to come!

During the evening the anchor chain snapped, allowing the *Mi Amigo* to drift. Those on board realised that things had gone wrong, and quickly lowered the emergency anchor, but this failed to stop the drift, such was the ferocity of the storm.

Radio Caroline recommenced broadcasts at 6 pm, but at 8.30 pm the DJ announced that the ship had run aground, on a sandbank, and that the ship was in need of assistance.

Transmissions continued with the DJ keeping anxious listeners informed of what was happening. Water was leaking in throughout the ship, hardly anything remained dry. Two SOS messages were broadcast, before the crew decided that they were not in dire trouble. It was agreed not to broadcast any more requests for assistance, unless the situation worsened.

The *Mi Amigo* was constantly bumping her hull onto the sandbank, with wave after wave crashing over her decks. Surprisingly, music continued on both frequencies until just after midnight. Without warning 192 suddenly went off the air and almost three hours later, also without warning, 259 fell silent, as a result of damage to the aerial.

Unlike the previous grounding in November 1975 when the ship had drifted right across the Thames Estuary, the ship had not gone so far before running aground. The captain was still in familiar waters, which is why Caroline had continued to broadcast. If the aerial feeder wire had not broken transmissions would not have stopped, as the ship was still in International waters.

On the Saturday morning another vessel approached, offering assistance. Marc Jacob (the announcer who had been soaked when the porthole smashed), and Jon van der Meer both decided to leave the radio ship. The captain of the *Mi Amigo* and his crew also decided to abandon ship, and left for the safety of the other ship.

With the ship's crew and Radio Mi Amigo staff gone there were only four men left on board, three DJs and one radio engineer. They realised that the ship could be lost, either to the elements or salvors, if they had decided to leave as well. In the worse case scenario, the *Mi Amigo* could have been towed into a British port and been impounded in accordance with an earlier court ruling after the previous drifting.

The other vessel stood by for a time, coming alongside again to see if the four had changed their minds. The four men were adamant that they would not leave, so the ship pulled away, but as it did so it collided with the *Mi Amigo*. This resulted in a large gash in the stern of the *Mi Amigo*, fortunately, although extensive, all the damage was above the water line.

During the night these four men, DJs Tom Anderson, Ed Foster and Marc Lawrence, with assistance from engineer Peter Chicago, kept the ship in Radio Caroline's hands. For much of the night the ship was in darkness, with the four men trapped in the wheel house by heavy seas crashing over the deck.

On Sunday morning the Trinity House vessel, *Ready*, arrived in the vicinity. The ship was anchored nearby, and a launch was lowered, which used a leadline to ascertain depth of water, as it approached the stricken radio ship.

The officer in charge of the launch asked if they could assist, but the offer, although appreciated, was declined. Naturally Radio Caroline personnel are suspicious of official ships, such as the *Ready*. This particular ship was quite powerful, as one of its duties was to tow lightships to and from their anchorages.

Not only were the four men suspicious, they were also concerned at the amount of water that had leaked in, and of possible hull damage. No doubt the *Ready* could have towed them off the bank, but the ship may have sunk. Having been thanked the launch returned to the *Ready*, which then continued on its passage.

The four men had to work long and hard to dry out the ship, especially the transmitter room. Peter Chicago managed to get a pump working, but for hours they had used buckets to bale out the water. The pump took over and was kept running day and night, only stopping if the pipe got clogged with debris.

The storm blew itself out, and the swell began to subside, making the work a little easier. Even with the improving weather conditions there was more then the four men could hope to achieve on their own. Welding equipment was needed for the stern damage and the aerial feeder needed repairs, or replacing.

It was long and tiring work, everything had to be dried out, floor coverings, bedding, broadcasting equipment, even the records and tapes. Virtually nothing had escaped the deluge, fortunately the weather remained fine, so the work could continue uninterrupted.

Eventually two tenders arrived on the scene carrying a replacement captain and crew, and announcers for Radio Mi Amigo. Welding equipment and a hull plate was brought out, so that repairs could be made to the stern and aerial feeder.

There was a replacement anchor and chain, the chain being much longer than the previous one. A mistake had been made with the previous chain: the anchor chain should be at least three times the depth of water, so that its weight acts as a flexible anchor, and thereby reduces the risk of the chain snapping. After the 1975 drifting the chain had just been measured to the depth of water.

In addition to the main anchor, a bracket was welded to the starboard side of the ship, which held a quick release emergency anchor. This anchor and chain were secured by a length of rope, so that if the need should ever arise, all that was required was to cut the rope, and the anchor would be released.

The *Mi Amigo* was towed back to her anchorage, where the repairs continued. On Thursday 16th September, six days after transmissions had ended, 259 metres came back to life with continuous taped music. Radio Mi Amigo commenced programmes at 9 am, with Radio Caroline returning at 7 pm that evening.

Although broadcasts had resumed, there was still a lot of work to be completed. The 10 kilowatt transmitter, used by Radio Caroline on 192, had to be overhauled as it had been soaked. Much of the equipment and many of the albums and tapes still had to be dried. The damaged porthole was replaced, and the ship cleaned and dried. Supplies of fuel and fresh provisions were loaded from the tenders.

It was not until Wednesday 22nd September that transmissions resumed on 192. Whilst this transmitter had been out of use, Caroline had been sharing 259 with Radio Mi Amigo. At 6 am, 192 returned with continuous taped music; repairs were still being made and it was too noisy to allow live broadcasts, however, by 5 pm it was quiet enough to resume live broadcasts.

Radio Mi Amigo was hugely popular not only in Holland and Belgium, but also parts of France and south-east Britain. Several new features were introduced, including a phone-in quiz. Participants had to telephone the Spanish studio, recordings were made of the answers, which were then taken out to the ship for broadcasting.

There was, however, increasing interference in Holland and Belgium, from a Hungarian radio station. Although Radio Mi Amigo was on full power, of 50 kilowatts, reception was made very difficult, at times, by the more powerful Budapest station. It was decided that Radio Mi Amigo would have to find a new frequency.

During November 1976, test transmissions were made on 312 metres, one of the frequencies used by Radio Atlantis. In spite of these tests, it was decided not to use this for regular broadcasts, instead Radio Caroline and Radio Mi Amigo exchanged frequencies. Broadcasts, on both 192 and 259, came to an end at midday on Friday 10th December, 1976, having announced that broadcasts were stopping for routine maintenance.

The *Mi Amigo* was fitted with a quick release emergency anchor after she had gone adrift in September 1976. The new anchor can be seen on the starboard side of the ship, with the chain fed through from the chain store in the bows.   *John Wilson*

Whilst the stations were off the air, the 50 kilowatt transmitter used on 259, was converted to 192 (1562kHz). The 10 kW transmitter, used by Caroline, was then converted to 259 (1187kHz). Radio Mi Amigo resumed broadcasts the next morning, with continuous music, and normal programming from midday.

Radio Caroline resumed broadcasting at 6 am on Sunday 12th December on 259, with 24 hour programming. Neither of these frequencies was very good any more, due to interference, so research was carried out to see if a new and clearer location could be found for both stations.

The interference, from Budapest, which had plagued Radio Mi Amigo was even worse for Radio Caroline. Caroline was only using a 10 kW transmitter, whilst Radio Mi Amigo had been using 50 kW. Inevitably some areas lost the broadcasts, but as Radio Mi Amigo was paying for the use of the radio ship's facilities, it had to have priority.

1977

Top 20 for week commencing Sunday 2nd January, 1977

1	(1)	When A Child Is Born	Johnny Mathis
2	(2)	Under The Moon Of Love	Showaddywaddy
3	(5)	Portsmouth	Mike Oldfield
4	(3)	Money Money Money	Abba
5	(9)	Living Next Door To Alice	Smokie
6	(4)	Somebody To Love	Queen
7	(8)	Dr Love	Tina Charles
8	(11)	Don't Give Up On Us	David Soul
9	(15)	Grandma's Party	Paul Nicholas
10	(12)	Lean On Me	Mud
11	(10)	Bionic Santa	Chris Hill
12	(19)	Things We Do For Love	10 cc
13	(17)	Wild Side Of Life	Status Quo
14	(13)	Fairy Tale	Dana
15	(6)	Livin' Thing	Electric Light Orchestra
16	(14)	Little Does She Know	Kursaal Flyers
17	(22)	I Wish	Stevie Wonder
18	(7)	Love Me	Yvonne Elliman
19	(24)	You Make Me Feel Like Dancing	Leo Sayer
20	(23)	Sideshow	Barry Briggs

In Breach of Bad Law

On 10th January, 1977, it was announced that the *MEBO I* (which had been renamed *Angela*) and the *MEBO II* had been purchased by the Libyan Government, for a total price of 6 million guilders (about £1,200,000 at the 1977 value of the guilder). On the same date the *MEBO II's* engines were tested, and stores were taken on board. It was announced that the ship would broadcast as People's Revolution Radio, and she would be tendered by the *Angela*.

Having gained Customs clearance, the two ships left Slikkerveer, where they had been impounded since 10th October, 1974. The plans to sail to the Italian coast and broadcast as Radio Nova International were abandoned.

As the *MEBO II* sailed down the River Maas, she collided with the 500 ton German vessel *Esterbrugge*, which was pushed into the British vessel *Hoocrest*, which in turn rammed the *River Taw*, another British ship. The journey had to be delayed by two days, whilst arrangements were made to pay the £3,000 of damages that resulted from the collisions.

At 10.30 am on 16th January the two ships sailed from Parkkade out into the North Sea, but it was found that the radar on the *MEBO II* was not working. At 2 pm that afternoon the ships anchored off the Hook of Holland and an engineer was taken out to make repairs.

On Monday 17th January, 1977 the *MEBO II*, accompanied by the *Angela*, left the Dutch coast for the last time. Three days later the ships had to anchor off Brest, to ride out a storm, which lasted for a week. On 28th January they continued their voyage, passing Gibraltar on 1st February.

From 2nd February, until the 9th, both ships were in the Moroccan port of Ceuta, where they took on supplies. They eventually arrived at Tripoli on Monday 14th February, where test transmissions commenced on 388 metres (773 kHz) and 6205 kHz in the 49 metre short wave band. On Monday 8th August, 1977 both ships moved to Benghazi, and then continued to Derna.

Test transmissions were broadcast but they were not very successful, so the ships moved back to Benghazi, arriving on Tuesday 1st November, 1977. Test transmissions were broadcast, whilst at anchor off the port on 12th December.

Further details of use of the two ships proved impossible to find, except that further tests were broadcast in the 49 metre short wave band. What is known is that both ships were used as target practice, and both were sunk by the Libyans in 1981.

Meanwhile, back in January 1977, Radio Caroline's very popular female DJ, Samantha, appeared in an Amsterdam court on Wednesday 12th. She faced charges of having made illegal broadcasts from the *Mi Amigo*. There were three witnesses for the prosecution, all ex-crew from the radio ship. She was found guilty, fined £200, and had a three week term of imprisonment, suspended for two years.

Two weeks later, on Thursday 27th January, the Magistrates court at Southend was the setting for another court case. The story of this prosecution began on Friday 6th August, 1976, when a boat trip to the *Mi Amigo* had been organised.

Unknown to the organiser, a plain clothes police officer was amongst those on the trip. The launch went alongside the *Mi Amigo* and the organiser threw newspapers and mail onto the radio ship. When the launch returned to Brightlingsea, it was boarded by police and Customs officers.

At this court case, the organiser of the trip was charged with supplying mail and newspapers to the ship, and for advertising Radio Caroline on a lapel badge! He was found guilty and fined £145. At the same hearing, the owner of the launch was fined £220.

Many thought that the courts were being too harsh on those who worked for, or supplied Radio Caroline; obviously they were breaking the law, but it does seem harsh to give such penalties for delivering papers, and wearing a lapel badge. A prospective Conservative candidate said at the time:

I believe that the 1967 Bill was wrong, its effect typical of socialism, was to restrict freedom, and further impose a State monopoly. Radio Caroline - an example of free enterprise at its most daring - should not have to operate (giving pleasure to thousands) in breach of bad law . . . It is not for me to encourage a body that is working outside the law, as I'm sure you will understand, but after the next election it will be, I hope, for me to change inefficient or obnoxious laws, like some of the provisions of the Marine Offences Act.

He did not win that election, nor did the Conservatives change that inefficient (or obnoxious) law.

In fairness, it was not just Britain that was trying to stop Radio Caroline by dealing harshly with anyone involved with the station. On Friday 25th February, 1977, five men were in court in Boulogne. They were charged with supplying food, wine and linen to the radio ship, in contravention of a 1969 French law. They were all found guilty and were fined from £100-£500.

Meanwhile, out on the *Mi Amigo*, March was chosen for a further change of frequency for Radio Caroline. The 259 wavelength was no longer suitable, because of interference to, and from, other stations. Radio Mi Amigo had already vacated that wavelength because of the interference, now it was Caroline's turn. The wavelength of 314 metres (953 kHz) was selected, using the callsign, 'Caroline on 319'.

The date for this change was deliberately chosen, 3rd March, as it was the ninth anniversary of the enforced closure of Caroline North and South, when tugs from the Wijsmuller Company had towed the ships away.

Radio Caroline DJs decided to make it a special day, as the countdown to the move continued. The last three hours included a walkabout tour of the *Mi Amigo*, presented by DJ James Brown. He described the various parts of the ship and talked to every other member of staff and crew that he met.

Marc Lawrence stayed in the studio, playing the music and providing the links. He also asked James questions that he thought listeners might have asked if they had been given the chance.

All too soon it was 6 pm, the chosen time for close down; listeners were reminded that the station would be off the air for six days. The final sounds on 259 were *On My Way Back Home* by The New Riders Of The Purple Sage, which had been adopted as Caroline's theme, due to the line 'Flying to the sun, sweet Caroline'.

At 6 pm on Thursday 3rd March, 1977, the transmitter was switched off, ending an association with 259 which had lasted since 17th April, 1966. It will be remembered that the *Mi Amigo* first used the frequency when it resumed broadcasts on that date, following its return from repairs in Holland after the ship had run aground at Frinton. The MV *Caroline* had commenced broadcasts on 259 from 31st October, 1966.

Over the next few days, whilst the station was off the air, the transmitter was tuned to the new wavelength and part of the complex aerial system was overhauled. The piece that needed attention was called a diplexer, and it was through this that both Radio Caroline and Mi Amigo could transmit through the same aerial using different frequencies.

On Wednesday 9th March, 1977, true to its word, Radio Caroline resumed broadcasts using the new wavelength. The transmitter was switched on during the early hours of the morning, for testing and final level adjustments.

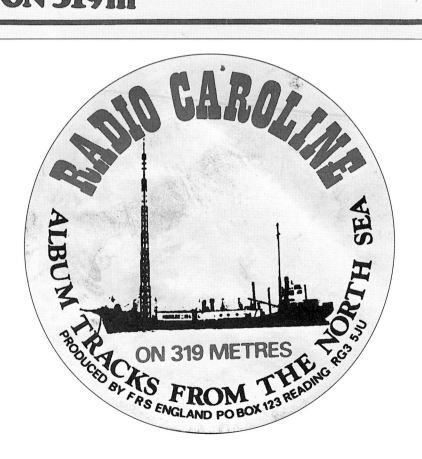

At 6 am DJ Marc Lawrence, who had closed 259, welcomed listeners to regular programming on 319, which went on 24 hours per day. Reception was stronger and clearer, freed as it was from interference from a nearby competitor. The Independent Broadcasting Authority station, Radio Orwell, had been allocated 257 metres (1169 kHz), whilst Caroline had been on 1187 kHz. Due to the interference in some areas caused by Radio Caroline, the IBA had to allocate an extra channel to Radio Orwell, 212 metres (1412 kHz). Now that Caroline had moved, there was no need to continue the use of the extra channel which closed down shortly afterwards, but 212 was not destined to remain silent for long as we shall see later.

On Thursday 17th March, 1977 the North Sea was proving that sometimes it can be a nice place to be, and that it was not always hostile. Conditions were so good that two staff from the *Mi Amigo*, decided to have fun in an inflatable dinghy. After a time they returned to the radio ship, and tied up alongside. They passed the outboard motor over to the *Mi Amigo*, but as they did so, the line securing the dinghy snapped and the current swept the inflatable away.

The radio ship called North Foreland Radio, telling them that two men had been seen drifting in an inflatable, but no mention was made of the fact that they had come from the *Mi Amigo*. A helicopter was tasked, from RAF Manston, and was soon over the area. The dinghy was quickly located and one of the helicopter crew was lowered, by winch. One by one, the two men were lifted to the safety of the rescue helicopter, but the dinghy was left to float away on the tide.

With both men safely aboard the crew asked how the men had got into their predicament, and where they had come from. They were told that the two men had come from the *Mi Amigo*, and were asked if they could return them to the radio ship, surprisingly the pilot agreed.

In a very tricky operation, the two men were lowered onto the deck of the *Mi Amigo*. Winching persons from, or to, any ship is a dangerous manoeuvre, but with the additional hazards of the aerial and all of the rigging, it was far from easy.

With the traditional skill that we sometimes take for granted, the highly trained rescue services completed the task. Both men were safely put aboard, none the worse for their adventure. The helicopter returned to its base, where the incident report must have made for interesting reading.

With Radio Caroline happily settled down on her new frequency, and Radio Mi Amigo still on 192, listeners thought that the future of both stations was assured. However, there was a shock announcement from Radio Mi Amigo which soon changed that.

On Monday 28th March, 1977 listeners were warned of the imminent closure of the station. It was stated that Radio Mi Amigo International had decided to close, due to pressure being exerted by the Dutch and Belgian Governments. Stunned listeners were told that the last programme would be broadcast on Friday 1st April, with the final close down at midday. There was shock and disbelief that the station would soon be gone. The statement was read every hour until normal close down on 31st March. There was no time left, after 3¼ years of broadcasting Radio Mi Amigo was to close.

On Friday 1st April listeners tuned to 192 to hear the final hours of their beloved station, but all they found was silence. Radio Mi Amigo had gone. Many quickly retuned to 319, to see if Radio Caroline would explain what had happened, but Caroline was not on the air either.

It was obviously the end, not just for Mi Amigo but also Radio Caroline, but was it? Out on the ship, engineers worked frantically to get the generator going. It was not until 12.15 pm that Radio Mi Amigo resumed broadcasts, when an apology was made for the breakdown.

A tape was then played to close the station; part way through the farewell, it was interrupted by laughter. Listeners were then informed that it all had been an April Fool's joke and the station was not going to close. It was a joke that almost went wrong, and it was definitely not appreciated by the listeners.

Radio Mi Amigo had upset its listeners with its closedown prank, and there was to be some unwelcome news for Caroline's audience. The 24 hour format was not destined to last for very long, in fact just 38 days. As from Saturday 16th April close down came at 7 pm. It was announced that this was to allow essential routine maintenance to be carried out.

On Wednesday 1st June the law was, once again, taking action against suppliers of the *Mi Amigo*. This case, being heard in a French Court, had arisen from the apprehension of a trawler at Calais. On board this vessel there had been three men, and the authorities had evidence that they had supplied the radio ship on at least 10 occasions.

Suspicions had been aroused when it had been noted that the trawler had taken on more food and water than the crew would have needed for a routine fishing trip. It was later discovered by French maritime police that special tanks had been constructed on the trawler to hold fuel and water, which was then delivered to the *Mi Amigo*.

The police made further enquiries, which led them to an English woman, living in France, who was being paid to supply the radio ship. The three men, and the woman, were charged with having contravened the French Marine Offences Act.

At the first hearing, held at Boulogne, they all pleaded guilty but one of the trawler crew was acquitted. The others had to wait until Wednesday 22nd June to find out what punishment they would receive. The woman was fined 4,000 francs, whilst the trawler skipper was fined 5,000 and the crewman 2,000 francs.

Keeping the stations an the air was becoming increasingly expensive and dangerous for those who operated the tenders. The equipment on the *Mi Amigo* was getting older, and less reliable, resulting in more breakdowns. Spares had to be paid for, as did the engineers who made the repairs. In an attempt to keep expenses lower, many of the engineering staff (and cooks and crew) took turns behind the microphone.

Operating costs were increasing, but income was not keeping pace and funds were becoming very low. Advertisers were not going to pay for campaigns on a radio station that spent a lot of time off the air. One of Radio Caroline's proudest claims was that it did not cost the listener anything to listen to her broadcasts.

As Johnnie Walker had said 10 years earlier in 1967, 'It is your station, even though it costs you nothing'. Nearly all of Caroline's income came from advertising contracts, but it was becoming harder to find existing clients, let alone new ones, as more prosecutions were taking place.

At the time, Radio Caroline was broadcasting sales promotions which advised potential advertisers how to contact the station. It went on to claim that the station had over 5 million listeners: 'Europe's biggest night time audience'.

With that claim in mind, it was decided to appeal to this massive audience for financial support, any amount large or small, to help keep the station on the air. The appeals were an obvious embarrassment to the station, but it did not seem like an unreasonable request. If you enjoy listening to Radio Caroline, why not help us to stay on the air?

Just think of what could have been achieved, if everyone of the claimed audience responded with just £1. Much of the ageing equipment could have been replaced, perhaps even a replacement for the 56-year-old *Mi Amigo*.

The request for financial assistance was very diplomatic, and low keyed, so as not to risk offending any of the listeners. This is how one of the first requests was made:

> It's five years since we brought Radio Caroline back to you - which is a hell of a long time, and those five years have been quite amazing. So many good things have happened, we have made so many nice friends, both working out here on the ship and also amongst you the listeners.
>
> In those early days, when we took the *Mi Amigo* out of Amsterdam harbour, and parked it out on the North Sea, off Holland we had no generators and no transmitters - nothing! It was great fun, everybody got in and had a go. A lot of people helped, and it all came together.
>
> Then that last day of September (1972), when everything happened, Veronica changed frequency and Radio Northsea came on with RNI 2, there was Caroline pumping away on 10 watts, zapping away, saying we love you.
>
> We have come along way since then, with our sister station, Radio Mi Amigo pumping out 50,000 watts, and we are here with our 10,000 watts. It's all going in the right direction.
>
> We have had so many letters from people, an amazing amount of feed back, especially in the last year since we have had our all day English service. One of the things that people have said to us is, please keep it up - please stay on, because you are the one thing in our life that we listen too, and we know it is Free. It's loving, it's caring, and is there every time that we want it.
>
> A lot of people have also written in and have said, can you do something about your signal? Well we try, we try and do the best that we can. At the moment we have a 10 kilowatt transmitter, maybe we can do something about that. Maybe we can get a bigger transmitter, and pump up a little more power, to give you a better service.
>
> Another thing that people have said to us is, 'How can we help?' People have written in and said, we want to be disc jockeys, or run tenders for you. And it's really nice.
>
> Other people have written in and asked, 'How do you exist financially?' Well we don't really need that much money. I suppose it's really a matter of how much you want. We are quite happy out here with what we have got, obviously the only thing that would be nice, is if we could get a new transmitter. Because that way we could put our love vibe out a lot further than it does at the moment.
>
> I know, for instance at night, say between 6 and midnight in a lot of places, the 319 signal is a total waste of time - you might as well not listen to it. It could be changed.

A lot of people have said, 'Could we help you financially?' Well Caroline's been here since 1964, which is a long time, and in that 13-14 years we have always said, Caroline comes to you free. NO charge.
We have always made a big thing of that, but, we have had a lot of people say, we want to help. It's taken a lot of soul searching, on our part, and a lot of very deep thought, but finally we have decided if you want to help - do, please. Maybe we can get that new transmitter and put out a whole new feeling. A bigger-stronger feeling,
So to those already who have written in and said, we would be prepared to actually put our hands in our pockets, and send you some bread, Thank you - do so.

This type of request did not last for long, Caroline's cry for assistance was a resounding failure! Just £400 was sent, how let down the staff must have felt. In spite of all the dangers that they had to face, to maintain broadcasts, the listeners were not bothered enough to help.

Radio Caroline had survived for 14 years, fighting against all of the odds, including the hostile North Sea, and the combined Governments of Europe. All of the staff faced prosecution, as did the operators of the tenders, the suppliers and the advertisers.

There was the risk of heavy fines, possible imprisonment, but all of these adversities were cheerfully met, to keep Radio Caroline alive. The spirit of Loving Awareness that Caroline had been broadcasting had not influenced the listeners, most of whom just could not be bothered!

It was later revealed that the reason most had not responded was that they were not going to pay for something over which they had no control! But surely that was against the very principles that Caroline had been fighting for. Radio Caroline was free of state control, DJs were free to select their own choice of music, and nobody told them what to say. Caroline was the epitome of Free radio. To help keep the station alive should have been the most important issue, not the fact that they were asking for help.

The decision to continue broadcasting, after such a dismal response, must have been a difficult one. This was an idea ahead of its time. Nowadays, nobody thinks anything of subscribing to satellite, or cable TV, in addition to the TV licence. Taken aback, but not deterred, the two stations did continue, but both stations were suffering from poor reception. They could not afford new equipment, so the decision was made to change frequencies, yet again.

During the early hours of Tuesday 5th July, Radio Caroline's transmitter was retuned from 953 kHz, to the adjacent 962 kHz (312 metres), although the station continued to identify as Caroline on 319.

Radio Mi Amigo was far from happy on its 192 slot, so the decision was taken to move to a new location. The station closed at 7 pm on Saturday 23rd July, ending the seven-month association with 192 (1562 kHz).

During that time there had been complaints, from Switzerland, claiming that Radio Mi Amigo had been causing interference. Closer to home, the station had been causing problems to Capital Radio, which broadcast on 194 metres (1546 kHz). In response, Radio Mi Amigo had lowered its output level, but it was obvious that it could no longer stay on 192. In fact, five years earlier, Radio Veronica had moved from 192, because of poor reception. So it was, on the face of it, a surprising frequency to have been chosen.

Radio Mi Amigo re-opened at midday, on Monday 25th July, on 212 metres (1412 kHz). This was, as we have already seen the frequency used by Radio Orwell whilst Caroline had been broadcasting on 259.

It seemed that things were now going smoothly for both stations. Caroline was broadcasting 24 hours a day, whilst Radio Mi Amigo was an the air for 13 hours. Whilst the music was being played, a potentially dangerous situation was manifesting itself below decks.

On Thursday 4th August, at 9.30 am, it was discovered that the engine room, record library and some of the cabins were flooded, to a depth of one foot. To their dismay, the water was still flooding in.

It was thought that the hull had sprung a plate and pumps were put into service whilst a search was made for the source of the leak. Both Radio Mi Amigo and Caroline were still on the air, however, taped music was being played, all live broadcasts having been suspended so that all hands could assist.

The ship had now taken on a pronounced list to port, as the pumps struggled to cope with the ingress of water. As a precaution, liferafts were launched, and tied alongside. The Coastguard was informed of the problem, and in response the Kent police launch arrived 1½ hours later.

Whilst the search for the leak was in progress the pumps suddenly stopped working; the search became more frantic, whilst engineers tried to get the pumps working again. Eventually they succeeded, and the water level started to drop. Engine room plates were lifted and the source of the leak was located, a 2½ inch pipe supplying water cooling to the generator had broken, it was not hull damage.

The generator was shut down, and the valve to the pipe was closed, which prevented any further flooding. The second generator was in service, powering the pumps, but this unit overheated and automatically shut down, at 3.45 pm, which forced both stations off the air. It was discovered that the supply of cooling water to the second generator had mistakenly been turned off. The plant was allowed to cool, before being re-started, and the pumps cleared the rest of the water.

Radio Caroline resumed broadcasts at 8pm, when a full description of the day's events was given by DJ and engineer, Roger Matthews. The opportunity was also taken to thank the emergency services, for their assistance throughout the drama.

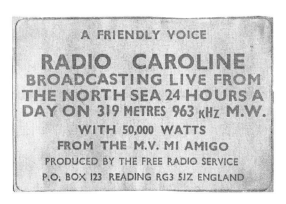

Flashback 67

August 1977 was a memorable month, for offshore radio devotees; it contained two anniversaries, and a special convention. The convention was entitled, 'Flashback 67', and it was to commemorate the 10 years since the introduction of the Marine Offences Act, on 15th August, 1967.

The convention was held at an hotel, at Heathrow Airport, over the weekend of 14th-15th August, and it was a complete sell-out. Hundreds of people attended, to watch special films, to see photographs and displays and listen to the talks. There were several celebrities, including Ronan O'Rahilly and ex-offshore radio DJs.

There was plenty to see and do, with offshore radio artefacts on sale, such as tee shirts, badges, stickers, records and tapes. Visitors came from far and near, from the UK and other parts of Europe. Interviews were recorded which were then sent out to the *Mi Amigo*, and were broadcast on Sunday 14th August on both frequencies (212 and 319) for the benefit of those who could not attend. Caroline also played jingles from those stations of the 1960s which had closed.

On Monday 15th there was a chance to see the *Mi Amigo*, a boat having been especially chartered for the occasion. It was no easy trip to reach the radio ship, because of the numerous sandbanks in the area, in fact the trip boat touched bottom, on more than one occasion. It all added to the excitement of the voyage, but doubtless gave the skipper and his crew a few anxious moments.

For many, this was the first time that they had seen the *Mi Amigo*, except in photographs, and there was a chance to talk to staff on the radio ship, well shout actually, and hundreds of photographs were taken. All too soon it was time to return to port, but all agreed that it had been an excellent experience.

The second anniversary date, which was just as unwelcome as the first, was 31st August. It was three years since the closure of the stations which had broadcasts from off the Dutch and Belgian coasts. To mark the occasion, Radio Caroline played jingles that had been used by Radio Northsea International, Radio Veronica and Radio Atlantis.

The very next day, Thursday 1st September, the Walton on Naze lifeboat was called to the *Mi Amigo*. Medical assistance had been requested for a Radio Caroline DJ who was suffering from a stomach bug, he was subsequently taken ashore.

It was later reported that the DJ had not been happy on the *Mi Amigo*, and the bug had just been an excuse to get off the ship, as soon as possible. When they returned to shore the DJ was interviewed by a national Sunday paper, in which he said that he never wanted to see the *Mi Amigo* again! The lifeboat coxswain was also interviewed about the incident, and said that the radio ship was in a very poor condition and that he feared for the safety of those still on board.

With one DJ gone, Radio Caroline had a few problems, as there were only two other DJs to present the 24 hour format. The DJs, Roger Matthews and Stuart Russell, were given assistance from Radio Mi Amigo staff, but the long hours were proving too much. It was decided to suspend the 24 hour programming, with a new schedule of 6 am until 8 pm, from Tuesday 13th September. However, both 212 and 319 transmissions came to an abrupt end at 6.30 pm on Sunday 18th.

The sudden closure was not due to a breakdown, in fact a tender had arrived with fresh supplies of food and water, programme tapes, and relief staff for both Radio Mi Amigo and Caroline. Transmissions, resumed the next morning, Caroline's new DJs being James Ross, Marc Lawrence and Martin Fisher.

Radio Caroline's engineer, and popular relief DJ, Peter Chicago appeared in a Norwich court on Friday 9th September. He had pleaded guilty to charges of having maintained wireless equipment, used for making illegal broadcasts.

The case had arisen from an incident on Thursday 4th August, at Gorleston, Norfolk. A Belgian trawler had entered the port and three men, including Chicago, were seen to come ashore. The men got into a taxi, which was later stopped by police, two men escaped but Chicago was apprehended.

He appeared in court, the next day, and was remanded in custody until bail, which had been set at £1,500, had been settled. The court found him guilty, as charged, and he was fined £170.

The trawler, from which Chicago had landed, was subsequently apprehended by Belgian officials. Three men, including two Radio Mi Amigo announcers, were apprehended. In spite of all of the risks, people were still prepared to run the gauntlet to keep the two pirate stations on the air.

The coming of the autumn usually heralds the start of the gale season, and the autumn of 1977 proved to be no exception. In fact there were more gales, and of greater intensity, than the norm.

Out in the North Sea the *Mi Amigo* and the staff rode out the worst storms that they had encountered in a long time. There were more breakdown, and of longer duration, than had happened for many years. The first such breakdown was on Tuesday 4th October, at 7pm.

Radio Caroline was off the air for 12 hours whilst the engineer cured the fault. Just 10 days later, more problems were encountered. On Saturday 15th the generator, which had been giving problems all day, failed at 6 pm, forcing Radio Caroline off the air yet again. The fault was eventually sorted, but it was not until the early hours of Wednesday 19th October that transmissions resumed.

The breakdowns, during that autumn, will long be remembered, especially one that occurred during November. Radio Mi Amigo, and Caroline, were off the air for 10 days; during that time the national press ran stories that the mast had collapsed.

It all started during the morning of Friday 11th November, when a generator fault forced the stations off the air at midday. Nature was also taking a hand in the proceedings, as system after system of storms smashed their way over land and sea.

On the shore, overhead cables were brought down, roofs were ripped apart, and trees and fences were blown down. Out on the North Sea, the *Mi Amigo* took a severe beating from heavy seas, pushed up by gale force winds, which were gusting up to storm force 10, at times.

To give the terms gale, or storm force, more meaning, the expected wind speeds during gale force 8, are expected to be between 39 and 46 mph. During storm force 10, the wind speeds can reach 53 to 63 mph.

The definition of the expected sea state, during such storms is described as very high waves, with overhanging crests. The resulting foam, in great patches, is blown in dense streaks along the direction of the wind. On the whole, the surface of the sea, takes on a white appearance. The tumbling of the waves becomes heavy and shock like. Waves in excess of 30 ft can be expected, behind which, small and medium sized ships may be lost to view for a time. Visibility is affected.

To experience this kind of weather on board ship is not pleasant, and not for the faint hearted, at times is can be quite frightening. When that ship is just 138 ft long, and weighing just 470 tons, with a huge mast, it could be positively alarming. Day after day the ship rode out the storms, remaining at anchor, when others had run for shelter. Throughout, the radio ship remained silent, both stations off the air. Not surprising when you consider the pounding the ship was taking, it was probably hard enough just moving around, let alone trying to repair the generator in cramped conditions.

As the storm abated, a tug skipper, for reasons best known to himself, told reporters that the mast on the *Mi Amigo* had collapsed. His story was accepted as being true, why should anyone doubt the word of a professional seaman? It just goes to show that the press should check out all the facts, before they publish.

Whatever his motive was for telling the story, Radio Caroline soon proved him wrong. Having sorted out the problematical generator, Caroline resumed broadcasting, during the early hours of Tuesday 22nd November. Further problems with the generator were experienced that month, but transmissions were only interrupted for short periods.

At the end of November it was announced that Radio Mi Amigo and Caroline were going to share the 962 kHz frequency. The reason for this move was that Radio Mi Amigo was suffering from very poor reception, especially at night.

The sharing of the one frequency also meant that Radio Caroline would lose its 24 hour service, which ended at 5 am on Thursday 1st December. Radio Mi Amigo then commenced broadcasts until handing back to Caroline at 6.30 pm.

Both stations were using the 10 kilowatt transmitter as the 50 kw one was still being used on 212 metres where listeners were informed to retune to the new frequency. Radio Mi Amigo finally left 212 at 6.30 pm on Sunday 4th December.

After the 50 kW transmitter was switched off, the engineers took the opportunity to service it, the work taking place over the next week. The transmitter was tested, during the early hours of Tuesday 13th December, on 953 kHz (314 metres). When Radio Mi Amigo opened, at 5 am, the transmitter had been retuned to 962 kHz.

During the morning a fault developed which forced the station off the air, but the fault was quickly rectified, allowing Radio Mi Amigo to return within the hour.

Radio Caroline had, once again, lost her all-day transmissions reverting to night time only, but she had gained use of the more powerful transmitter. This greatly improved her reception, and widened her listening greatly. I was stationed in Cornwall, at the time, and her signal was very clear.

It was also on Thursday 1st December that the official Radio Caroline Roadshow started. It was presented as the Disco Lights, and the venues were advertised nightly, every hour, on Caroline. The Roadshow toured London and the South-East, proving to be very popular with all venues packed to capacity. The organiser was former Caroline DJ, Robb Eden, and one of the first guest DJs was Simon Dee.

1978

Top 20 for week commencing Sunday 1st January, 1978

1	(1)	*Mull Of Kintyre/Girls School*	Wings
2	(2)	*Floral Dance*	Brighouse & Rastrick Brass Band
3	(3)	*How Deep Is Your Love*	Bee Gees
4	(6)	*Love's Unkind*	Donna Summer
5	(4)	*I Will*	Ruby Winters
6	(7)	*It's A Heartache*	Bonnie Tyler
7	(8)	*Daddy Cool*	Darts
8	(18)	*Don't It Make Your Brown Eyes Blue*	Crystal Gayle
9	(14)	*My Way*	Elvis Presley
10	(19)	*Dance Dance Dance*	Chic
11	(21)	*Who Pays The Ferryman*	Yannis Markopoulus
12	(11)	*Belfast*	Boney M
13	(17)	*Let's Have A Quiet Night In*	David Soul
14	(10)	*Put Your Love In Me*	Hot Chocolate
15	(12)	*Dancin' Party*	Showaddywaddy
16	(5)	*White Christmas*	Bing Crosby
17	(13)	*Love Of My Life*	Dooleys
18	(34)	*Uptown Top Ranking*	Althia & Donna
19	(24)	*Only Women Bleed*	Julie Covington
20	(25)	*Rockin' All Over The World*	Status Quo

Zee Zenders 20

On Sunday 1st January, 1978, Radio Mi Amigo celebrated its fourth birthday, with special programming. Unfortunately the celebrations did not last for long. The North Sea was ravaged by storm force winds, which gave the *Mi Amigo* a beating.

At 11 pm, on Tuesday 10th January, a generator fault forced Radio Caroline off the air. Due to the effects of the stormy weather, it took the engineer five days to rectify the problem. Radio Mi Amigo returned to the air at midday on Sunday 15th, followed by Radio Caroline at 6. 30 pm.

On Tuesday 28th March Radio Caroline celebrated her 14th birthday, with special programming. The proceedings were started by Radio Mi Amigo, who paid their own tribute. This included special items such as Simon Dee describing the equipment aboard the MV *Caroline*, from a recording made in 1964.

The Beatles sang *All You Need Is Love*, as they had done on two previous occasions, when Radio Caroline had continued (1967 and 1974). Other musical tributes were played, such as *My Way Back Home* by The New Riders of the Purple Sage.

As a tribute to Radio Northsea International, *Peace* by Peter was played, which was the last record to be played before the closure of the English language programmes. There was also a recording of Andy Archer, as he broadcast for Radio Seagull. The Radio Mi Amigo staff sang 'Happy Birthday Sweet Caroline', which was followed by a recording of Johnnie Walker's, 'Let no man ever forget'.

At 6.30 pm Radio Caroline took to the air with the Beatles singing *Going to a Party*. The DJ then went on to explain how they were planning to spend the evening: 'Right it's our birthday, we are 14 today, Happy Birthday to us. What we are going to do, until midnight, is have a top 50 chart compiled from your personal Top 30s, that you have sent in.'

One of the regular weekend features on Radio Caroline at that time, had been the listeners top 30 album tracks. The listeners sent in their all-time favourites, in order of merit, to the office in Spain. These were then sent out to the ship, and the lucky listener would have their selection played.

To compile this top 50 the DJs had sifted through all of the lists, and by using a points system the top 50 had been selected. This chart got underway with *Brown Sugar* by the Rolling Stones, at number 50. The programme had been scheduled to end at midnight, but it actually finished at 1.30 am. The No. 1 record in this chart was *Stairway to Heaven* by Led Zeppelin.

With the birthday celebrations over, for another year, Radio Caroline prepared for yet another successful year of operations. It was a tribute to the engineers, one in particular, Peter Chicago, that the station had survived for so long.

Ronan had paid the ultimate accolade to Peter by saying that he was 100 per cent certain, that if it had not been for Peter, Radio Caroline would not have lasted as long as it had. It had been Peter and DJ Chris Cary (Spangles Muldoon) that had done so much for the station, since its dramatic return in 1972.

Peter had been the chief engineer, throughout the intervening years, and it was his skill and dedication that had kept the station going. To enable routine maintenance to be undertaken Radio Caroline would close early, one night a week.

This year was the 20th anniversary of offshore radio, in Europe, and for 14 of those years Radio Caroline had been a part of it. Not only had she given pleasure to countless millions of listeners, she had also broken the monopoly of the BBC and been the main reason for the restructuring of broadcasting in Britain. Quite an achievement, in anyone's book.

During August 1977 there had been a conference, at Heathrow, to commemorate 10 years since the passing of the Marine Offences Act. This had been so successful that a second conference was held, over the weekend of 29th-30th July, 1978.

Entitled 'Zee Zenders' the conference was held at the Leeutiennorst Congress Centre, Noordwijkershout, Holland. This was to celebrate 20 years of offshore radio, since that first broadcast, by Radio Mercur, on 11th July, 1958. All of the European pirate stations were featured, and there were films, photographs, lectures and the sale of memorabilia.

The agenda also featured New Zealand's only offshore station, Radio Hauraki, which broadcast from the radio ship *Tiri*, anchored in the Hauraki Gulf to the north-east of Auckland.

Test transmissions, on 1480 kHz, commenced at 4 pm on Friday 2nd December, 1966. 'This is Radio Hauraki, the station for young New Zealanders, broadcasting test transmissions from the *Tiri*, in the Hauraki Gulf.' The station officially opened on Monday 5th December.

On Saturday 27th January, 1968 Radio Hauraki suspended broadcasts, so that the radio ship could assist in the search for a person missing from a small launch. Unfortunately, the *Tiri's* engine failed, and the ship ran aground just before 11.30 pm. The ship was subsequently salvaged but the cost of repairs amounted to more then the value of the ship.

A replacement ship was purchased, and renamed *Tiri II*, having previously been named *Kapuni*. This ship had been built in 1909, it was 101 ft in length, and weighed 194 tons. The *Tiri II* was just 11 ft longer, 25 tons heavier, but 22 years older than the *Tiri*. The ship was quickly fitted out, commencing broadcasts at 5 am on Wednesday 28th February, 1968. On Tuesday 9th April the ship lost its anchor, and was driven ashore by storm force winds, and a heavy sea.

Little damage was sustained, but the 170 ft mast collapsed; the ship was successfully salvaged, and towed into port. The ship was fitted with the mast from the *Tiri*, which had been retained for just such an emergency. Just six days later the *Tiri II* was back at sea, from where Radio Hauraki resumed broadcasts on Monday 15th April.

The station proved so popular that the New Zealand Government decided to invite Radio Hauraki ashore, to broadcast legally. The *Tiri II* broadcast the last seaborne programme on Monday 1st June, 1970, the transmitter being switched off at 10 pm.

The anchor was raised, and the *Tiri II* started her journey to Auckland, during the early hours of Tuesday 2nd June. During the passage the ship rolled sharply, throwing disc jockey Rick Grant into the sea. The radio ship was joined by several other vessels in a desperate search, but the DJ could not be found. In worsening weather conditions the search was reluctantly called off.

Radio Hauraki commenced broadcasts from studios in Auckland, at 6 am on Saturday 26th September, 1970, using the new callsign of '1XA'. The year would certainly hold many memories for the station: the loss of a well respected colleague, and the honour of being the first pirate invited ashore.

Also on the agenda was the Voice of Peace, an offshore station that broadcast from the white painted ship, the MV *Peace*. The 570 ton coaster had been built in 1940 as the *Cito*, she was 170 ft in length. The radio ship anchored off the coast of Israel, near Tel Aviv, commencing broadcasts at 8 pm on Saturday 26th May, 1973. This station, as its name suggests, broadcast messages of love and peace to the war torn Middle East, on 195 metres (1540 kHz).

Programming was in English, Hebrew, Arabic and French, with some of the DJs who had worked on Radio Northsea and Caroline. The owner, Abie Nathen, even went on a hunger strike in an attempt to get Israel and Egypt to sign a peace treaty.

When the two countries went to war, in October of that year, the ship moved to a location off Suez, to broadcast messages to the soldiers to stop fighting. However, during November the ship was escorted into port by an Israeli gunboat.

Radio Free America was also mentioned, which broadcast from the MV *Columbus*, anchored off the New Jersey coast. This station opened on Wednesday 12th September, 1973, broadcasting on 259 metres (1160 kHz). Just two days later the ship lost its anchor, and had to enter port to collect a replacement.

The station reopened on Saturday 19th September, but complaints of interference to legal stations had been received. Radio Free America went off the air that evening, at 10 pm. The *Columbus* returned to port where the transmitter was converted to 186 metres (1608 kHz). A test was broadcast, but the station did not reopen.

Broadcasting to the Middle East from somewhere in the Mediterranean.

The 570 ton MV *Peace* broadcasts messages of love and peace to the war torn Middle East, from somewhere in the Mediterranean during 1973. The initial broadcasts were short-lived, but the station did return to the air during the mid-1970s.

Zee Zenders 20 was an outstanding success, but to my knowledge no further conferences were organised. Radio Caroline relayed special broadcasts of the event during the weekend, so as to be a part of the proceedings.

Say Hello, Wave Goodbye

The summer of 1978 will be remembered for the start of a new radio station. It seems incredible that anyone would think of doing such a thing, after all that Radio Caroline had been through.

In the Dutch port of Scheveningen, under strict secrecy, and on an even tighter budget, a 250 ton coaster was being equipped and prepared for its new role as a radio ship. As the work progressed many tactics were employed to try and mislead the Dutch authorities.

The *Aegir* frequently went out to sea, so as to appear as though she was actively involved in fishing; even the name of the ship was changed, on several occasions. All of this subterfuge was necessary because the Dutch were quick to stop illegal broadcasters.

With the conversion work well in hand the Dutch authorities, acting on a tip-off, raided the ship. The officials seized the transmitters (2) and other equipment, as well as over 10,000 records and 200 tapes. The three men who were found on the ship were detained by the police, but released after questioning.

In spite of the raid, which had taken place on Friday 23rd June, the work continued, and in August the *Aegir* put to sea. Sailing south, she anchored 12 miles from Goeree, off the Dutch coast. Transmissions commenced on Monday 21st August, and although the signal was low powered, it could be heard on both sides of the North Sea.

Radio Del Mare broadcast on 192 metres (1570 kHz), using ex-Belgian army issue transmitters, manufactured by Marconi, with the signal fed to a long wire antenna supported by two 36 ft masts. The transmitters were not crystal controlled, so the signal tended to be a bit erratic, but with some adjustments the signal started to improve. Transmissions continued throughout August, with listeners in Holland and the south-east of England. Unfortunately the North Sea can be a very dangerous place, for professionals, let alone ill-equipped and ill-trained amateurs.

During the second week of September, storms raged through the North Sea. Radio Del Mare was set to be the latest victim of the hostile environment. On Monday 11th September the 115 ft *Aegir* took a severe pounding, which proved too much for the anchor chain.

The chain finally parted, leaving the little ship to the mercy of the elements. Only three persons were on board the *Aegir*, and it was not until 8 am that they realised their dire predicament. None of the men knew how to start the ship's engine; as they neared the Dutch coast they broadcast Mayday calls on 192 metres, and on an amateur radio band.

Listeners were amazed to hear the DJ broadcast details of the ship's plight, and so that there could be no doubt as to who was making the broadcast the station's theme tune, *The Eve Of The War* (from Jeff Wayne's *War of the Worlds*), was played throughout the drama.

On receipt of the distress call, a full scale rescue operation was mounted, by the Dutch Coastguard, a tug and two lifeboats being dispatched. The tug *Smitbank*, was the first on the scene, and the crew soon managed to get a line onto the stricken radio ship, which by this time was just 400 yards from the shore. The *Aegir* was towed to the port of Maasluis, where the crew were detained for questioning by the local police. The ship was impounded, and taken to the Customs Harbour at Rotterdam.

The man responsible for the Radio Del Mare project was none other then Gerrard van Dam, who had purchased the *Mi Amigo* in 1972. He was a well known free radio activist, who had worked for a time as a DJ on Radio Atlantis. Unfortunately, he could not afford to pay for the salvage operation, and as a result he lost his ship. He was interviewed by a Dutch newspaper, stating that the station was not finished and that it would be back on the air during 1979.

During October 1978, Radio Mi Amigo and Caroline were facing problems of their own. The troublesome generator was once again playing up, forcing Radio Mi Amigo off the air on the morning of Friday 20th. Caroline was unable to resume broadcasts that evening.

This was not an uncommon occurrence, but as the days of silence spread into weeks and then months, doubts about the station's future became evident. These doubts were later confirmed when newspapers reported that the owner of Radio Mi Amigo, Sylvain Tack, had decided to close the station.

Radio Mi Amigo made its first test transmission on Saturday 6th October, 1973, the *Mi Amigo*'s mast collapse prevented further testing until 28th December. The station officially opened at noon on Tuesday 1st January, 1974, making its final broadcast from the *Mi Amigo* on Friday 20th October, 1978.

John Wilson

It was reported that this was to allow him to concentrate on his other business activities. The papers also carried a copy of a letter, sent to Mr Tack, by the Spanish Government. The letter stated that as Spain was making stronger bonds with Europe, the Government had decided to ratify the Strasbourg Treaty even though Spain was not a signatory to that Treaty.

The letter also required assurances that all activities, connected with Radio Mi Amigo and Radio Caroline, would cease as soon as possible, to avoid action being taken by the Spanish Government. So that was the end of Radio Mi Amigo, broadcasting from the ship from which it had taken its name.

For five years the two stations had 'Sailed on an Ocean of Love' sharing the hazards of the North Sea, and the animosity of European Governments. For millions of listeners in Belgium, Holland, France and the UK it was a very sad occasion.

The daytime programmes from Radio Mi Amigo had offered a very high quality alternative to what many considered the mundane output from land-based stations. Not only did the station play good music, it was famous for its jingles which were used far more than on most stations.

There had been good and bad times, moments of pleasure and times of high drama. Unfortunately, the partnership that had been so beneficial to both stations ended at 10.54 am on Friday 20th October, 1978.

Having lost her partner, and facing even more pressure to silence her, Radio Caroline was determined to continue broadcasting. There was even a contingency plan, to move the office from Spain to Morocco, if the Spanish authorities took any action against the premises at Apartado 321, Rosas, Gerona.

Radio Caroline was confident that it could find a new partner, given the immense interest generated by the station, both in Holland and Belgium. There was, however, the more immediate problem of getting Radio Caroline back on the air. The radio ship had been silent for almost two months, mainly due to financial problems, which meant that repairs and fuel could not be financed.

In December, a small vessel slipped quietly out of the Dutch port of Scheveningen with a new generator on board. The vessel made its clandestine voyage across the North Sea, to rendezvous with the *Mi Amigo*. Once alongside, the generator, and other essential items of stores and equipment, were transferred, the tender returning to Holland.

Radio Caroline was going through a cash crisis, made worse by the fact that she could not find a new partner. The loss of income from Radio Mi Amigo was very nearly a fatal blow.

Unfortunately, an already bad situation was about to turn decidedly worse. The weather conditions deteriorated, with strong winds and a heavy sea pounding the ship. On Sunday 31st December the *Mi Amigo* received damage to the hull, and began leaking. Far from celebrating the start of a new year, those on board were fighting to keep the ship afloat!

1979

Top 20 for week commencing Sunday 7th January, 1979

1	(1)	*YMCA*	Village People
2	(6)	*Hit Me With Your Rhythm Stick*	Ian Dury & The Blockheads
3	(3)	*Lay Your Love On Me*	Racey
4	(5)	*Song For Guy*	Elton John
5	(18)	*September*	Earth, Wind & Fire
6	(4)	*A Taste Of Aggro*	Barron Knights
7	(2)	*Mary's Boy Child*	Boney M
8	(7)	*You Don't Bring Me Flowers*	Barbra Streisand
9	(10)	*Le Freak*	Chic
10	(8)	*Too Much Heaven*	Bee Gees
11	(9)	*I Lost My Heart To A Starship Trooper*	Sarah Brightman & Hot Gossip
12	(21)	*A Little More Love*	Olivia Newton-John
13	(24)	*Hello This Is Joanie*	Paul Evans
14	(15)	*I'm Every Woman*	Chaka Khan
15	(13)	*Greased Lightning*	John Travolta
16	(16)	*I'll Put You Together Again*	Hot Chocolate
17	(12)	*Always and Forever/Mind Blowing Decisions*	Heatwave
18	(28)	*One Nation Under A Groove*	Funkadelic
19	(14)	*Shooting Star*	Dollar
20	(11)	*Do Ya Think I'm Sexy*	Rod Stewart

Survival of the Fittest

The New Year arrived, but it did not bring any respite for the weary staff or the crippled radio ship. For 18 days the pumps had kept the water at bay, but the generator providing power to those pumps failed on Thursday 18th January. A standby generator was put into service, but this was not powerful enough to cope with the ingress of water. The new generator, which had been delivered in December, which was still out on the deck and could not be started.

The situation was becoming desperate, the wind was still blowing a near gale, and there was so much water entering the ship that she had begun to settle deeper into the water. Fearful that the ship was going to sink, the men finally admitted defeat and called for assistance. During the afternoon of Friday 19th January, the Harwich lifeboat and an Air Sea Rescue helicopter from RAF Manston, responded. The Coastguard requested other ships in the area to standby, in case they were needed.

The five men on board the *Mi Amigo* decided against being winched off by the helicopter, opting to wait for the lifeboat which took 2½ hours to battle its way out to the stricken radio ship. Reluctantly, all of the men transferred to the lifeboat, leaving the *Mi Amigo* to her fate. The Coastguard was reported as saying that if nothing were done to prevent it, the *Mi Amigo* would probably sink within 24 hours!

The plight of the famous radio ship, fighting for her life, was given nationwide coverage on TV, radio and in the press. All of the appropriate authorities were notified. Trinity House responded by sending its lighthouse tender, *Winston Churchill*, into the area to ensure that the *Mi Amigo* posed no threat to safe navigation.

Everything seemed to have been lost. After nearly 15 years it seemed as though Radio Caroline had perished, yet another victim of the cruel North Sea. Contingency plans were put into place, ready to deal with the inevitable, but somebody forgot to tell the *Mi Amigo*, because she was not ready to give up the fight. The *Mi Amigo* had not sunk, even though she had settled deeply in the water, fortunately she had settled on an even keel. The salvage operation commenced on Saturday 20th January, when several people went back to the ship.

As soon as they had got on board, they started to bale out the ship, using buckets or similar containers. It was all done by hand, but later in the day, a generator was taken out to the ship. The engineer managed to get two pumps operating and lighting was restored, using paraffin lamps.

At the end of the day, all of the salvors, with the exception of the engineer Peter Chicago, left the ship. Overnight he managed to place one working pump in the engine room and the other pumping out the cabins.

On Sunday 21st another vessel took a new generator out to the *Mi Amigo*. This was quickly put into service, providing power for light and heat. The rest of the staff also returned to the ship and assisted in the mopping-up operation. The immediate danger was soon over, with repairs being made to the hull. 'Lady Luck' stayed with the ship, as the silent transmitters had not been damaged.

The dramatic events were widely reported; many thought that Radio Caroline had finally perished, others were amazed to hear that the station was still around. Due to the almost total lack of any coverage in the media, those living outside Caroline's reception area had no idea that the station had survived for so long.

Radio Caroline has what can only be described as an incredible survival instinct. She had survived beaching, driftings, aerial collapses, mutiny and enforced closure. No matter what happened, there was no shortage of people to help keep her on the air.

Over the following weeks work continued apace to clean the ship. Repairs were carried out and much of the equipment was overhauled. Fuel oil was delivered, everyone was working with one aim: to restart broadcasting in time for her 15th birthday.

Due to the immense amount of work involved, it was not until Sunday 18th March, 1979 that Radio Caroline was able to make a test transmission. The test was broadcast on 539 metres (557 kHz), and lasted for almost six hours; however, the new frequency proved unsuitable. Over the following weeks, engineers continued to work on the equipment in preparation for resuming broadcasts. There was a slight change in the frequency, from 962 to 963 kHz, but retaining the callsign Caroline on 319.

Everything was now ready; apart from the aforementioned test, Radio Caroline had been silent for 176 days, but on Sunday 15th April she finally returned to the air. Once again the station had triumphed against all of the odds.

The first 30 minutes were in English, then Caroline started its own Dutch language service. The contact address, for the new service, was given as Alta Mira, Avenida Ansol, Marbella, Spain. That evening, at 5 pm, Tom Hardy welcomed listeners back to the English service, which closed at midnight.

On shore, Caroline's listeners were thrilled to have their favourite station back on the air. News of the return spread like wildfire. In spite of the split with Radio Mi

Amigo, Caroline showed no signs of faltering. The new Dutch service carried a mix of genuine and fake advertisements, in an attempt to protect clients from prosecution.

A new series of religious programmes were broadcast, on both services, being sponsored from America and Canada, and later from the UK, Holland, and even South Africa. These contracts helped to keep the station going, with a regular source of income.

Just two weeks after Radio Caroline had resumed broadcasting, a second radio ship sailed quietly out of a Dutch port and out into the North Sea. The 270 ton, 120 foot MV *Martina* anchored off Goeree on Sunday 29th April, in a location near where the MV *Aegir* had been anchored.

The owner of this ship was none other than Gerrard van Dam, who was determined to restart his Radio Del Mare station after its enforced closure. It will be remembered that his first ship, the *Aegir*, had gone adrift on 11th September, 1978. The ship had subsequently been impounded, because Mr van Dam could not afford the salvage fees.

He had purchased this ship and fitted it out in total secrecy, so as to evade possible pre-emptive action, by the Dutch authorities, to prevent the ship from sailing. Radio Del Mare commenced broadcasting, on 192 metres, on Saturday 2nd June, after a silence lasting 262 days.

Incredible though it may seem, a third radio ship was being fitted out, prior to commencing broadcasts from the North Sea. The 200 ft MV *Magdalena*, had been equipped with a long wire antenna, which was supported by two masts, rather than a tall mast like Caroline. The long wire system had also been adopted by Radio Del Mare.

The *Magdalena* anchored off Knokke, near the Thornton Bank, during June, and commenced test transmissions almost straight away. Testing on 273 metres (1098 kHz) continued through the last week of the month. On Sunday 1st July, the station officially opened, Radio Mi Amigo was back!

The station broadcast for 24 hours per day, using a 10 kilowatt transmitter, and could be heard in Holland, Belgium and parts of the south-east of England. In the south-east some areas experienced interference with BBC Radio 1, which was broadcasting on 275 metres (1089kHz).

Against all sound judgement (excuse the pun!), a mini offshore radio boom had started, which proved very popular with the listeners. Radio Mi Amigo rapidly regained its former popularity, and many new listeners, by strategically using the frequency alongside Radio 1. It was a situation that was not destined to last for very long.

On Sunday 12th August there was a mutiny aboard the MV *Martina*, by DJs and crew of Radio Del Mare. They were not satisfied with the way that the ship was being run. They decided to let their feelings be known and took over the organisation and running of the ship themselves. Radio Del Mare continued to broadcast, but some of the staff left the ship and were not replaced.

It was not all smooth sailing for Radio Mi Amigo either, the 24 hour format had been dropped, but there was worse to come. The station suddenly went off the air, just after starting normal broadcasts at 5 am on Tuesday 18th September. Strong winds had produced a heavy swell and, unable to cope with the strain, the anchor chain snapped. The silent radio ship drifted helplessly, until running aground near Goeree. The *Magdalena* suffered hull damage, but was successfully towed off the sandbank on Sunday 23rd September. The ship was placed under arrest, and eventually sold for scrap, meeting its end in a Dutch scrap yard.

Meanwhile, things were not going too well for Radio Del Mare. The station had continued to broadcast, after the August mutiny, but standards had dropped. During the evening of Friday 28th September the station closed down, and it has remained silent. The *Martina* remained at sea, until late October, when it sailed into port and was immediately arrested by Dutch officials.

Once again, Radio Caroline was the sole survivor, and she seemed to be going from strength to strength. The regular income, from the religious broadcasts, was financing repairs to the overworked equipment.

The 10 kilowatt transmitter had been in service, but at the end of August, almost like an act of defiance, the 50 kilowatt transmitter was put into service.

After just two weeks the transmitter developed a fault, forcing Caroline off the air on Friday 14th September. It was not until the next afternoon that broadcasts resumed, but the 10 kilowatt transmitter had to be used.

The mini offshore radio boom of 1979 proved that the pace and interest in offshore radio had not diminished, in spite of all the BBC and IBA local radio stations. Its popularity is hard to define, but for millions of devoted listeners there was no substitute.

Offshore radio in general, Radio Caroline in particular, epitomise freedom that no legal land based station could hope to emulate. Not only did the little ships have to fight the elements, they had to endure the wrath of officialdom. The very law, designed to silence that freedom of speech and choice, had made martyrs of the pirates. Radio Caroline was the sole representative of that freedom, as she continued to broadcast love, peace and good music.

1980

Top 20 for week commencing Sunday 16th March, 1980

1	(2)	*Together We Are Beautiful*	Fern Kinney
2	(1)	*Atomic*	Blondie
3	(3)	*Take That Look Off Your Face*	Marti Webb
4	(8)	*Games Without Frontiers*	Peter Gabriel
5	(10)	*All Night Long*	Rainbow
6	(12)	*So Lonely*	Police
7	(25)	*Do That To Me One More Time*	Captain and Tennille
8	(18)	*Turning Japanese*	Vapors
9	(16)	*Hand's Off, She's Mine*	Beat
10	(5)	*And The Beat Goes On*	Whispers
11	(7)	*Carrie*	Cliff Richard
12	(4)	*I Can't Stand Up For Falling Down*	Elvis Costello
13	(9)	*Rock With You*	Michael Jackson
14	(23)	*Dance Yourself Dizzy*	Liquid Gold
15	(6)	*Coward Of The County*	Kenny Rogers
16	(19)	*Cuba/Do It Salsa*	Gibson Brothers
17	(13)	*Riders In The Sky*	Shadows
18	(15)	*At The Edge*	Stiff Little Fingers
19	(11)	*So Good To Be Back Home Again*	Tourists
20	(31)	*Working My Way Back To You/Forgive Me Girl*	Detroit Spinners

The Lady Retires

1980 had arrived, it was Radio Caroline's 16th year, and the *Mi Amigo's* 59th. As the new decade dawned, the question in the back of the minds of the listeners was, how much longer could Caroline continue? No one could have imagined that the end was so near.

In spite of a lack of cash, the engineers had restored the 50 kilowatt transmitter and most of the country could hear her broadcasts. Both the station, and the ship, had survived the worst of the winter storms, and preparations were underway to celebrate her birthday.

With the changing of the clocks to British Summer Time came strong to gale force winds, with most of the country having showers or longer periods of snow. Winter was leaving with a sting in its tail.

To the men on the *Mi Amigo*, it was nothing new, they had seen it all before. The wind swung into the north-east, which was the most feared direction, as the ship was now fully exposed to the effects of the wind and the swell which it generated.

Throughout the day of Wednesday 19th March the *Mi Amigo* was pounded by the heavy swell, and winds gusting up to gale force 9. At approximately 2 pm the main anchor chain snapped, leaving the *Mi Amigo* to drift helplessly with her engine not working.

For nearly 2½ hours the ship drifted, before anybody realised that anything was wrong. Disc jockey Tom Anderson discovered their predicament, and alerted his colleagues. The emergency anchor was lowered at about 3.30 pm, but it was too late, the ship was aground on a sandbank known as Long Sand.

At this stage they were not unduly worried, but they did inform the Coastguard, adding that they were not in need of assistance. The weather conditions worsened, prompting the Coastguard to request the launch of Sheerness lifeboat, which battled its way to the stricken radio ship.

The lifeboat crew urged the men to leave the *Mi Amigo*, but they refused, so the lifeboat just stood by in case it should be needed. As the tide began to rise the *Mi Amigo* started to bounce up and down on the hard sand, causing holes to appear in the hull.

In spite of the seriousness of the situation Radio Caroline remained on the air, broadcasting continuous music which was interrupted at the top of each hour by coded messages. The pumps were unable to cope with amount of water flooding in and, with the lifeboat crew urging them to come off, the decision was made to abandon ship. DJs Stevie Gordon and Tom Anderson went back to the studio, to make this dramatic final broadcast from the good ship *Mi Amigo*.

Well we are very sorry to tell you that due to the severe weather conditions, and also to the fact that we are shipping quite a lot of water, we are closing down, and the crew are at this stage leaving the ship. Obviously we hope to be back with you, as soon as possible, but we would just like to assure you all on land that there is nothing to worry about, we are all quite safe. Just for the moment we would like to say goodbye, Tom?

Yes it's not a very good occasion really, I'll have to hurry this as the lifeboat is standing by. We are not leaving and disappearing, we are going into the lifeboat hoping that the pumps can take it. If they can we will be back, if not, well I don't like to say it?

I think we will be back, one way or another Tom.

Yes I think so.

DJ Stevie Gordon closed the station down by saying 'From all of us, for the moment, Goodbye and God bless'. Just after midnight, on Thursday 20th March, 1980, the theme tune *Caroline*, by the Fortunes, was played and then there was silence.

In a very dangerous operation the four men, Nick Richards, Tom Anderson, Steve Gordon and a Dutch crewman, and the ship's canary Wilson, managed to transfer to the lifeboat. The pumps were left running on the *Mi Amigo* in the hope that they would stop the ship from sinking. The navigation lights were also left on, so that the *Mi Amigo* would not be a hindrance to other shipping.

The lifeboat took the four men ashore, where they were taken to a police station and made comfortable. Under instructions from the Home Office, the men were interviewed and warned that they were liable to prosecution, but in the event no charges were made. In a separate case, one DJ was charged with drugs offences and later fined £75.

During the early hours of Thursday 20th March, the *Mi Amigo* was overwhelmed by the heavy sea, and it sunk in 25 ft of water. Trinity House were informed, and they laid a warning buoy, appropriately named 'Mi Amigo', near the wreck.

On Tuesday 25th March, Trinity House issued a Notice to Mariners which gave the position of the *Mi Amigo* as 51 degrees 35 minutes north, 01 degrees 17 minutes 20 seconds east. Under sections 530 and 531 of the 1894 Merchant Shipping Act, Trinity House claimed the wreck and warned, 'that nothing may be taken therefrom, without permission'. This was a standard procedure, to prevent looters raiding the ship.

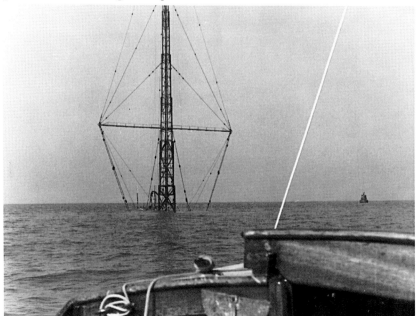

A final act of defiance the *Mi Amigo's* mast continues to stand, even though the ship has sunk.   *A.C. Stock*

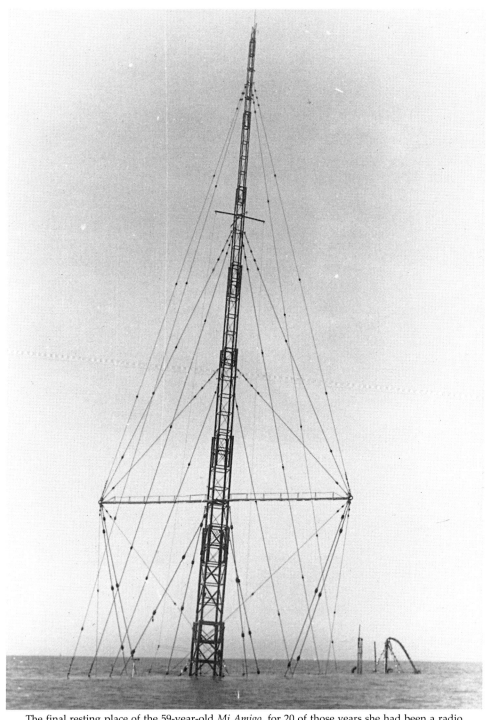

The final resting place of the 59-year-old *Mi Amigo*, for 20 of those years she had been a radio ship. This lattice mast was the fourth to have been fitted to her, it collapsed in 1986. *A.C. Stock*

NOTICE TO MARINERS

(No.48 of 1980)

EAST COAST OF ENGLAND

THAMES ESTUARY

WRECK

"MI AMIGO"

Latitude 51° 35' 00" N., Longitude 01° 17' 20" E.

The Wreck "MI AMIGO", which lies sunk in the position defined above, has been marked by means of a Lighted Buoy, as follows:-

MI AMIGO LIGHTED BUOY :

Position : 320° about 450 feet from the Wreck

Description : Can: Red: Exhibiting a Very Quick Flashing Red Light.

Notice is hereby given to all concerned in the Ship and Cargo that the Corporation of Trinity House has taken possession of the Wreck under Sections 530 and 531 of the Merchant Shipping Act, 1894, and that nothing may be taken therefrom without permission.

By Order,

L.N.POTTER

Secretary.

TRINITY HOUSE,
LONDON, EC3N 4DH.

25th March, 1980.

560/13/7

It was a devastating blow for everyone connected with Radio Caroline, and all of the dedicated listeners. Just eight days before her 16th birthday, Radio Caroline's home had sunk; the *Mi Amigo* had finally succumbed to the incessant pounding from wind and sea. There was, however, slight comfort in the knowledge that she had been the victim of the elements, rather than of Governmental action.

Not only had they lost their beloved *Mi Amigo*, Radio Caroline had lost a priceless collection of records and tapes, and an estimated £100,000 worth of equipment. Interviewed for TV News, Stevie Gordon, the last voice to be heard from the *Mi Amigo*, had this to say: 'The records and tapes are always replacable, but the losing of the Caroline is the bit that hurts at the moment. One day, one way or another, I'm sure that Caroline will be back.'

The North Sea has the reputation of being amongst the most hostile waters in the world, and within days it had more than lived up to that reputation. Not only was the *Mi Amigo* lost, but there was far worse to come, the unimaginable horror of the worst tragedy in North Sea oil and gas exploration.

Within hours of the loss of the *Mi Amigo*, plans were being made to see if the radio ship could be salvaged. Ex-Caroline DJ, Robb Eden, who had organised the highly successful Caroline Roadshow, spearheaded the plans to raise the ship. It was his intention, if the plans succeeded, to convert the *Mi Amigo* into a museum dedicated to offshore radio.

He went on to say that if the plan failed, all of the money that had been collected for the project, would be donated to the RNLI. Divers went down to inspect the hull and it was decided to try and raise the ship, using very large balloons tied to the hull, which would be inflated with compressed air.

The plan to bring the ship into harbour, should the salvage attempt succeed, met with considerable approval. Thanet Council said that they were searching for a suitable location and the local MP was very enthusiastic about having a new tourist attraction in his constituency.

There was some local opposition to the project, but in the end there was no need for any arguments. The salvage attempt was called off, in early April, as the hull had become firmly embedded and the ship was filling with sand.

That is where this chapter in Caroline's eventful life comes to an end. Her partnership with the *Mi Amigo* had finished, after 16 very eventful years. It may have been the end of the ship, but it most certainly was not the end for Radio Caroline.

The purpose of this book was to describe the partnership, between Caroline and the *Mi Amigo*, that had now ended. The end of part one, if you like, but there is a part two and it started like this . . .

Chapter Five

The Legend Lives On!
1980-1983

1983

Top 20 for week commencing Sunday 7th August, 1983

1	(5)	*Give It Up*	KC & The Sunshine Band
2	(1)	*Wherever I Lay My Hat (That's My Home)*	Paul Young
3	(2)	*I.O.U.*	Freeez
4	(3)	*Double Dutch*	Malcolm McLaren
5	(10)	*Club Tropicana*	Wham!
6	(6)	*The Crown*	Gary Bird & The GB Experience
7	(4)	*Who's That Girl*	Eurythmics
8	(-)	*Long Hot Summer*	Style Council
9	(24)	*I'm Still Standing*	Elton John
10	(16)	*Everything Counts*	Depeche Mode
11	(15)	*Big Log*	Robert Plant
12	(-)	*Gold*	Spandau Ballet
13	(8)	*Cruel Summer*	Bananarama
14	(11)	*It's Late*	Shakin' Stevens
15	(25)	*Rockit*	Herbie Hancock
16	(12)	*Moonlight Shadow*	Mike Oldfield
17	(20)	*Right Now*	Creatures
18	(7)	*Wrapped Around Your Finger*	Police
19	(9)	*Come Live With Me*	Heaven 17
20	(14)	*Don't Try To Stop It*	Roman Holiday

Robbers of the Airwaves

After all that they had been through, Radio Caroline was not going to let a simple thing, like losing their ship, stop them from broadcasting. With the confirmation that the *Mi Amigo* was beyond help, behind the scenes those involved with the station were far from inactive.

The search was on for new sponsors, and a new ship. Within months rumours of Radio Caroline's imminent return spread like wild fire. The story circulated that the most likely date for her return was Monday 15th December, 1980, but in the event nothing materialised.

On Tuesday 23rd December, 1980 an article was published in the *Irish Times* which said that a new ship was being prepared, and that broadcasts would commence in early 1981. It went on to say that over £300,000 had been invested in the new station, and that Caroline would broadcast on a new frequency at the top end of the medium wave.

On Saturday 3rd January, 1981, the ITN News, at 9.15 pm, reported that Radio Caroline was back on the air, which was not the case. The next evening a Caroline spokesman denied the story, adding that it was premature. This was a carefully worded statement with the adjective, premature, being the most important part of the statement.

Radio Caroline resumed broadcasting on 20th August, 1983 from the *Ross Revenge* anchored in the Knock Deep Channel. *Fotoflite*

It took two years to find the necessary funding, and locate a suitable ship. That ship was called the *Ross Revenge*, a converted trawler which had been built in 1960. She was the product of the Bremerhaven yard of Seebeckwerft AG, for an Icelandic company, who named her *Freyr*. She was a well found vessel of 238 ft, capable of 16 knots.

She was sold to Ross Trawlers Ltd, in 1963, who renamed her *Ross Revenge* and registered her in Grimsby. In 1969 she passed into the ownership of British United Trawlers Ltd, when that company took over the Ross fleet.

The vessel was sold again, two years later, and converted for use as a wreck recovery ship, employed in the North Sea oil and gas industry. In 1983 she was sold to the Grotham Shipping Lines who re-registered her in Panama and she sailed to Santander on the northern coast of Spain.

The Spanish Authorities did not hinder the conversion work, as the ship was prepared for her new role, not even when it was fitted with a 300 ft aerial mast. The living accommodation was refurbished, and the large hold, of some 9,000 square metres, was used for the transmitting equipment.

With the work almost complete, the *Ross Revenge* was towed out of the port by a Spanish tug, on Thursday 4th August. The two ships sailed across the Bay of Biscay, turning east into the English Channel, the voyage lasting four days.

During the early evening of Monday 8th August the radio ship was anchored in the Knock Deep Channel, close to where the *Mi Amigo* had anchored. Within hours of arriving in the Thames Estuary, test transmissions commenced just after midnight on 9th August, using the old 319 (963 kHz) frequency. Caroline's revenge came in 1983.

Radio Caroline officially reopened at midday on Saturday 20th August, after a period of silence which had lasted for 3 years and 5 months. The very first record to be played, at that time, was *Caroline* by the Fortunes. Caroline had returned, against all the odds, and that return was given wide coverage by the media, on TV and in the press, resulting in millions tuning to the broadcasts of the world's most famous offshore radio station.

Some people had thought that with the increasing number of legal local radio stations there would be no room for Radio Caroline, how wrong they were! The station soon regained a large audience, and all the time that the listeners want the station, Ronan will do his best to give it to them.

The Government was far from happy with the situation, but did not know at the time that there was worse (as far as it was concerned) to come.

During that same month of August 1983, talks were taking place with a view to commencing an offshore radio station. The project got underway, led by Irish and English businessmen, with a budget of £500,000.

A suitable ship was located, the *Guardline Seeker*, which was being sold in Aberdeen by Guardline Shipping. The 489 ton vessel was moved to Lowestoft, from where it was purchased for £60,000. The deal would only be completed if the ship sailed from the port that day.

In spite of appalling weather conditions, the ship did sail, taking 25 days to cross the Atlantic, to Fort Lauderdale. The ship was renamed *Communicator*, and was equipped with two 25 kilowatt, CSI transmitters. With most of the work completed, she sailed to New Ross in the Republic of Ireland. To conceal her true identity, port officials were told that the vessel was to be used in oil research, seeking out new deposits. It was not long before rumours started that she was actually going to be used for broadcasting, so the ship again set sail.

The voyage took her around the Cornish peninsula, encountering very rough weather through the English Channel, and into the Thames Estuary. The MV *Communicator* dropped anchor in the Knock Deep Channel, close to the *Ross Revenge*, in January 1984.

This proved to be a very stormy month. Radio Caroline was forced off the air, at 9.20 pm on Friday 20th, when the *Ross Revenge* lost its anchor. The ship drifted onto a sandbank, but fortunately no damage resulted and she was able to return to her anchorage the following Wednesday.

The ship had to use the emergency anchor, which proved too light, allowing the ship to drag anchor during rough weather. A new, and heavier, anchor was dispatched from Spain, being delivered by a tug. The tug was used to relocate the radio ship in its proper position, on Monday 5th March.

Meanwhile, the *Communicator*, had commenced test transmissions, giving MMI, East Madison Avenue, New York, New York, 10017, USA, as a contact address. The ship did not have a large aerial, like on the *Ross Revenge*, it had been decided to use a helium balloon to lift the aerial wire into the air.

A balloon was launched, which allowed broadcasts to commence on 729 metres, but the balloon quickly broke adrift. A second balloon was inflated, which allowed the tests to resume, but during a storm this balloon also broke free.

The owner of the station, Philip Smythe, was furious as each balloon cost in the region of £10,000. After two months at anchor, only four hours had been spent broadcasting. Mr Smythe threatened to pull out of the project if the station did not start proper broadcasts; he had already invested 1½ million US dollars.

The MV *Communicator*, home of Laser 558, anchored in the Knock Deep Channel in January 1984.   *Fotoflite*

The engineers rigged a conventional T aerial, which allowed testing to recommence, these tests proved to be successful. It was agreed that the tests would finish at the end of February, to allow a new system to be constructed. Listeners were told that the station would be back in 10-15 days, but that it would broadcast on a new frequency.

Construction of the aerial mast commenced, on land, but after a short time the yard was raided by the DTI and all the equipment was impounded. Using riggers from the Republic of Ireland, a new system was constructed on board the ship.

During the morning of Thursday 24th May, 1984, the station officially opened, using the new callsign, 'Laser 558'. The station was broadcasting on 538 metres (558 kHz). Presenter Rick Harris opened the proceedings.

Good morning, I'm pleased to introduce you to a brand new radio station. All Europe Radio, Laser 558, broadcasting live from International waters, from the MV *Communicator*. We promise to bring you at least 54 minutes of International hit songs, each hour we broadcast. All hits, all of the time. Plus,we keep you informed of the news of the world, hourly. Welcome to Laser 558, where you are never more than a minute away from music, starting NOW!

At 11 am in the UK (12 o'clock in central Europe), Jessie Brandon read the news headlines, which included:

- Talks at settling the strikes, in the West German car industry, start in Bonn today.
- Cuba has withdrawn from the Olympic Games, in Los Angeles.
- Iraq has pledged to step up attacks on shipping, in the prohibited zone, in the Gulf.
- President Regan's third defeat, on his 1985 defence budget. The House of Representatives have voted to stop testing anti-satellite weapons.

Laser 558 went on on to be one of the most successful pirate radio stations of all time, much to the annoyance of the authorities. The station did not have a long life, it became a victim of its own success,

Faced with losing droves of listeners to this new upstart, the IBA local radio stations wanted the Government to take swift and decisive action against this 'Robber of the airwaves'. The Government responded by stationing the MV *Dioptric Surveyor* in the vicinity of the radio ships, in what became known as 'Euro Siege 85'.

During 1986, the mast which had marked the *Mi Amigo's* watery grave, came crashing down. The mast had survived for for 13 years, and six of those had been spent partially submerged.

The collapse of the *Mi Amigo's* fourth mast, as opposed to any temporary structures, brings our story to a close. The story of Radio Caroline, from the *Ross Revenge*, and Laser 558 from the *Communicator* will, I hope, form the basis for a separate book.

The good news is that Radio Caroline is now a legal radio station. It broadcasts on the internet and on satellite. In the UK tune Sky recievers to 11623 Ghz. H polarity. 27.5 Symbol rate. FEC 2/3.

Caroline continues

NOTICE TO MARINERS

(No.68 of 1986)

EAST COAST OF ENGLAND

THAMES ESTUARY

WRECK

"MI AMIGO"

Latitude 51° 34'.95N., Longitude 01° 17'.35E.

The Wreck "MI AMIGO", which lies sunk in the position defined above, has been marked by means of a Buoy, as follows:-

MI AMIGO BUOY :

Position   : 320° about 450 feet from the Wreck.

Description : Can: Red.

Mariners are warned to give the Wreck and Buoy a wide berth.

Mariners should note that the lattice mast of the Wreck is no longer visible.

By Order,

J.R. BACKHOUSE,

Secretary.

Appendix One

Harry's Story

Having had a chequered career, shipyard apprentice, yacht hand, lifeboat deliveries, yacht yard foreman, mate on coastal vessels, delivery skipper, shipwright, sailmaker, etc., etc., etc., I finally found myself married and self-employed.

I was effecting rigging work, both yacht and commercial, I also did spar making, carving, and skippering a 12 metre racing yacht. I have undertaken some unusual jobs too, such as lifting and replacing the fog signal structure at St Catherine's Lighthouse. I raised the entire roof of a large boatyard.

I lifted some cannons, from the sea, up a 350 ft cliff. During the evenings, instead of taking it easy, I made very accurate models of ships, tugs and patrol craft, for test tank purposes. Then I would eat, drink, and take part in the normal activities that newly married couples do!

My workshop, where I employed three or four people had an impressive address, 3 Bank Chambers, and an even more impressive telephone number, Cowes 15. Three or four times down that phone line, came the request to talk about a big mast for a weather ship from a man in London called Allan Crawford.

Eventually I found enough time, and took the train to London. I then went to an address in Soho, not for the usual activities for which young men went (and still go) to Soho! I went to visit this persistent Crawford, at the offices of Merit Music, this turned out to be one door, between two strip clubs.

Once inside I was asked, by a young receptionist, to take a seat. People kept passing through this little office, just nodding, or politely saying, 'Good morning'. I supposed that I was being checked out, anyway, I was eventually shown into a much larger office upstairs. I sat there alone, then in came a man, who introduced himself as Mr Thomas.

His opening question was, 'What height of mast can you put on this ship?'. I replied, 'What ship?' 'Oh, don't you know, well it's a small coaster, of some 300 tons.'

I asked him, 'What's the mast for?' 'Oh, God', he said, 'It's a transmission mast, I'm a transmission engineer, just left the BBC'. I replied, 'Some 160-200 feet'. Incredulously, he took out a slide rule, and murmured something about 199, and then he left the room.

After a short time, in came a young Irish man who introduced himself as Ronan O'Rahilly. He was accompanied by a large man, with steel-rimmed glasses. He had an enormous stomach, divided by a belt which was completely enveloped by the overhang! 'I am Captain de Jong Lanau, Chief Superintendent of the Wijsmuller Towing Company.' His next statement took me by surprise. 'Mr Thomas tells me that you say you can put a 200 foot mast on this ship. rubbish! We have had 100 foot masts that have failed.' With the rolling we will break the wires, and the eggs (insulators). 200 foot, impossible, you know nothing!'

'Sir', I said, 'You are a sea Captain?'

'Ja, I have been in charge of salvage and rescue operations, from Scotland, during the war.'

'Do you come from a seafaring family?', I asked.

'Ja, my father and my grandfather.'

'Well', I said, 'Your predecessors probably were in ships of this size, not with a slender mast, but masts with many square feet of sail. They sailed around the world, this is just a transmission mast.'

'Ja, but it's not the same. This is not a yacht, not a square rigged ship. You either know something, or you know nothing.'

At this point we adjourned for lunch.

Sitting next to Captain de Jong, we continued our conversation.
'Where will this ship dock.'
'She will never dock', he replied.
'So this weather ship has to be tended with supplies?'
'Ja, it is not a weather ship, but a radio ship, and she will be supplied by a trawler.'
'So how tall is the mast on the trawler?', I asked.
'I don't know, maybe 10 metres or so, why, what are you saying?'
'Well you have the ship's length, to give good staying, but not the beam. To increase the beam you need to spread the shrouds (side rigging) outboard, by means of a spreader beam. If the ship cannot dock, and the tender's mast is 10 metres, then I suggest spreaders at some 14-15 metres.' I scribbled this on a paper serviette, and at the same time I noticed that he was becoming both agitated, and interested.
'Perhaps you do know something, perhaps nothing, but I want you to come to Holland.'
'Well perhaps next week', I replied. His fist crashed down onto the table, 'No today', he shouted. 'Look I've only come up today like this, I'm making an important model of an icebreaker, I have no passport with me.'
'No passport, no problem, you come with me now.'
'OK, if we go now, I must come back tomorrow, and I must buy a razor and a toothbrush.'
We went to the nearest shop, but the only sponge bag that I could buy was bright red, with a little handle (I was to curse that bag later!).
Some phone calls were made, then we went back to Sloane Street, and from there we went to Heathrow. The flight was uneventful, and on landing we were taken through immigration, where the Captain vouched for me, and I was issued with a temporary receipt, and told to report back the next day, on return to London.
A large black Mercedes collected all the Captain's numerous, and voluminous baggage, and my little red sponge bag! We swept through the streets, to the Park Hotel, in Amsterdam. A line of bell hops were waiting to show us to our rooms. The bell hop insisted on carrying my little red bag, at chest height, right out in front of him. (I could have killed him, I was so embarrassed!)
My room was a double suite, two bedrooms, two toilets, two bathrooms, dressing room, and another large room, with a table, which was big enough to have a Board meeting! Each room, including the toilets, had telephones.
I cleaned my teeth, shaved, then went down to dinner. In the morning we had breakfast, then the Captain ordered the Mercedes. The luggage was carried out to the car, and once again, the bell-hop descended the stairs swinging my little red bag in front of him.
We were driven to the de Jong shipyard in Rotterdam, where I threw that little red bag, as far as I could, out into the harbour. We were taken to the Boardroom where several men were sitting around a large table.
The conversation (all in Dutch) went on for about an hour, I was getting rather bored, when the Captain suddenly slapped me on the shoulder. 'This is Mr Spencer, he builds yachts and masts in England, please now all speak in English.'
Spread out on the table was a drawing of a ship, with a large mast, completely covered with struts, and diamond shaped wire rigging. There were several insulators, but only a few side shrouds (wires).
Captain de Jong said. 'Mr Spencer, what is your opinion of this mast?'
'Well', I replied, 'It's a good rig, but not for a ship.'
'Why not!', he demanded.
'Well the shroud angles are not wide enough.'
'So?'
'The wires, and the attachments on the mast and the ship will have to to be massive to take such loads.'

'So?'
'Then all of these diamonds will be dangerous.'
'Why?'
The question was asked by another man, presumably from the company who had submitted the drawing. I was getting embarrassed at all the attention that was now coming my way, but I pressed on.

Gentlemen, I presume some here are mariners? Well suppose you were in the wheelhouse, in a gale, and you can't see the top of the mast, because it is too high, much higher then any normal mast.
Suppose that on one of these wire diamonds an insulator breaks, this means there will be a slack wire, it will happen where there is the most stress, such as at the top of a shroud. If nothing is done you may lose the mast. Are you, or you, or you [pointing at each Master in turn] going to send two men to secure that slack wire, knowing full well that the mast may fail, and the two men might be killed?

Silence ensued, the man who had submitted the drawing looked uncomfortable. Captain de Jong broke the silence, 'So, you are saying that this is rubbish?'
'No, it is not rubbish, but it is impractical for this ship.'
'So it is rubbish.'
With that he said, to the representative of the contracting firm, 'We don't want this, you may go'. He then screwed up the drawing.
The second drawing was very similar, and my comments were similar, another prospective contractor was sent on his way. 'Now, Mr Spencer, tell them what you told me in London', said Captain de Jong.
I was given a pencil and some paper, on which I drew a 60 cm vertical line, which represented 200 feet. On one side of that line I started at the top, giving a commentary as I drew,

It's all a matter of angles. I like nothing less than 11 degrees, but 13 is better. Obviously we cannot increase the ship's beam, so if we come down, say 10 or 12 metres, then we insert a 3 or 4 foot spreader.
From that spreader root, draw another 13 degree, down to another spreader, some 15 metres above the water line. That will give us the spreader to increase the beam, and still leave the ship's side clear for the tender to come alongside.
At 10 metre intervals bring another wire, to the end of the big spreader, and return all wire shrouds back to the ship's side. You will then have a stable, accessible rig. There will be no problems with the fore and aft rig, due to the ship's length.

'But with this length of wire, there will be too much stretch, and we could lose the mast', said a concerned Captain de Jong. Feeling more in command of the situation, because of my specialised training I was able reassure them.

No Captain, even the longest wire will not stretch more then 30 centimetres, and you will have battle screws to take up the slack. If you think that there is a risk that one of the insulators will break, we will use fully enclosed insulators, which cannot break. As an extra precaution we could use two bottle screws.
You could then send two men on deck, even in bad weather, with life lines, to use the bottle screws to take up any slack. If we use 110/115 tensile 7 x 7 galvanised wire, you will have no trouble?

'Can you get that wire quickly?'
'Yes, I have a supplier.'

Merit Music Co Ltd

CABLES: "AYCEEMUSIC, LONDON W.1"

47 DEAN STREET, LONDON, W.1
TELEPHONE: REGENT 7451-2-3

30th January 1964.

Mr. Harry Spencer,
3 Bank Chambers,
Cowes,
I. O. W.

Dear Mr. Spencer,

<u>Re: Rajah Anstalt, Vaduz</u>

This is to confirm, on behalf of the above Company, that you
will be required to carry out all Rigging work in connection
with the installation of a new Mast for the vessel "Mi Amigo"
during the course of the next few weeks.

It is understood that you are already ordering the necessary
wirerope and fittings, which, together with your own fee, will
be payable by Rajah Anstalt as above.

Capt. de Jong has asked me to write you this letter as a favour,
and when you meet with him during his next visit to England
you can arrange directly with him as to the method of presentation
of your invoice, which I am sure will be paid promptly.

With kind regards,

Sincerely,

Allan Crawford

'Then phone him now, and confirm its availability.'

'Now then', continued the Captain, we have another ship which will need a lighter mast, where can we get that quickly?'

'I think I have a supplier for that'. So I made another phone call. Halls Barton Ropery was the wire supplier, and John Powell of Sparlight, was the mast maker.

'We need all of these things within 14 days, can you supply them?' asked Captain de Jong. With my heart thumping, I knew that it was going to be very difficult, as we did not have the facilities to terminate the wires, but I knew who could. 'Yes, I can supply.'

It was arranged that the MV *Fredericia*, a 700 ton ex-Danish ferry, would sail down the English Channel, passing close to the Isle of Wight, where we could transfer all of the rig. They would have to take the mast, and the two spreaders.

I was also told that the *Fredericia* was to be renamed *Caroline*, after the daughter of President Kennedy. The name Caroline also rhymed with 199, which was the frequency on which this radio station would broadcast.

I returned to Cowes, to get things moving. I only had four people working for me, Derek Whitehead, an apprentice, John and Charlie Alder, Ben Bradley was in the office, he had just left the drawing office of John Samuel White's (the local ship builder's yard).

J.S. White's had just purchased a comparatively new machine, a hand operated hydraulic Talurit machine, which was used for terminating wires with alloy ferrules.

Ben had the job of obtaining the wire, and persuading the shipyard manager that our little firm had the credibility to undertake such an order, and use the machine, in such a short time scale. Ben did succeed in both of his allocated tasks.

In the meantime I had driven to Tamworth, in my old Austin A95 estate, where I met Jim Patey, at the entrance to Dalton's Industrial Porcelains. Jim was an ex-school colleague, which was a great help. He searched through the stores, and filled my car with about a ton of insulators. I then drove back to the Isle of Wight.

The next day I had a phone call requesting me to take John Powell, the mast maker, and fly to Madrid. Everything had been laid on, cars, air fares, hotels, etc. Suddenly I found myself caught up in this project, which was full of secrecy and intrigue.

On arrival at Madrid we were met, and instructed to take the train to Coruna, and then to El Ferrol, on the north-west coast. We were taken to an hotel, in the centre of El Ferrol, which is a naval port. At the hotel we were met by a tall, 80-year-old, Dutch surveyor. He told us that the ship we had come to see had not yet arrived.

That ship was called the *Mi Amigo*, she was underpowered, and could only make about 4 knots. The northern route is the fastest way to cross the Atlantic, but it was felt that it would be safer to use the southern route. She had sailed from Galveston, Texas and had called in at Cuba. The ship then called at Las Palmas, in the Canary Islands. The Spanish authorities were interested in the fact that she had called in at Cuba, so we kept a low profile, whilst we waited her arrival. The ship eventually arrived on Wednesday 5th February, 1964; we measured her for an alloy mast, then returned to England.

Meanwhile, Ben had organised the standing rigging for the *Fredericia*, which had sailed from Rotterdam on Thursday 13th February. The next day, during the afternoon, Ben had a phone call to say the ship would not now stop to collect the mast. The ship was going to remain in International waters, during her passage to Greenore, in the Irish Republic.

Ben was instructed to organise road transport to take all of the equipment to Liverpool, where it would be loaded onto a Dutch coaster. Charlie Alder and I loaded up the 'Green Goddess' (my old Austin A95), with tools wires, bottles screws, and our luggage. We then drove to Holyhead, and took the ferry to Dun Laoghaire, we then drove north to Greenore, on the southern shores of Carlingford Lough.

The O'Rahilly family had purchased the port from British Railways, and when we got there the *Fredericia* was moored alongside the quay. We were given cabins on board the ship, and I well remember two of the crew, a seaman called Piet, and Peter who was a cook.

Right: The mast designed and rigged by Harry Spencer, the upper section of the MV *Caroline's* mast. Close examination will show how the rigging is passed over the spreaders. The rigging then descends from the root to the spreader, at an angle of 13 degrees as stipulated in Harry's sketch.   *E. Varley*

Below: The stump of the *Fredericia's* original mast can be seen just behind the catwalk.   *E. Varley*

Peter always amazed us, with the food that he prepared. His galley was only 8 foot by 8 foot, but he produced fresh bread daily, and a variety of delicacies. There were about 16 people on the ship, there were Dutch crew, and members of the O'Rahilly family. No matter how many came aboard, Peter always had a meal for them.

We worked really hard, joining up the mast, we then rigged it, and prepared to step it on the next low water. Measuring up, we found it was only just within the capacity of the dockside crane, for height and outreach, at dead low water.

The Dutch shipyard had prepared the *Fredericia's* foremast to take the long steel mast, much as I had designed whilst I was in Holland. The joint was just a socket, of some 25 centimetres, with two flanges.

I was at the top of the mast, with Piet, the Dutch seaman, on the *Fredericia's* foremast. The new 120 ft top mast was lifted, and swung over. Hands led the bare ends of the rigging forward, and aft, and over each end of the big, 50 ft spreader. Obviously, because the mast was slung from the midway point, the mast did not hang exactly plumb.

Piet and I could not get the new mast into the stump of the foremast, no matter how we got the crane to move it, it just would not line up. My mind suddenly swung into gear, and I shouted down to the crew to swing out a lifeboat, or two. The extra weight, over the side, gave the ship a slight list, which was enough for us to line the new mast up.

Whilst Piet and I secured the flange bolts, other members of the crew, made the rigging secure, but only with temporary fixings. Work complete we climbed down to the deck, for a well deserved cup of tea and a smoke.

Yells, coming from the crane driver, alerted us to a developing problem. The tide had turned, and the hoist wire was still hanging from the sling, instead of having been moved to the top sheave. I had to frantically climb the mast, to detach the sling, before any damage was done to the mast.

Climbing back down again, I realised that there was another serious problem. As I have already said, the mast was only secured with temporary fixings. There was 120 feet of mast, with about 10 tons of rigging. The fore stays had also been temporarily secured, but the chain links were stretching!

At any moment the links could have snapped, bringing the whole assembly crashing down. It took some frantic effort on my part, to secure those stays with bulldog clips, and run them through the bottle screws. I don't think I have ever worked so fast!

We spent our evenings in the local pub, establishing a rapport with the locals who tried to find out what the mast was for. We told them that one of the ships would be a weather ship, and the other was for marine research. We even formed our own dart team, to take on the locals.

The local Post Office was run by a little old lady, every time I asked her to ring Cowes she would crank away on the little handle that rang the bell at the other and of the line.

'Cove you say?'

'No Cowes.'

'Right you are then Cove it is.'

We then found out that Cove was the Irish for Cork!

Eventually I was asked to go for a meal with the customers, it was mainly the O'Rahilly family, two sons and the father. Mr O'Rahilly senior was a definite republican, he was a product of the 1916, and the 1922, problems and solutions. He would not speak to me, or even look at me, in fact he sat with his back to me. I could hear him ask his son, 'What's the English man saying now, or what is he doing?'

The Dutch part of the project was also represented, as the *Mi Amigo* had since arrived, and the *Fredericia*, which had now been renamed *Caroline*, was nearing completion. The captain, and some of his crew, wanted a good night out before the ship sailed, so we all went to Dublin. Plenty of alcohol was consumed, and some of the crew dallied with the ladies of the night.

We had some German generators to fit on the MV *Caroline*, I had made some suggestions where we could site them, I marked out areas of steel bulkheads that would have to be cut, and marked out on the deck where the plant would be sited.

Harry and his friend attended a social evening, where a chance conversation with a priest ended a work embargo.   *Author's Collection*

I needed extra staff for this work, about half a dozen in all including engineers, welders, burners, etc., which we got from the Dundalk Engineering Works. The work continued apace, but when the company discovered that this was to be a radio ship, the workers did not return.

Two social events took place, around this time; firstly we were invited to the crane driver's house, to watch a Cassius Clay fight. We drove half way up a mountain to his little cottage, inside were photographs of the Pope, President Kennedy, with an American flag. The fight only lasted for a few minutes, but the drinking went on, from a good supply of Guinness, and his wife provided us with some food. A good evening was had by all.

The second event, was a social evening, with food and dancing. During the evening I had a conversation with the captain of the *Mi Amigo*, who was Polish. It transpired that the captain knew Cowes, as J.S. White's shipyard had built two Polish warships, the *Gram* and the *Blyyskawica* (thunder and lightning).

I then entered a conversation with a local Catholic priest who asked me how the work was progressing. I told him that we were having a problem, because the Dundalk Engineering would not allow their men to work on the ships, once they had found out what they were going to be used for.

'Well now, when would you be wanting these Dundalk men to come?', he asked.

'Ideally tomorrow, but I don't think that they will be allowed to come.'

'Ah well, we will see about that', he smirked. The next day the workers duly arrived, such was the power of the priest, in Ireland, at that time.

Prior to sailing, the MV *Caroline* broadcast a test transmission, from Greenore, this put the cat amongst the pigeons! Cars had been hired, and they drove off in all directions, to see how far the signal would reach. We even had cars over in England using their radios, to see how far it would reach.

Blasting out music, with a 20 kilowatt transmitter, at the end of the road in Greenore, was not the best thing to do. Everything, and I mean everything, was picking up the signal. It interfered with other radio and television broadcasts, no other transmissions could be heard

We were no longer the most popular people in the town, in fact we were drummed out of the local pub, From that time we were watched, I'm not sure by whom, but on one evening one of the Customs officers came into the saloon of the *Mi Amigo*. He was obviously very shaken, he told us that he had run over a man with a tall stovepipe hat, and strange clothing. When they had searched for the man, they found nothing!

The MV *Caroline* was preparing to sail, but there was some problem with the transmitter, which had to be sorted before it could be handed over to Caroline from Continental Electric. Then Piet went berserk.

He took a cleaver from the galley, and smashed down a cabin door. He then went and sat down; the Garda had to be called. Piet and I had become friends, and he trusted me. Although I am not the bravest person, I did manage to persuade him to give himself up.

John Alder helped me to rig the mast on the *Mi Amigo*, but now that the purpose of the radio ships had been leaked to the press we had reporters everywhere. We had them pestering us outside the compound, we even had a helicopter hovering over the harbour, taking photographs.

I saw my photograph, with one of the seamen, leaning over the ship's rail. It was front page on the *Daily Express* (I think), with the headline, 'THE PIRATES ARE HERE!' Luckily it was the Irish edition, or I think I would have been in trouble, if not with the English police, then certainly with my bank manager.

We were driving all over the place, up to Shannon to meet someone from Houston, who delivered a part for the transmitter. Then we would race back to the ship, being chased by the reporters. We would run up the gangway on to the ship, where we were safe, under either the Polish or Dutch flag.

RADIO SCOTLAND

Please reply to

T.V. Shields
Managing Director

Head Office:—
38 BATH STREET
GLASGOW, C.2
Telephone: DOUglas 5726-7-8

WALMAR HOUSE
296 REGENT STREET
LONDON, W.I
Telephone: Langham 9401

TVS/BI

13th October 1965

H.R. Spencer, Esq.,
The Loft,
3 Bank Chambers,
High Street,
Cowes,
Isle of Wight.

Dear Mr. Spencer,

Further to your letter of September 23rd, and the various discussions we have had on the telephone since then, I confirm acceptance of your quotation for work detailed in your letter of September 30th for the final figure of £4,217 with an additional £200 and travelling expenses as incurred.

In reaching our decision, we bear in mind the high recommendations we have had concerning your work and we are confident that you will execute all work on the "Comet" to our entire satisfaction and with a minimum of delay.

Yours sincerely,

T.V. Shields
Managing Director.

CITY AND COUNTY COMMERCIAL RADIO (SCOTLAND) LTD.

Directors:—
Sir Andrew Murray, O.B.E., K.C.J., LL.D., D.L., J.P., (Chairman), T. V. Shields, (Managing Director), Alan Carr, Stanley Jackson, (Joint Deputy Managing Directors), James Donald.

I had to go to Belfast, where I bought a huge anchor, a massive chain and some swivels, which would be used for the ship's mooring. From there I went to Dublin airport, where I purchased a double red runway light, for the ship's masthead.

The work was now completed, so I returned to the Isle of Wight. The *Mi Amigo* eventually sailed on Monday 20th April, 28 days after the *Caroline*. Two days later I got a phone call, from the ship. Something on the rigging had broken, the ship had been given permission to enter the port of Falmouth, and would I get down to join them, as soon as possible.

I kicked the 'Green Goddess' into life, and caught the first ferry out of Cowes. By midday I had arrived at the Cornish port, and made my way to the Harbour Master's office, where I was questioned by Customs officers.

The local TV and press reporters were there, so I gave them an interview, then I was taken out to the *Mi Amigo* on the Customs launch. Once on board the radio ship, the damage was clear to see.

The ship's original mast had four shrouds, which were attached to the side of the ship. One of these shrouds had broken one of the side plates, putting extra strain on the new wires, that we had fitted.

I was able to purchase all that I needed, from a Falmouth ship yard, and made the necessary repairs. The work took 1½ days to complete, after which the *Mi Amigo* continued on her passage and I returned to the Isle of Wight.

The two radio ships were often in the news, especially when Caroline and Atlanta merged in July 1964. The *Mi Amigo* was anchored outside of the number 4 buoy, in the Wallet Channel, on the north side of the Thames Estuary. The MV *Caroline* sailed around the south coast, to a new anchorage off the Isle of Man.

During the summer of 1965, I got a phone call from Mr Shields, the Managing Director of City and County Commercial Radio (Scotland) Ltd. He wanted to start a radio station, which was to be called Radio Scotland.

'I understand you know about radio ships?'

'A little', I replied.

'What do you think would be a good vessel to convert?'

'A lightship', I answered. 'They are designed to remain at sea, for long periods'. Mr Shields then asked me to find a suitable for ship, for the project.

Laying in Dun Laoghaire harbour were three redundant lightships, which were being offered for sale by the Commissioners of Irish Lights. I was asked to go there and look into the possibility of purchasing one of them.

I travelled up to London, and whilst there I purchased a new briefcase, for the princely sum of £18. It has to be said that I had not made much money whilst working for Radio Caroline.

On the train to Holyhead I carefully inscribed my initials, with a black biro, with diamond dots between the H.R.S. It looked very professional, and gave the briefcase a more important look.

Having crossed the Irish Sea, we all met at the offices of the Irish Lights. Accompanied by the Superintendent, we went out to view the ships. The middle ship was named *Comet*, a small ship built in 1880, of Loadmore iron, in Scotland.

There were two watchmen living aboard and, after putting my new briefcase on the saloon table, we went to look around the ship. Whilst in the next cabin , I heard one of the watchmen say, 'Who's the little fella with the Super?'

'You can see who he is', came the reply, 'Look at those initials on his case, H.R.S., it's obvious he's Her Royal Surveyor'. We all were doubled up laughing on the other side of the bulkhead.

We purchased the *Comet* for £10,000, and she was towed to the Liffy Dockyard. I was asked to supervise the conversion, design the rig, and see her on station by Hogmanay, New Year's Eve, 1965.

The *Comet* was a converted lightship which was officially described as a 'hulk' as it had no propulsion equipment. It is seen here under tow through the Dover Straits.   *Fotoflite*

I stayed at the Adelphi Hotel, and then drove down to the yard, only to find that the workers were on strike! I was informed, by one of the pickets, that I would be allowed into the Yard. I would have no skilled workers, but they would allow labourers and apprentices to work for me.

We cut up the air receivers, that had been used for the fog signal, and the scrap was put into the hull for additional ballast. I worked out, that if we removed the lantern structure, we could replace it with a 200 foot mast, and still maintain stability.

The strike was soon over, which allowed skilled workers to cut off the lantern. We then moved the ship into drydock, where two lorry loads of flag weed were removed from her hull, some 8-10 tons. Some of the fronds were 15 feet in length, with stalks as big as my arm.

She was then given a sonic test which revealed that there was one inch thickness in her hull plates, not bad after a 60 year career. There were just two places where she had lost $\frac{1}{16}$th in., and they were where the rudder chains had caused wear. She was a sound vessel. John Powell made the mast, using some discarded sections from the masts of the sail training ship, *Winston Churchill*, which was lying at Goole. We made applications to the shipyard to rig the mast, but they refused to give us permission. The *Comet* was, however, issued with a certificate of seaworthiness, which meant we could tow her to another port.

It cost me a £2,000 deposit for a tug to sail round from Hull and tow the *Comet* to Hamburg, where we had gained permission to rig the mast. I saw the tow commence, then made my way home.

I was then informed that the authorities at Hamburg would not allow the ship to come alongside a quay, the mast would have to be fitted with the ship tied to a mooring buoy. This meant that we would have to hire barges, and a floating crane, which would have been very expensive. Fortunately, I had some previous dealings with a yard in St Sampson's Harbour, on the Channel Island of Guernsey. I phoned my contact, and found that it was a viable option and we would be allowed alongside. There were some large dockside cranes and the yard could assist us.

The *Comet* was diverted, arriving in tow of the tug *Foreman*. The work then proceeded, but we were running out of time as we had to be ready for the ship to be towed to Scotland, and broadcasting by the end of the year.

John Powell had the mast ready, in sections, so that it could easily be moved. We had all of the rigging wires ready, everything was loaded onto two Bristol aircraft, and flown to Guernsey. We had two lorries waiting, which we used to transport the equipment down to the harbour.

Eventually we were ready to put the mast onto the ship, the sections were laid out on the quay, but we had to move the *Comet* from across the other side of the harbour. As the tide fell, the *Comet* rested on the floor of the harbour, which gave us maximum height to step the mast.

On that day it was blowing a gale but fortunately we had plenty of workers to assist us. The crane lifted the mast from off the quay into an upright position. The wind was blowing so hard the mast was swaying, about 6 feet, making it difficult to control.

Gradually we manoeuvred the mast into position, and it was made secure to the remains of the lantern tower. The rigging was secured, and on 22nd December, we ordered a tug.

The tug berthed in St Peter Port on Christmas Eve and the next morning I went aboard to discuss the tow. Some of the crew were asleep on the deck, still feeling the effects of the night before. Apparently this was their first spell ashore after sailing from Haifa.

The tug was called *Rifleman*, part of the fleet of the United Towing Company who had also supplied the tug *Foreman*. The tug sailed from St Peter Port the short distance to St Sampson's.

Two lines were passed from the *Comet* to the tug, but both snapped as the tow commenced. I could do nothing except watch in horror as the *Comet* collided with the

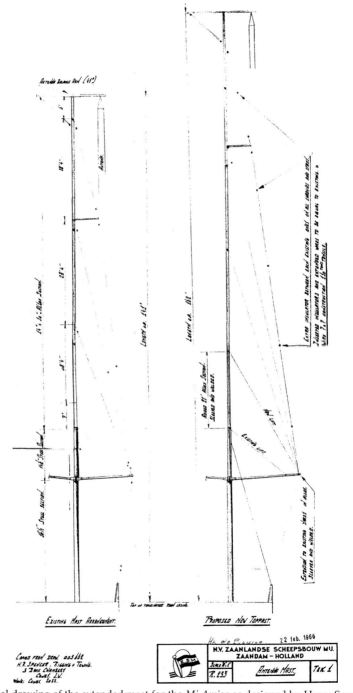

An original drawing of the extended mast for the *Mi Amigo* as designed by Harry Spencer. The 22 ft extension was fitted in Zaandam.

south-west wall. She hit the quay, then rose up about two feet, then slid back down again. The ship and the mast survived the impact but there was about 8 feet of the quay damaged, which fell into the harbour.

The ship was re-secured and then towed to St Peter Port, where there was to be more drama. We were tied alongside, the spreaders of the mast increasing our beam by about 13 feet. The tide went out, dropping us some 28 feet, with some of the rigging hard against the wood of the quay.

The *Rifleman* commenced the tow as soon as we let go our mooring ropes, but as we moved the rigging wires were gouging along the whaling timbers of the quay. We shouted at the tug, but they could not hear us. The wires cut right through the timbers to the securing bolts. We thought that the mast would come crashing down. but instead the wires cut through the bolts, and a large section of timber crashed into the harbour.

At last we were out in open water, the weather was fine, just a force three wind blowing. After a few hours we were being forced backwards by an easterly gale, which abated as quickly as it had started. We experienced more strong winds, this time from the north, as we rounded Flamborough Head off the coast of Yorkshire.

Eventually we arrived off Bass Rock, some four miles from Dunbar, on the southern side of the Firth of Forth. We were met by a launch, which I boarded with two other men, ready to lay out the mushroom anchor. The tug helped us position the ship, then it sailed to Hull to give the crew some shore leave.

We were joined by radio personnel, and someone accepted the ship from me, at which time I was taken ashore. I spent the night in the Roxborough Hotel, in Dunbar. The next morning I took some urgently required parts to the *Comet*, then returned to the Isle of Wight.

Towards the end of 1965 we were requested to visit the *Mi Amigo*; they were planning to increase power, which meant increasing the height of the mast and the antenna. John Alder went out to the ship, where it was decided to try a telescopic extension from the masthead.

The work had to be done at night so as not to interrupt transmissions. Imagine working up that mast in the dark, bolting on the tube with its associated rigging and pump. Increasing the height also meant that extra rigging would have to be fitted.

The job was not an easy task to complete, but eventually John was ready. The extension was pumped up to its full 20 feet, and was then secured, but it did not last for long. The pump leaked, the extension destroyed itself, and John had to go back up to clear the tangled mess.

In January 1966 the *Mi Amigo* ran aground, was subsequently refloated, and towed to Zaandam for repairs. Whilst this work was being undertaken I was asked to join the ship, as they wanted to install a 22 ft extension to the mast.

I made drawings of the proposed extension, it would mean that the mast would have to be lifted, extended and then re-rigged. I was also representing the insurance company, and I felt that it was not necessary to bring extra staff from England. I approached a Dutch rigging company to supply the extra lengths of wire and the workers. They had the drawings, and specifications, so I returned to England, leaving instructions that I was to be informed when the ship was ready to sail, as I would have to undertake a survey.

In early February whilst the work on the *Mi Amigo* was progressing I was contacted by Ellambar Investments Ltd. They were planning an offshore radio station and informed me that they had a Dutch trawler, and asked if I could rig it.

The *Oceaan VII*, arrived in Scarborough on 26th February, so I went up to view the ship. I agreed to undertake the work, with the rigging being made in Cowes and the mast fitted in St Sampson's Harbour.

We used one section of mast, that had been intended for Radio Scotland, and I also used parts of the mast from the *Norsaga*. This was a 12 metre yacht that we had been doing trials with, prior to it competing in the America Cup races.

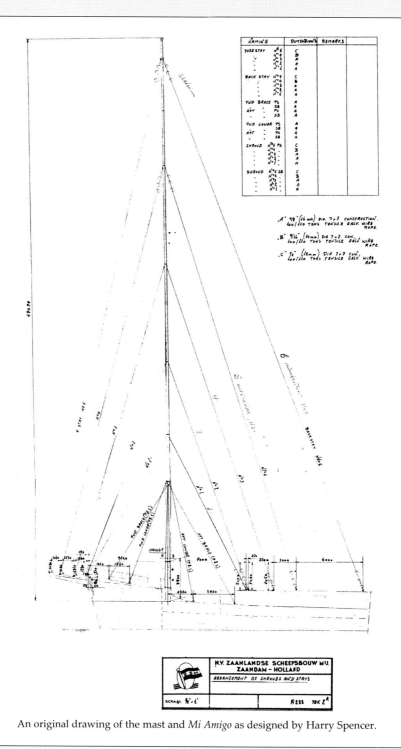

An original drawing of the mast and *Mi Amigo* as designed by Harry Spencer.

RADIO-270

COMMERCIAL RADIO FOR THE NORTH EAST, YORKSHIRE AND MIDLANDS

From the office of The Technical Director,
10 Neville Street,
Newcastle.

WESTMINSTER BANK CHAMBERS
ST. NICHOLAS STREET, SCARBOROUGH, YORKSHIRE
TELEPHONE SCARBOROUGH 701—
TELEGRAMS TOSEVENO SCARBOROUGH
YOUR REF: OUR REF: PD/PAD

24th February 1966.

H.R. Spencer,
The Loft,
3 Bank Chambers,
High Street,
Cowes,
Isle of Wight.

Dear Sirs,

Further to your letter of 14th February, I have pleasure to inform you that your tender for the project has been accepted.

The ship should soon be in Scarborough, and as soon as it arrives you will be informed in order that you may inspect it.

Yours faithfully,

P. A. Duncan

Peter Duncan.
Technical Director.
ELLAMBAR INVESTMENTS LTD.

Harry had to rejoin the *Mi Amigo* off the Essex coast. The radio ship was still off the air, with Radio Caroline being broadcast from the *Cheeta II*. He is seen here checking new support wires.

Author's Collection

John Alder and I had sailed the *Norsaga* for six days a week, for almost a year. She had been fitted with strain gauges and instruments, computers were installed, and we had a team of technicians. When the tests had been completed, the mast was no longer required.

We shipped everything out to Guernsey, where we installed the mast in a similar assembly to that on Radio Scotland. The ship then sailed, with a Dutch crew, and anchored off the Yorkshire coast, where she was to broadcast as Radio 270.

I joined the ship off Scarborough to find that the Dutch crew were not happy having such an unusual mast on their ship. They asked many questions about the tension of the rigging, they did not seem to be convinced when I told them to just leave it alone. A last minute check was made, then I returned ashore.

The *Mi Amigo* in the meantime had been made ready, so I went to Zaandam to inspect the ship. The first thing that I saw were two metre lengths of long link chain on the lower part of the rigging. I asked why this had been done, and was told: 'It was easier for us to get the final lengths'.

I knew that this chain would not have an equal breaking strain to the high tensile rigging wire that I had used. I asked them to show me a test certificate, but they could not as one had not been issued. It meant that I would have to inspect all of the rigging from top to bottom.

When we had rigged the mast we had used galvanised shackles, all of which had been tested. This firm had changed them for rusty, ungalvanised ones. I told them that the ship could not return to sea, until all of the shackles had been replaced. I was not very popular.

At the beginning of April, whilst I was still in Zaandam, I had a phone call from the owners of Radio 270. The ship had lost the top section of her mast, which was now lying on the bottom of the sea. They wanted me to meet thousands of pounds for wages and lost revenue.

I flew to Yorkshire, and joined the ship at Grimsby. On board I found that the massive deck eyeplates and the bottle screws were all still in place. The bottle screws, which were more than adequate for the job, showed signs of strain. It subsequently came to light that the Dutch crew had tightened the rigging; as the ship rolled the tension tore out the tangs, aloft, and the rig collapsed. Lloyds asked for my drawings, and a week later, they authorised a new rig. Phew!

Within days, the *Mi Amigo* returned to her anchorage, but there was a fault on the masthead lights. I was asked to go out to the ship and try and sort out the problem. 'Surely you don't need me to change a light bulb?' I was told that someone (I believe it was Tony Blackburn) had tried to fix it, but could not.

I was taken out to the *Mi Amigo*, by a fishing vessel, which sailed from Brightlingsea. Once on the radio ship I had to wait until 8 pm, when the station closed for the night.

At the top of the mast I found that one of the covers (there were two) had been removed and the screws were rolling around in that cover. I replaced both of the lamps and re-assembled the fittings, I then called down to the engineer to switch them on.

The next thing that I knew was that 220 volts were passing through my arm and my knee. That was a big punch! I'm sure that the engineer saved my life, he heard a loud buzz so he switched them off immediately.

I found that there was an abrasion in the cable insulation where it entered the lamp housing. Shaken, but none the worse for this shocking experience, I repaired the cable which solved the problem.

The *Mi Amigo* resumed test transmissions, but it was found that the increased power caused radiation through the upper rigging. We had to make all new wires, which were sent out from Harwich after it had been cleared by Customs.

I went back out to the ship with the new 180 ft wires, which had a string of six insulators in the top, and more down each wire. It weighed about 250-300 kilos, so we had to rig a hoist wire to winch them to the masthead. It was very hard work, but at least the weather stayed fine.

Radio Caroline

SOLE SELLING AGENTS

PLANET PRODUCTIONS LIMITED - 6 CHESTERFIELD GARDENS - LONDON W.1 - HYDE PARK 9721

Overseas Cables & Telegrams : Palairwave London W1   Telex 261816

ALM/D.

H. R. Spencer Esq.
The Loft.
3 Bank Chambers.
High Street. Cowes.   3rd September, 1966.

Dear Mr Spencer,
                        Thank you for your letter of the 31st August, regarding the
Aluminium lengths belonging to Sparlight Ltd of Emsworth.
These are in store at Harwich and I have today given instructions to Mr Scaddon
our Agent in Harwich to dispatch as soon as transport can be arranged to
Sparlight Ltd.

Please dispatch the new Sausage Aerial to Radio Caroline, C/0 Ramsey Shipping Co
The Quay, Ramsey, Isle of Man as soon as possible.

                With regards,
                         Sincerely

                                A. L. Morphy.

I was up that mast for 17½ hours without a break. For safety reasons I had a wire, covered in red tape, which I could clearly see from my position aloft. This wire was clipped from the transmitter terminal to the ship's side, there was no way that I was going to get electrocuted again whilst I was up that mast.

Whilst this work was progressing the *Mi Amigo* was off the air, the *Cheeta II* was transmitting programmes for Radio Caroline on low power. The hoist wire was twice the height of the mast, it was the longest wire in the rig, without insulators, and I kept getting RF burns on my arms and a couple on my face.

I shouted down to the deck, and asked them to ensure that everything was switched off. They checked around, and confirmed that there was nothing live. It was later discovered that the wire was picking up radio frequency from Radio London, such was the output power of their transmissions. That is why we had to ensure that all of our wires, in the mast rigging, had to be insulated lengths of 35-39 feet.

With the work completed, the *Mi Amigo* resumed test transmissions, on her new frequency, and with increased power on 25th April, and two days later regular broadcasts resumed.

In the meantime, Radio Scotland had found that they were not getting a good signal into Glasgow. It was decided that the *Comet* would be moved to a new anchorage off Troon, on the west coast of Scotland.

There was great difficulty in retrieving the mushroom anchor, so the *Comet* was towed around the north coast, and a heavy lift vessel had to recover the gear which was then sent overland to join the ship.

A fault developed on one of the generators, which had to be replaced. A new unit was taken out to the *Comet*, on a fishing boat, with the intention of lifting the generator with the boat's lifting crane.

The whole lifting operation was a disaster; the crew of the boat had obviously never lifted anything this heavy before, but they took no notice of the advice that we offered. The generator was, by this time, swinging in the air and it crashed into the deckhouse of the *Comet*.

Luckily I jumped out of the way just in time, otherwise it would have crushed me. I don't often get overheated, but the skipper of that trawler was very near to being hospitalised for a very long time.

Eventually we got the unit onto the *Comet*, and it was taken to the engine room, where it had to be lifted over the other equipment at about head height before it could be installed.

In August 1966 we were contacted by Radio Caroline because the copper antenna on the MV *Caroline* had broken. Charlie Alder and I went over to the Isle of Man, where we constructed the new antenna on the quay at Douglas. The antenna was made of 180 ft lengths of copper wire seized onto 12 inch diameter rings, which were placed at four foot intervals. We then took the assembly out to the Caroline and installed it.

The next visit was at the request of the insurance company. I had to survey the whole rig, every wire from top to bottom. Every insulator had to be checked, there were over 80 of those. They were 250 mm in length, 150 mm in diameter, and made of brown porcelain.

As I was to undertake this survey I was asked, by Radio Caroline, to grease all of the wires whilst I was up there. It was impossible to work anywhere in the rigging whilst the station was on the air. Even at deck level you could light a 220 volt lamp between any of the wires!

Caroline was broadcasting from 6 am until 8 pm, so it meant that all of the work had to be done at night. I used a bosun's chair to haul myself aloft, it had a wooden seat and was not comfy. I would haul myself to the top of the mast, where I shackled onto my chosen wire, then I would work down that wire, to deck level. For lighting I had a miner's lamp around my head, with the battery in my pocket.

This was no easy task, the masthead could describe a 15 foot arc, even when the ship was just gently rolling. If there were any waves it could be as much as 30 feet, with the mast vibrating as much as 6-9 feet, fore and aft.

MV *Mi Amigo*

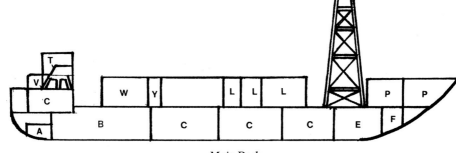

Main Deck

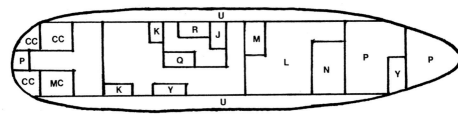

Lower Deck

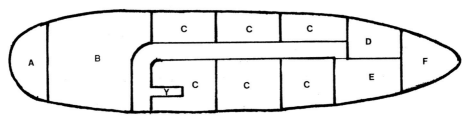

A	Water & Fuel	F	Transmitter Room	N	Radio Mi Amigo's Studio
B	Engine Room	Y	Stairs	Q	Toilets
C	Cabins	J	Shower	R	Wash Room
CC	Crew Cabins	K	Refrigerators	T	Bridge
MC	Master's Cabin	L	Mess Room	U	Deck
D	Album Library	M	Television Lounge	V	Generator
E	Caroline Studio	P	Storage	W	Galley

If the weather stayed good, the most I could do was three wires each night. The work went on for about one week, I was up that mast every night, for which I was paid just £1 per hour.

I was working on the last forestay wire, the wind had been blowing quite fresh, when there came a sudden squall, combined with the change in the tide. The ship rolled violently, the motion spinning me twice around that forestay. The line had become tangled, I was stuck aloft, where no one else could help me.

I had to lash myself to the stay, whilst I attempted to untangle the rope of my bosun's chair. It meant hauling through 180 feet of rope. Just as I thought I had succeeded, the wind wrested the rope from my grip. I had to start all over again, my arms were getting very tired, as I fought to control my precarious position.

The time ticked by, and all too soon it was time for Caroline to go back on the air, but they dared not transmit or they would have fried me. The DJs were shouting at me, but there was little I could do, it took me almost five hours to free myself. As soon as my feet hit the deck, the station opened.

We had no further contact with the radio ships, until one day some 17 years later I got a phone call from Ronan O'Rahilly. He asked me if I would meet him at the Dorchester, in London. During our meeting he informed me that he had purchased another radio ship,which was being converted in Spain, and he wanted me to go and do some rigging work.

I went down to Santander with Joe Henderson, and we found the *Ross Revenge* in a very chaotic state. The work was well in hand, but the decks were covered with black sand which had been used to grit blast the paint work.

The lattice mast had been erected by a Dutch company, but they had not finished it properly. We found that wires had been cut short and held with just one Bulldog grip. We turned each wire into Flemish eyes, for extra security, and measured up the fore and aft guys from the spreaders. Ian McCully and Joe took a truck down to the ship, loaded with winches, and records. For two days the Spanish impounded that truck, at Bilbao, but eventually we got the work completed but we never did get paid, ah well, such is life!

The last time I saw the *Ross Revenge*, it was moored in the River Blackwater, Radio Caroline was silent, and there were no more radio ships. Radio Caroline did break the BBC monopoly, and was responsible for the introduction of local commercial radio - was that a good thing?

REFERENCES

Monitor Magazine: Roland C. Pearson. (Various issues)
Hapy Birthday Radio Caroline: Roland C. Pearson. (Monitor Special 1984)
Radio Caroline:John Venmore-Rowland. (The Landmark Press 1967)
Offshore Radio: Gerry Bishop. (Iceni Enterprises 1975)

Appendix Two

Broadcasting Staff

MV *Caroline*

Radio Caroline: 28th March-2nd July, 1964

Carl Conway	Simon Dee	John Junkin	Doug Kerr
Jerry Leighton	Tom Lodge	Chris Moore	Gerry Duncan

Caroline North: 3rd July, 1964-3rd March, 1968

Mike Ahern	Don Allen	John Aston	Nick Bailey
Freddie Beare	Lord Charles Brown	Errol Bruce	Carl Conway
Gordon Cruz	Rick Dane	Roger Gale	Stevie Gee
Jim Gordon	Dee Harrison	Mel Howard	Ric Johns
Martin Kayne	Doug Kerr	Jerry King	Paul Kramer
Jerry Leighton	Tom Lodge	Mike Luvzit	Mike Marriott
Jim Murphy	Tony Prince	Roger Scott	Mark Sloane
Jack Spector	Bob Stewart	Dave Lee Travis	Ray Teret
Ripley Torne	Alan Turner	Jason Wolfe	Dave Williams
Ed White			

MV *Mi Amigo*

Radio Atlanta: 27th April-2nd July, 1964

Richard Harris	Johnnie Jackson	Ted King	Keith Martin
Ed Moreno	Colin Nichol	Mike Raven	Bob Scott
Bryan Vaughan	Tony Withers		

Caroline South: 3rd July, 1964-3rd March, 1968

Glen Adams	Mike Ahern	Don Allen	Mike Allen
Herb Anderson	Andy Archer	John Aston	Nick Bailey
Bud Ballou	Colin Berry	Tony Blackburn	Ross Brown
Errol Bruce	Gerry Burke	Cary Clarke	Carl Conway
Ray Cooper	Gordon Cruz	Robbie Dale	Rick Dane
Roger Day	Simon Dee	Gerry Duncan	Tom Edwards
Roger Gale	Stevie Gee	Keith Hampshire	Bill Hearne
Mel Howard	Peter James	Gary Kemp	Doug Kerr
Kilroy	Jerry King	Mike Luvzit	Ian MacCrea
Keith Martin	Stevi Mericke	Carl Mitchell	Christopher Moore
Ed Moreno	Henry Morgan	Spangles Muldoon	Mitch Murray
Colin Nichol	Paul Noble	Tony Prince	Emperor Rosko
Ray Sebastian	Keith Skues	Mark Sloane	Jack Spector
Norman St John	Richard Swainson	Jon Sydney	Tony Symonds
Dave Lee Travis	Bryan Vaughan	Tommy Vance	Johnnie Walker
Robert Walton	Graham Webb	Tim Yale	Steve Young

Radio Caroline: 29th September, 1972-20th March, 1980

Robin Adcroft	Alan (cook)	Paul Alexander	Dickie Allen
Tony Allen	Brian Anderson	Tom Anderson	Andy Archer
Robin Banks	Simon Barrett	Mike Barrington	Norman Barrington
Jeremy Bender	Michael Benjamin	Bert Bennett	Stephen Bishop
Jeff Bolan	Dr Boogie	Kees Borrel	Ted Bouwens
Paul Brandt	Dave Brown	Peter Bryan	Kelvin Carter
Jeremy Charlton	Peter Chicago	Clive Corell	Jonathan Day
Roger Day	Tom Dekkler	Steve Diamond	Ron Dolman
Chris Drummond	Paul Dubois	Samantha Dubois	Robbie Duke
Robb Eden	Nigel Elgin	Ellen (cook)	Chris Elliott
Debbie England	Steve England	Martin Fisher	Ed Foster
Emile Garrett	Graham Gill	Steve Gordon	Dave Gotz
Mike Hagler	Tom Hardy	Peter Haze	Rob Hudson
Mark Jacobs	Jimmy James	Kenny James	Johnny Jason
Jolly J.	James Kay	Lion Keezer	Steve Kent
Dennis King	Mark Lawrence	Sane Leone	Michael Lindsay
Michael Lloyd	Will Luikinga	John B. Mair	Brian Martin
Roger Matthews	Hank Meeuwis	Mickey Mercer	Sue Mercer
Hugo Meulenhaff	Phil Mitchell	Jos Mulder	Spangles Muldoon
Bob Noakes	Cliff Osborne	Dave Owen	Kenny Page
Dick Palmer	Paul (cook)	Ad Peerson	Sebastian Peters
Brian Richards	Nick Richards	Ad Roberts	James Ross
Stuart Russell	Cyril Scott	Crispian St John	Don Stevens
Mike Stevens	Mike Storm	Alan Symonds	Theo
Richard Thompson	Tom (cook)	Jan Troost	Dominique Vautrin
Joop Verhoff	Joost Verhoevan	Johan Visser	Mike Wall-Garland
Dave West	Alan Wheeler	Jeroen Woelwater	Peter Zonneveld
Herman de Graff	Leo de Later	Peter de Vries	Paul de Wit
Moniek van Dijk	Peter van Dyken	Peter van Elst	Pierre van Gent
Jerry van der Loo	Frank van der Mast	Pierre van der Steen	Tom van der Velden
Gerard van der Zee			

Radio Seagull: 24th July, 1973-23rd February, 1974

Tony Allen	Brian Anderson	Andy Archer	Baas
Norman Barrington	Peter Chicago	Barry Everett	John Farlow
Mike Hagler	Johnny Jason	Mickey Mercer	Bob Noakes
Hugh Nolan	Dick Palmer	Phil Randall	Charlotte Ribbelli
Peter van Dyken	Rene van de Snoek	Russell Tollerfield	

Berlin Service: 11th August-29th December, 1975

Dennis King	Jack O'Brien

Appendix Three

Masts and Frequencies

Masts

Mi Amigo Masts

		From	To
1. Radio Nord	125 feet	1960	1963
2. Radio Atlanta/Caroline	168 feet	1964	1966
2. Radio Caroline	*180 feet	1966	1972
3. Radio Caroline	180 feet	5/73	10/73
4. Radio Caroline	165 feet	1973	1986

* Mast number 2 was increased in height by 22 feet.

Frequencies

MV *Caroline*

		From	To
201 m	1495 kHz	27th March, 1964	
197 m	1520 kHz	28th March, 1964	17th December, 1966
257 m	1169 kHz*	18th December, 1966	2nd March, 1968

*Tests on this frequency commenced 31.10.1966.

MV *Mi Amigo*

		From	To
197 m	1520 kHz	9th May, 1964	
201 m	1493 kHz	12th May, 1964	20th January, 1966
256 m	1169 kHz	17th April, 1966	25th April, 1966
253 m	1187 kHz	26th April, 1966	3rd March, 1968
253 m	1187 kHz	29th September, 1972	17th December, 1972
197 m	1520 kHz	17th December, 1972	30th December, 1972
253 m	1187 kHz	2nd January, 1973	3rd March, 1977
388 m	773 kHz	13th May, 1973	26th June, 1973
388 m	773 kHz	24th August, 1975	15th October, 1975
197 m	1520 kHz	31st March, 1976	31st March, 1976
192 m	1562 kHz	5th April, 1976	23rd July, 1976
312 m	962 kHz	9th November, 1976	9th November, 1976
314 m	953 kHz	5th March, 1977	5th July, 1977
312 m	962 kHz	5th May, 1977	20th October, 1978
212 m	1412 kHz	23rd July, 1977	4th December, 1977
539 m	557 kHz	18th March, 1979	18th March, 1979
319 m	963 kHz	15th April, 1979	20th March, 1980

Appendix Four

Advertising Rates *circa* 1966

It was estimated that it cost Radio Caroline in the region of £700,000 to get both ships on the air. The cost of running both ships was in the region of £28,000 per month. At that time advertising contracts were earning Caroline £50,000 per month.

	RCN	RCS	RCN	RCS	RCN	RCS	RCN	RCS	RCN	RCS
	60 secs		45 secs		30 secs		15 secs		7 secs	
	£	£	£	£	£	£	£	£	£	£
0600-0700	30	50	23	38	15	25	10	15	7	10
0700-0830	60	100	45	75	30	50	20	30	15	20
0830-1200	80	120	60	90	40	60	25	40	17	25
1200-1500	60	100	45	75	30	50	20	30	15	20
1500-1630	45	70	35	50	23	36	15	25	10	15
1630-2100	60	100	45	75	30	50	20	30	15	20

RCN Radio Caroline North.
RCS Radio Caroline South.

The revenue, from advertising, was the life-blood for the pirate radio stations. The possibility of gaining lucrative contracts led to the increase in stations, each trying to out do the other. It led to an increase in output power, extended transmission hours, and ultimately to the outbreak of hostilities.

Each station had its own rate, with a peak period payment between 8 am and midday. Off peak payments were usually for early morning, or late evening. The following list shows a comparison, listed by the highest peak rate, per minute.

Station	Peak	Off Peak
Radio London	£152	£112
Caroline South	£120	£50
Radio 270	£120	£40
Caroline North	£80	£30
Radio Scotland	£56	£20
Radio City	£40	£20

Index